EX MACHINA
EX CATHEDRA

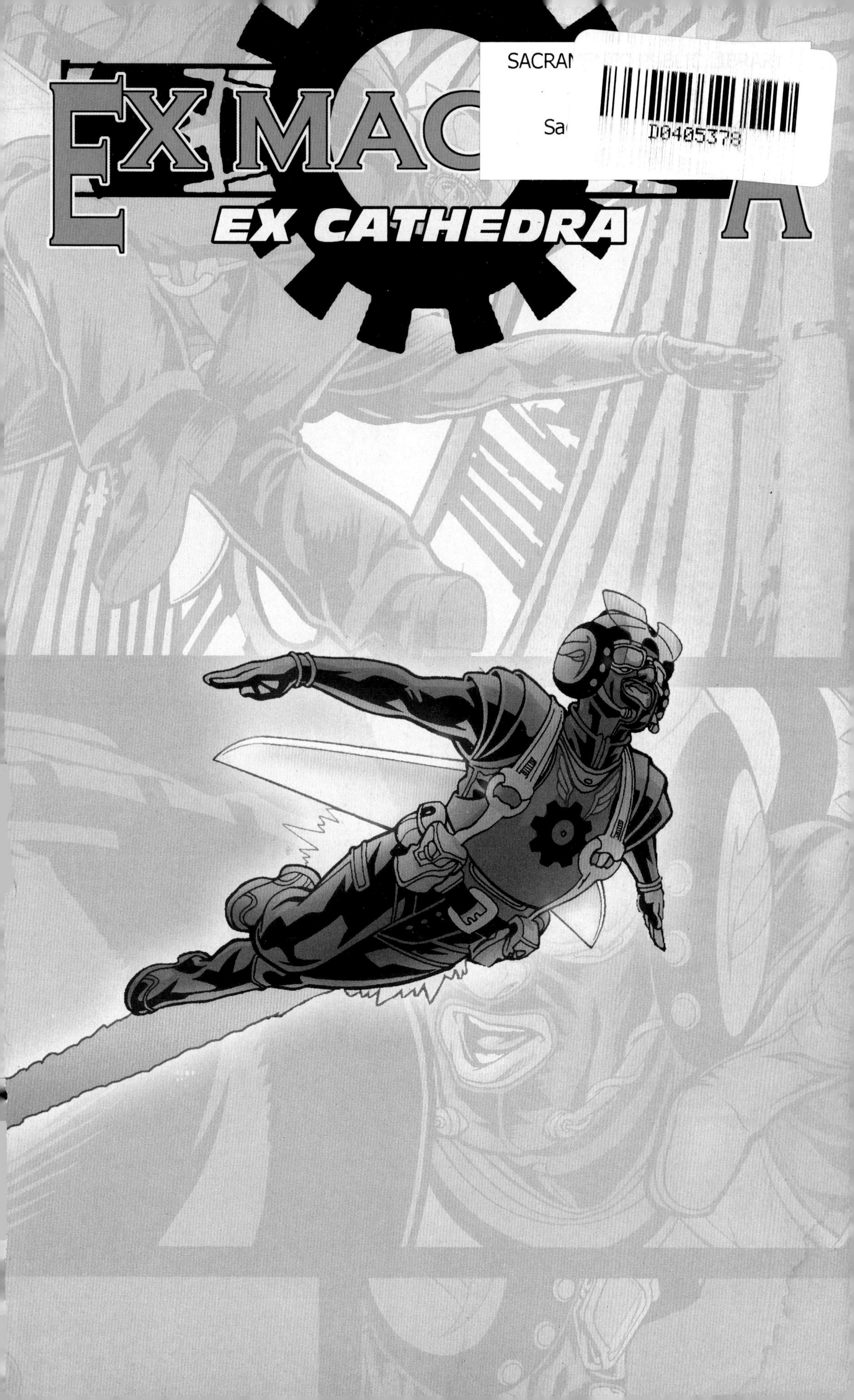

CREDITS

BRIAN K. VAUGHAN: WRITER
TONY HARRIS: PENCILS
JIM CLARK: INKS
JD METTLER: COLORS
JARED K. FLETCHER: LETTERS

Jim Lee, **Editorial Director**   Ben Abernathy, **Editor**   Kristy Quinn, **Assistant Editor**
Ed Roeder, **Art Director**   Paul Levitz, **President & Publisher**
Georg Brewer, **VP—Design & DC Direct Creative**   Richard Bruning, **Senior VP—Creative Director**
Patrick Caldon, **Executive VP—Finance & Operations**   Chris Caramalis, **VP—Finance**
John Cunningham, **VP—Marketing**   Terri Cunningham, **VP—Managing Editor**
Amy Genkins, **Senior VP—Business & Legal Affairs**   Alison Gill, **VP—Manufacturing**
David Hyde, **VP—Publicity**   Hank Kanalz, **VP—General Manager, WildStorm**
Gregory Noveck, **Senior VP—Creative Affairs**   Sue Pohja, **VP—Book Trade Sales**
Steve Rotterdam, **Senior VP—Sales & Marketing**   Cheryl Rubin, **Senior VP—Brand Management**
Alysse Soll, **VP—Advertising & Custom Publishing**
Jeff Trojan, **VP—Business Development, DC Direct**   Bob Wayne, **VP—Sales**

EX MACHINA: EX CATHEDRA. Published by WildStorm
Productions, an imprint of DC Comics. 888 Prospect St.
#240, La Jolla, CA 92037. Cover, compilation Copyright ©
2008 Brian K. Vaughan and Tony Harris. All Rights Reserved.
EX MACHINA is ™ Brian K. Vaughan and Tony Harris.
Originally published in single magazine form as EX MACHINA
#30-34 © 2007, 2008 Brian K. Vaughan and Tony Harris.

DC Comics,
a Warner Bros. Entertainment Company.

ISBN: 978-1-4012-1859-1

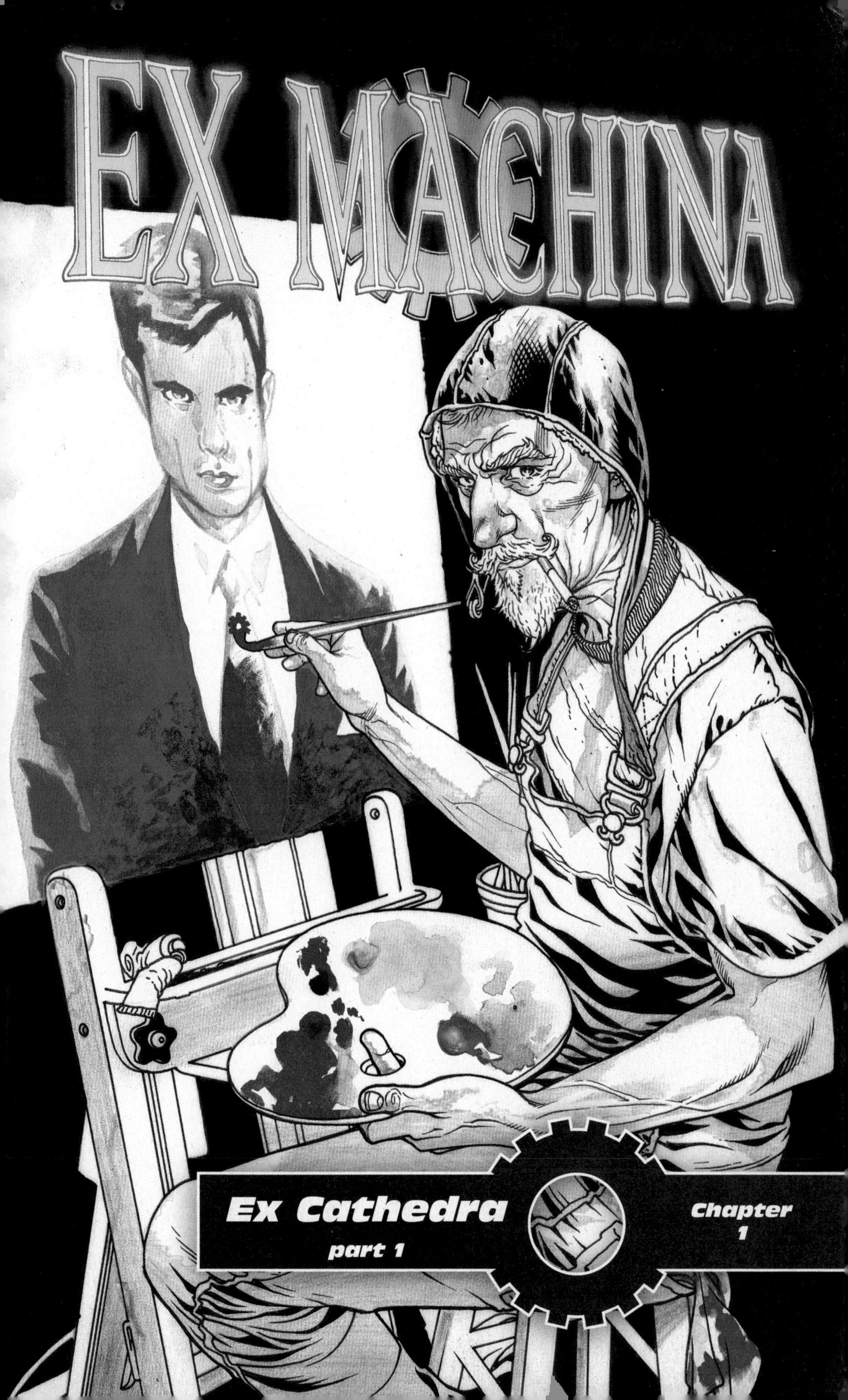
EX MACHINA
Ex Cathedra
part 1
Chapter
1

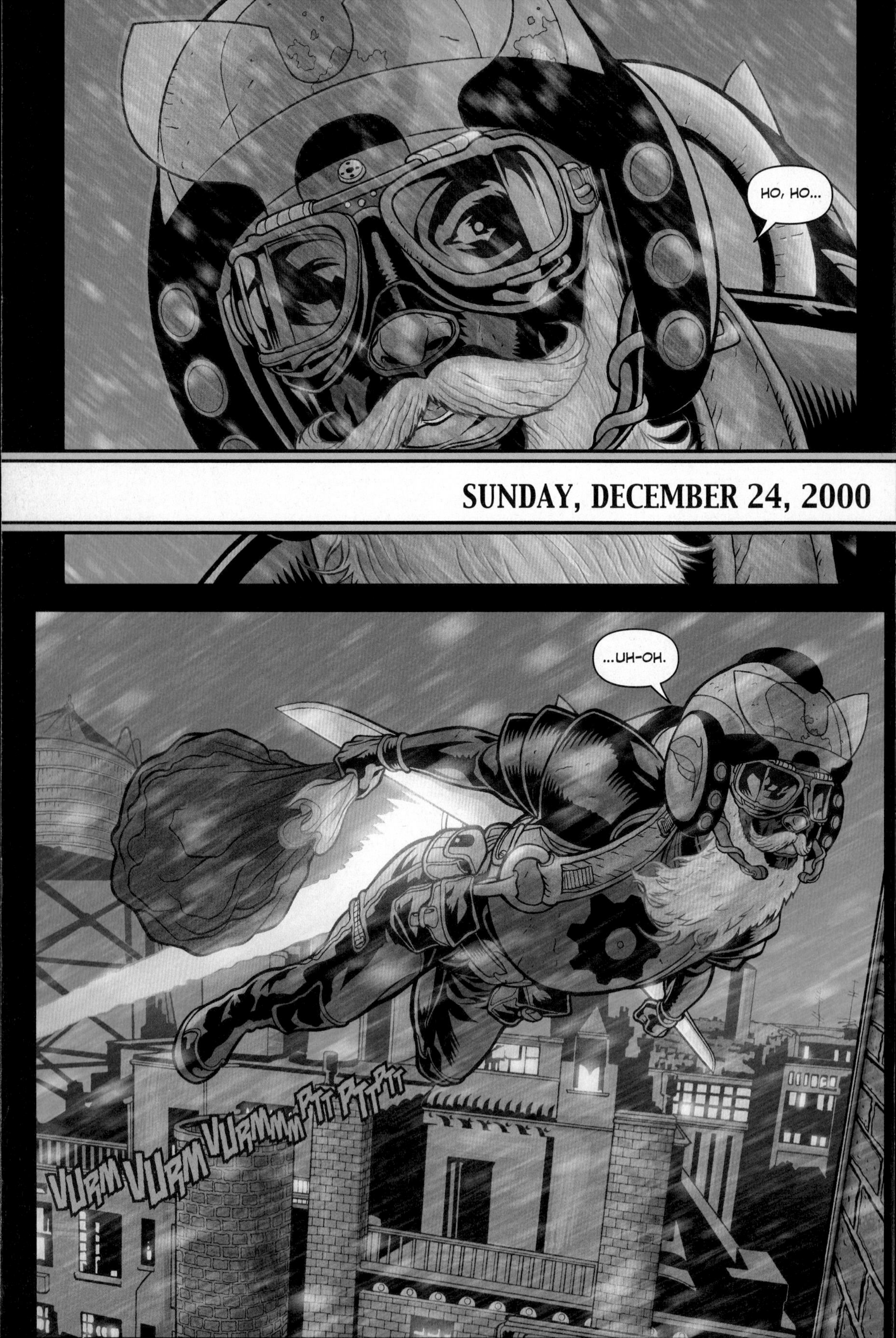
HO, HO...
SUNDAY, DECEMBER 24, 2000
...UH-OH.
VURM VURM VURMMMMPTT PTTPTT

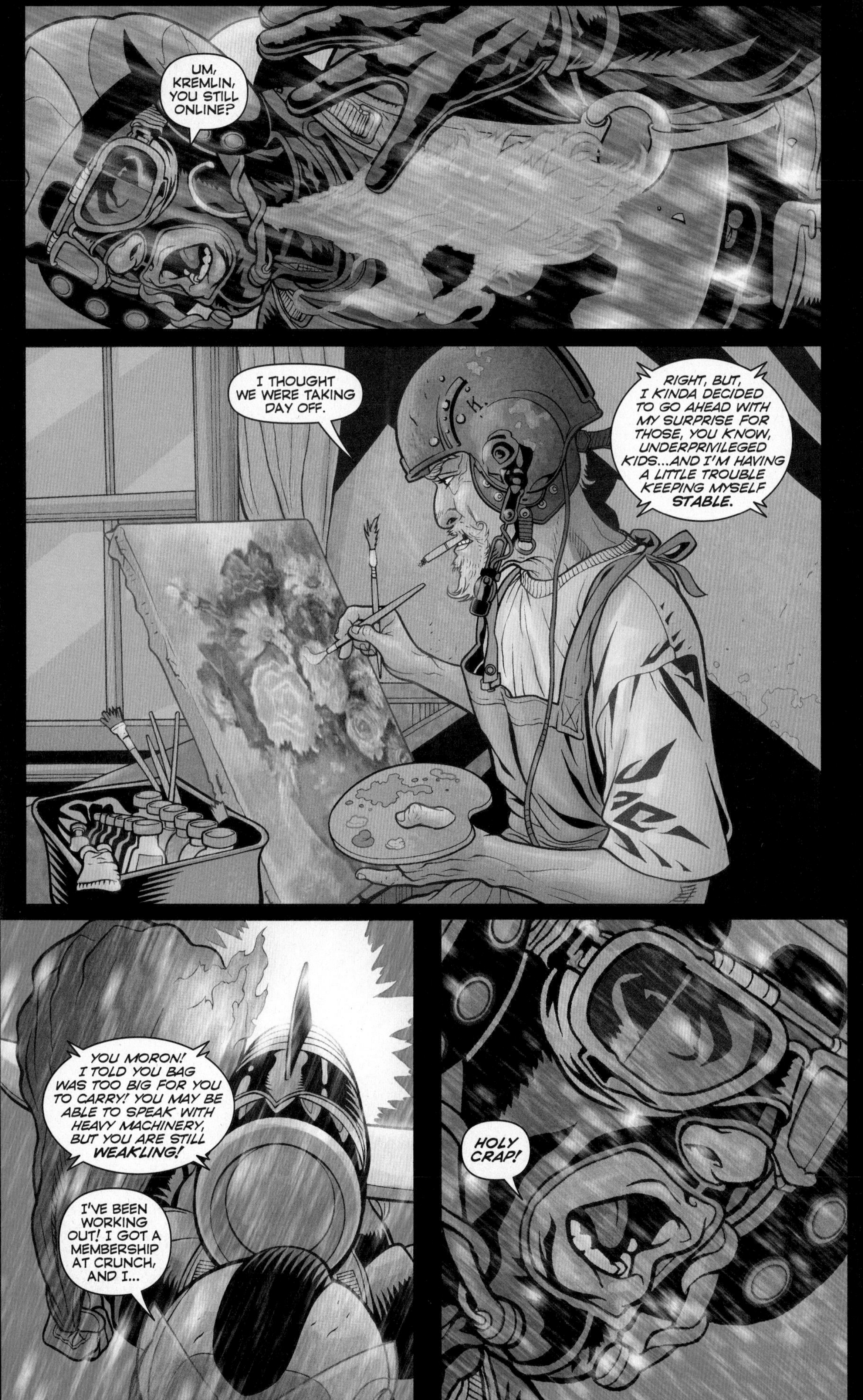
UM, KREMLIN, YOU STILL ONLINE?
I THOUGHT WE WERE TAKING DAY OFF.
RIGHT, BUT, I KINDA DECIDED TO GO AHEAD WITH MY SURPRISE FOR THOSE, YOU KNOW, UNDERPRIVILEGED KIDS...AND I'M HAVING A LITTLE TROUBLE KEEPING MYSELF STABLE.
YOU MORON! I TOLD YOU BAG WAS TOO BIG FOR YOU TO CARRY! YOU MAY BE ABLE TO SPEAK WITH HEAVY MACHINERY, BUT YOU ARE STILL WEAKLING!
I'VE BEEN WORKING OUT! I GOT A MEMBERSHIP AT CRUNCH, AND I...
HOLY CRAP!

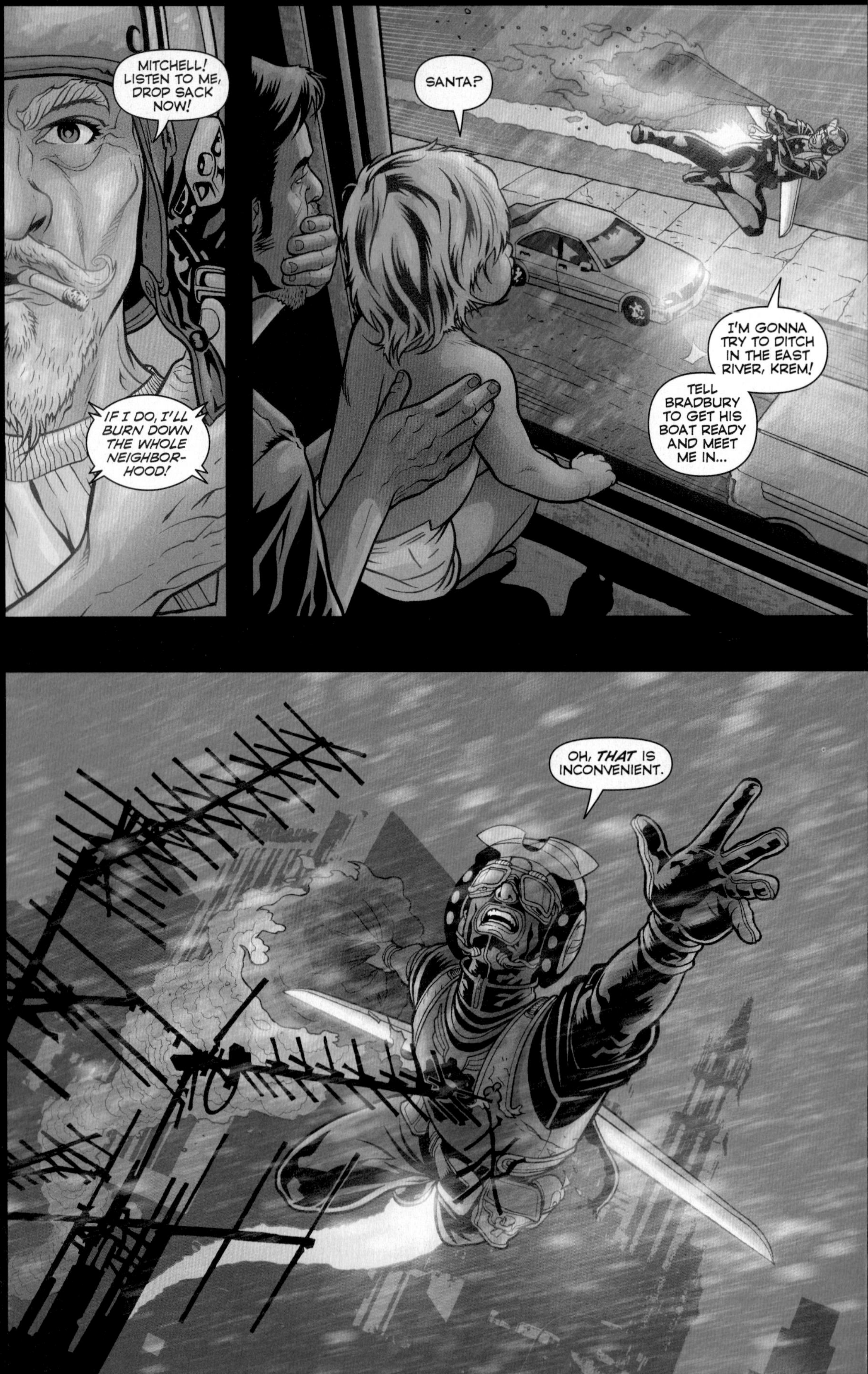
MITCHELL! LISTEN TO ME, DROP SACK NOW!
IF I DO, I'LL BURN DOWN THE WHOLE NEIGHBOR-HOOD!
SANTA?
I'M GONNA TRY TO DITCH IN THE EAST RIVER, KREM!
TELL BRADBURY TO GET HIS BOAT READY AND MEET ME IN...
OH, THAT IS INCONVENIENT.

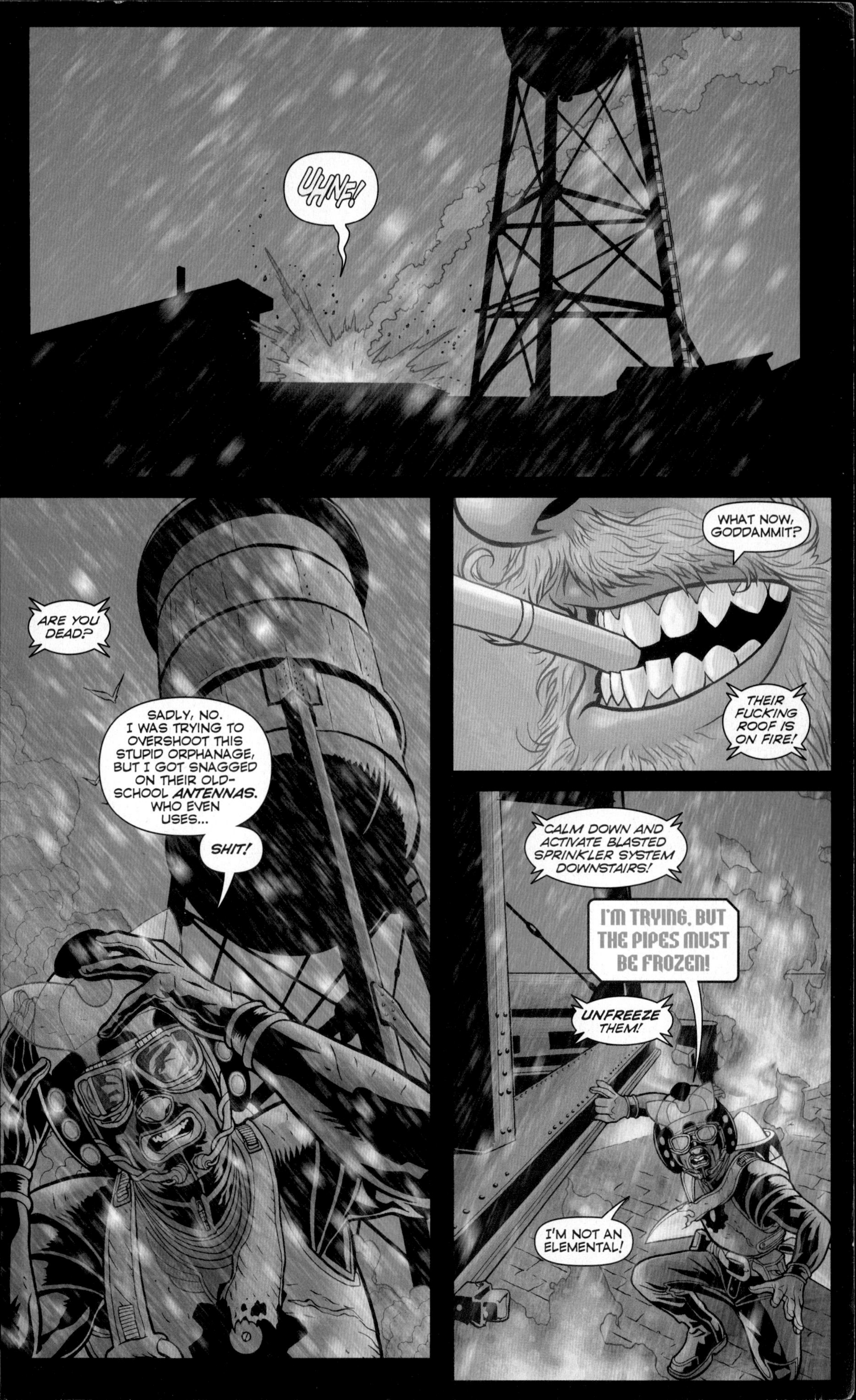
UHNF!
ARE YOU DEAD?
SADLY, NO. I WAS TRYING TO OVERSHOOT THIS STUPID ORPHANAGE, BUT I GOT SNAGGED ON THEIR OLD-SCHOOL *ANTENNAS.* WHO EVEN USES...
SHIT!
WHAT NOW, GODDAMMIT?
THEIR FUCKING ROOF IS ON FIRE!
CALM DOWN AND ACTIVATE BLASTED SPRINKLER SYSTEM DOWNSTAIRS!
I'M TRYING, BUT THE PIPES MUST BE FROZEN!
UNFREEZE THEM!
I'M NOT AN ELEMENTAL!

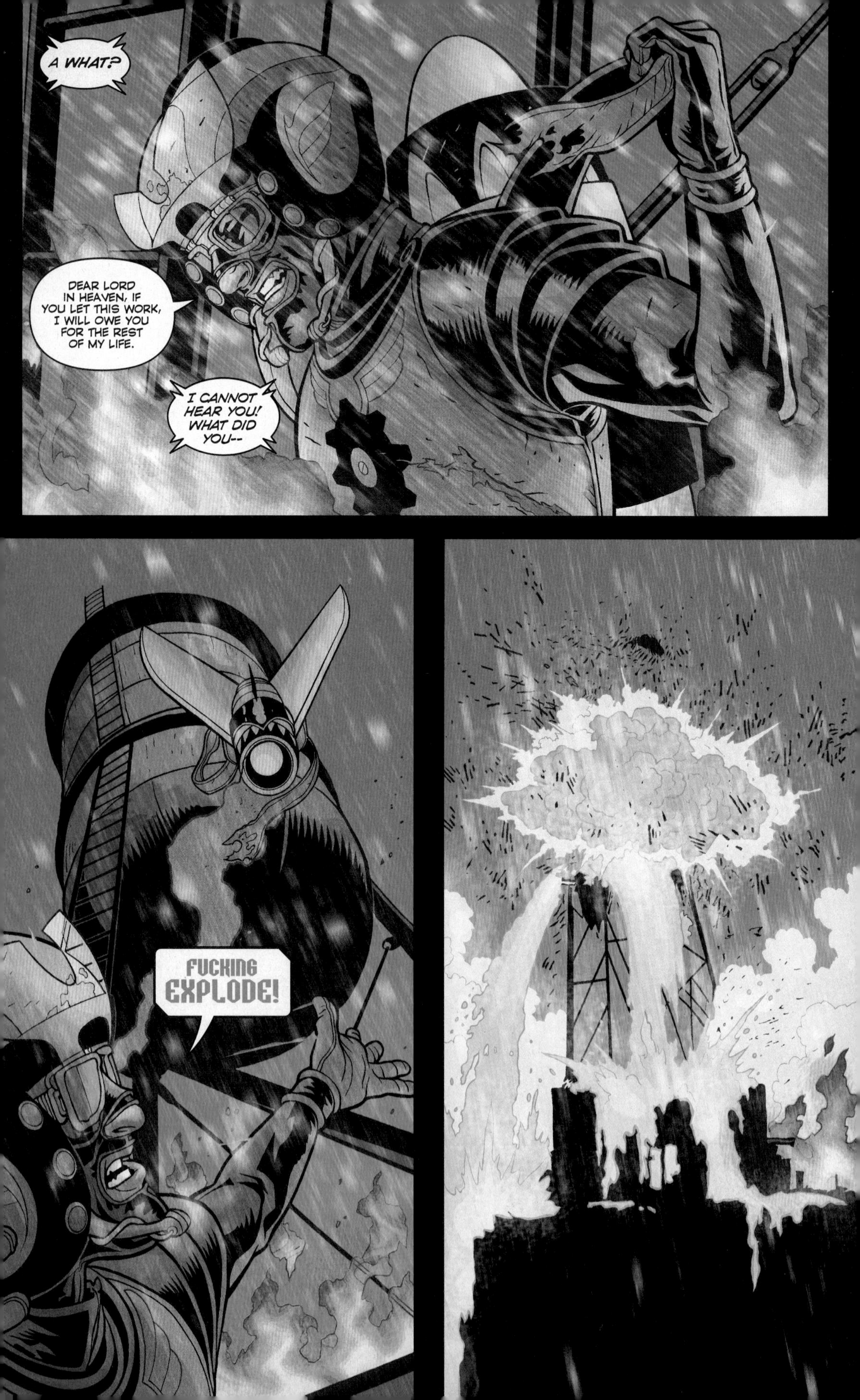
A WHAT?
DEAR LORD IN HEAVEN, IF YOU LET THIS WORK, I WILL OWE YOU FOR THE REST OF MY LIFE.
I CANNOT HEAR YOU! WHAT DID YOU--
FUCKING EXPLODE!

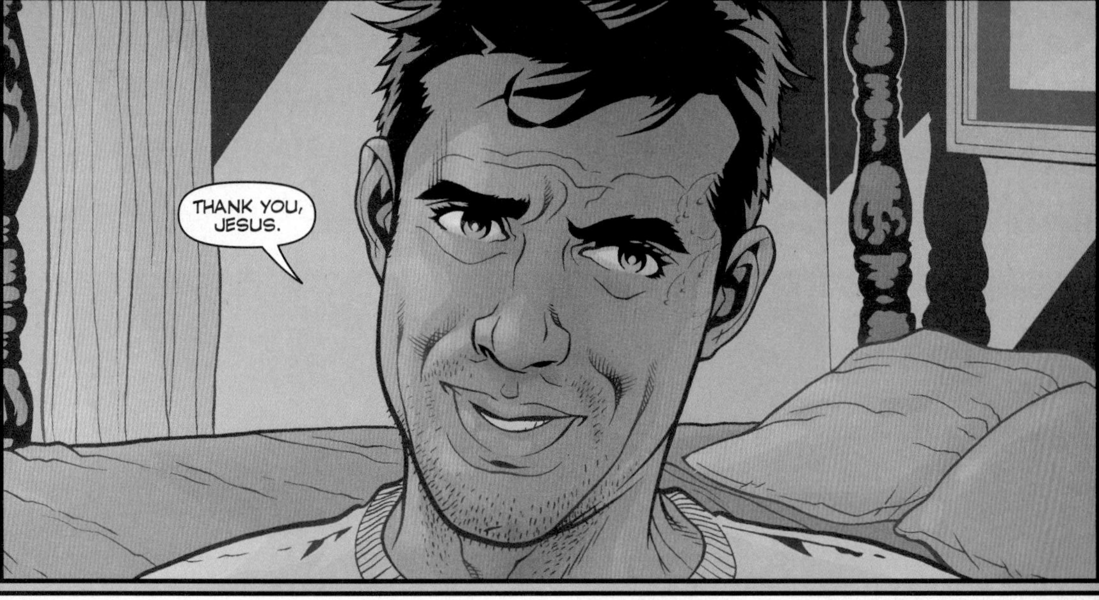
THANK YOU, JESUS.

TUESDAY, DECEMBER 9, 2003

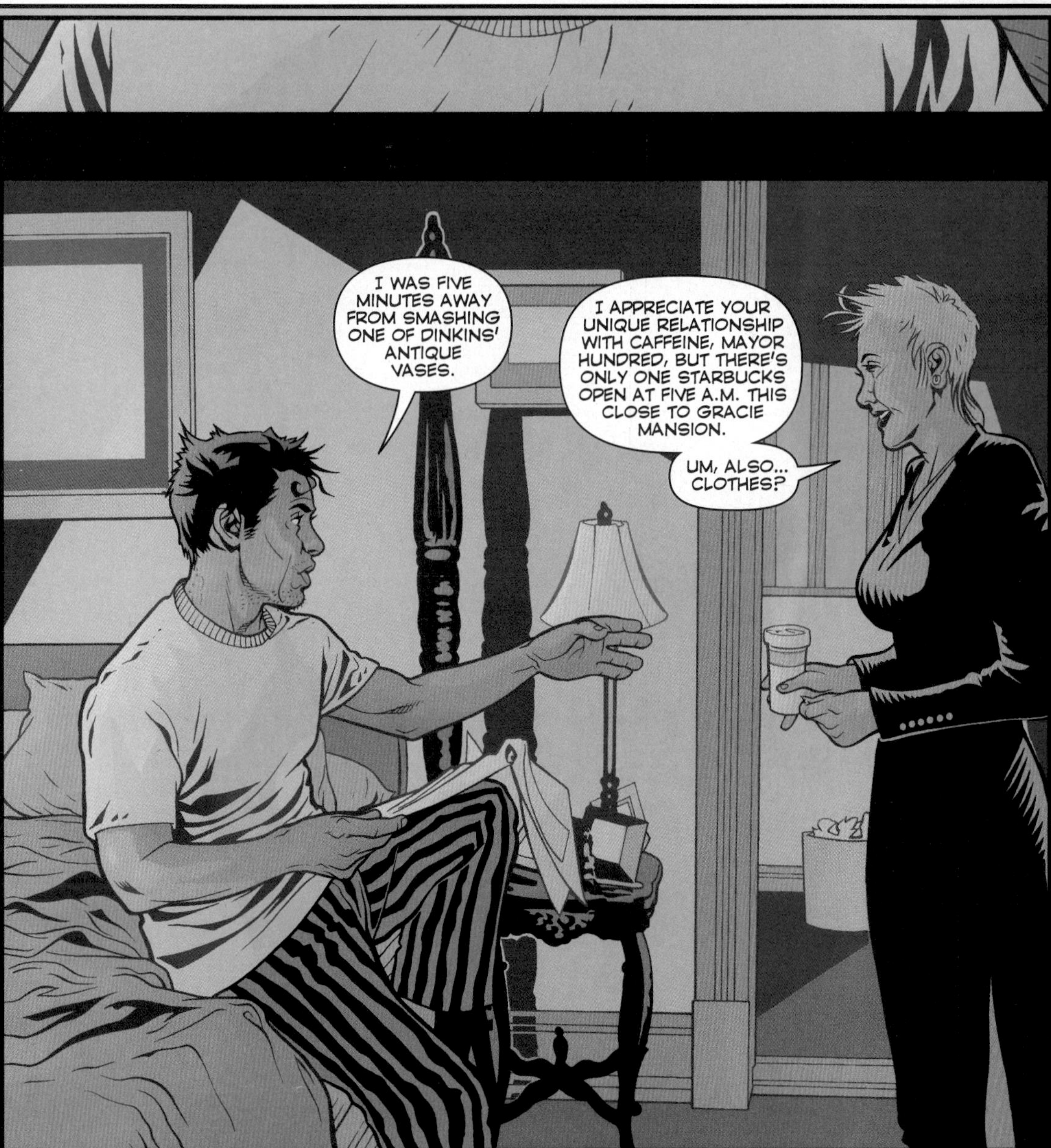
I WAS FIVE MINUTES AWAY FROM SMASHING ONE OF DINKINS' ANTIQUE VASES.
I APPRECIATE YOUR UNIQUE RELATIONSHIP WITH CAFFEINE, MAYOR HUNDRED, BUT THERE'S ONLY ONE STARBUCKS OPEN AT FIVE A.M. THIS CLOSE TO GRACIE MANSION.
UM, ALSO... CLOTHES?

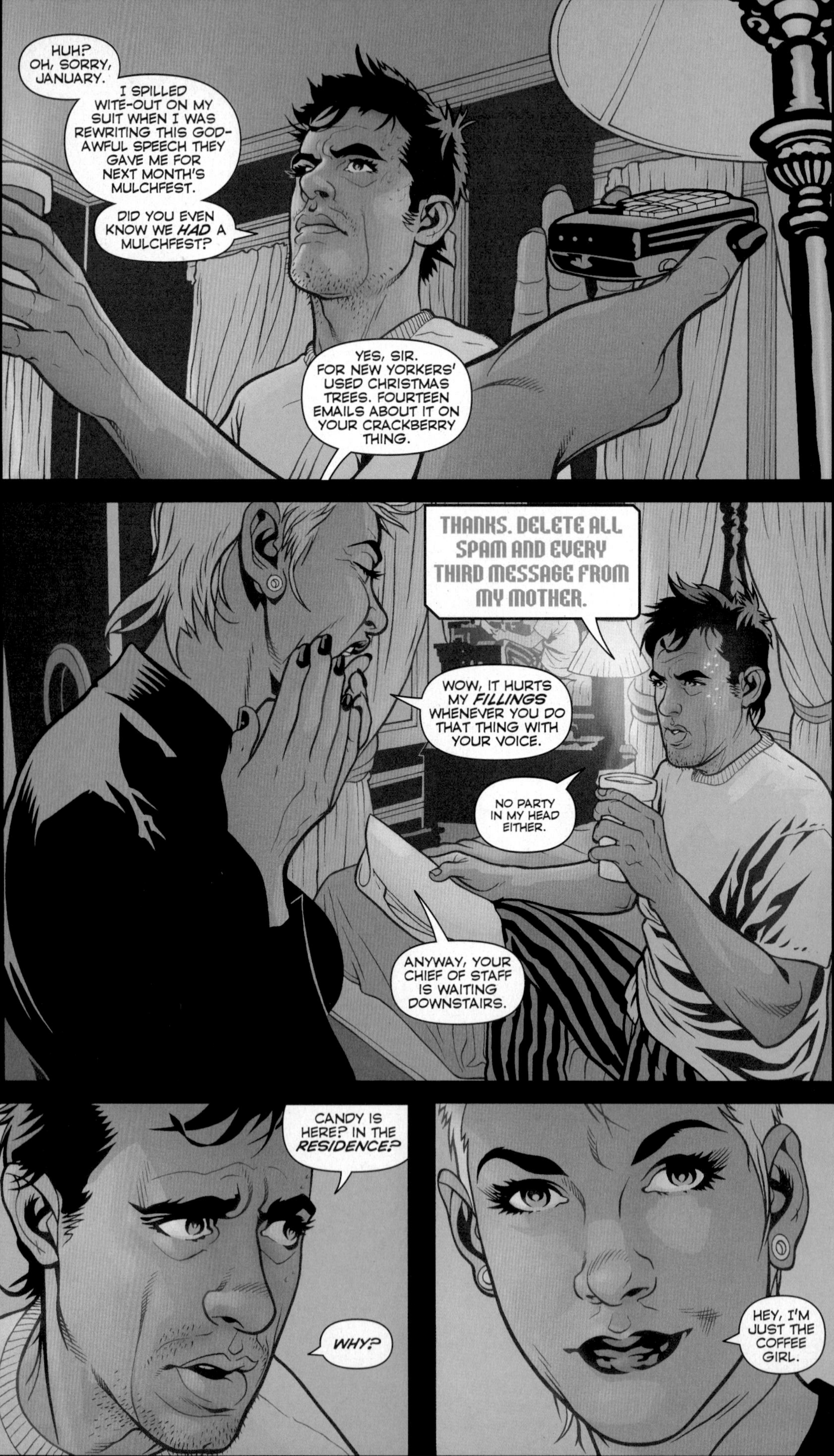

HUH? OH, SORRY, JANUARY.
I SPILLED WITE-OUT ON MY SUIT WHEN I WAS REWRITING THIS GOD-AWFUL SPEECH THEY GAVE ME FOR NEXT MONTH'S MULCHFEST.
DID YOU EVEN KNOW WE *HAD* A MULCHFEST?
YES, SIR. FOR NEW YORKERS' USED CHRISTMAS TREES. FOURTEEN EMAILS ABOUT IT ON YOUR CRACKBERRY THING.
THANKS. DELETE ALL SPAM AND EVERY THIRD MESSAGE FROM MY MOTHER.
WOW, IT HURTS MY *FILLINGS* WHENEVER YOU DO THAT THING WITH YOUR VOICE.
NO PARTY IN MY HEAD EITHER.
ANYWAY, YOUR CHIEF OF STAFF IS WAITING DOWNSTAIRS.
CANDY IS HERE? IN THE *RESIDENCE?*
WHY?
HEY, I'M JUST THE COFFEE GIRL.

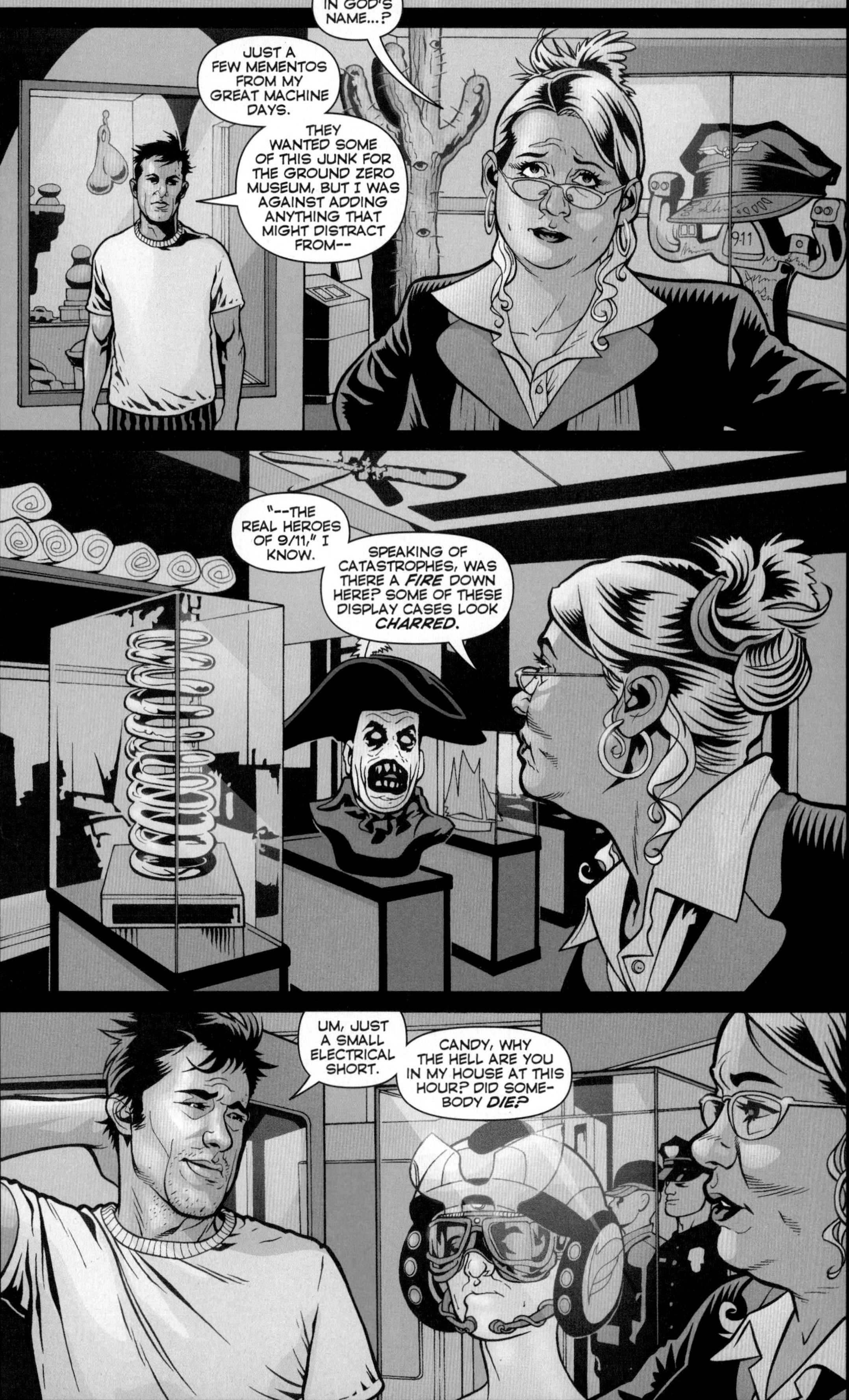
WHAT IN GOD'S NAME...?
JUST A FEW MEMENTOS FROM MY GREAT MACHINE DAYS.
THEY WANTED SOME OF THIS JUNK FOR THE GROUND ZERO MUSEUM, BUT I WAS AGAINST ADDING ANYTHING THAT MIGHT DISTRACT FROM--
"--THE REAL HEROES OF 9/11," I KNOW.
SPEAKING OF CATASTROPHES, WAS THERE A *FIRE* DOWN HERE? SOME OF THESE DISPLAY CASES LOOK ***CHARRED***.
UM, JUST A SMALL ELECTRICAL SHORT.
CANDY, WHY THE HELL ARE YOU IN MY HOUSE AT THIS HOUR? DID SOMEBODY ***DIE?***

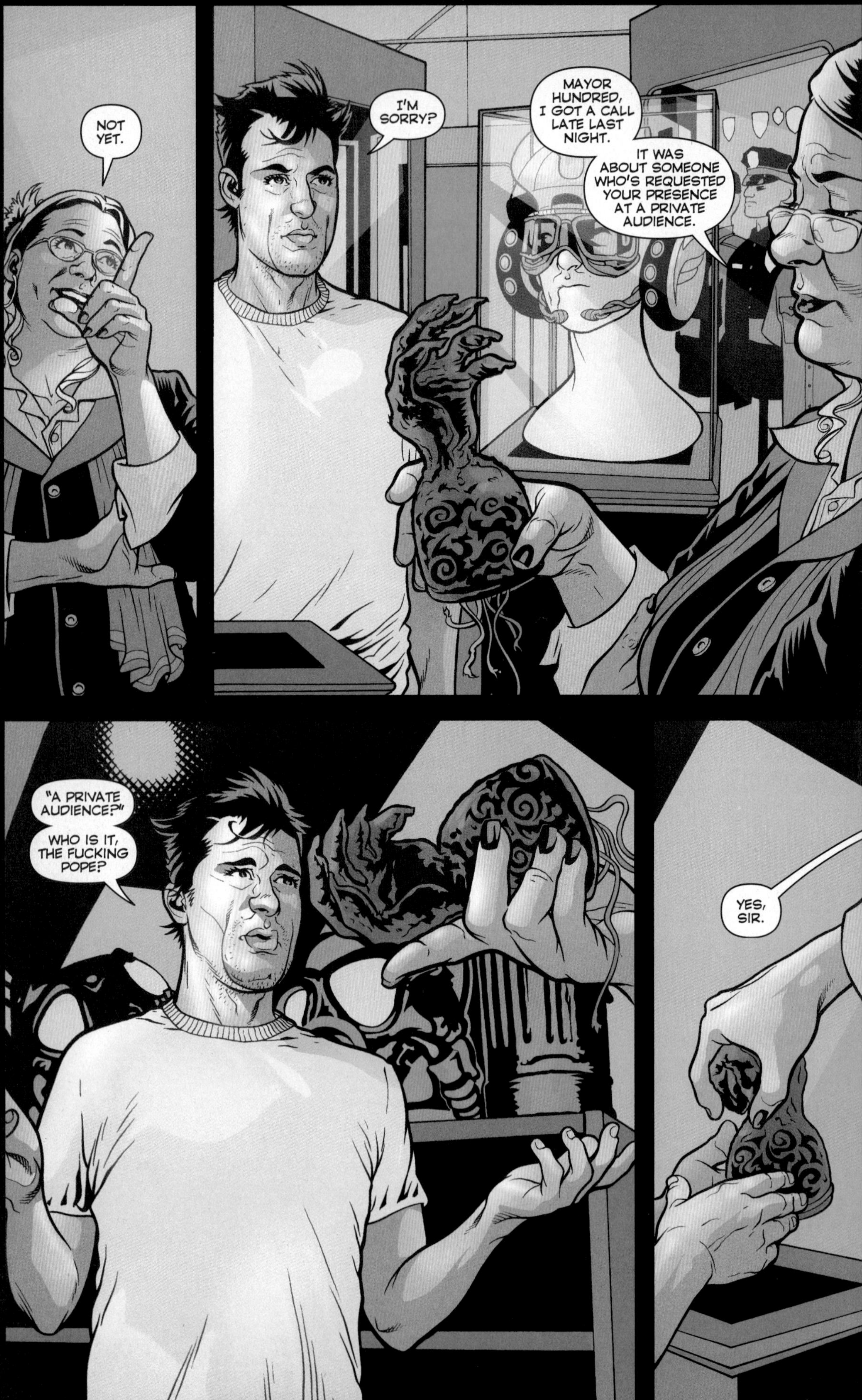

NOT YET.
I'M SORRY?
MAYOR HUNDRED, I GOT A CALL LATE LAST NIGHT.
IT WAS ABOUT SOMEONE WHO'S REQUESTED YOUR PRESENCE AT A PRIVATE AUDIENCE.
"A PRIVATE AUDIENCE?"
WHO IS IT, THE FUCKING POPE?
YES, SIR.

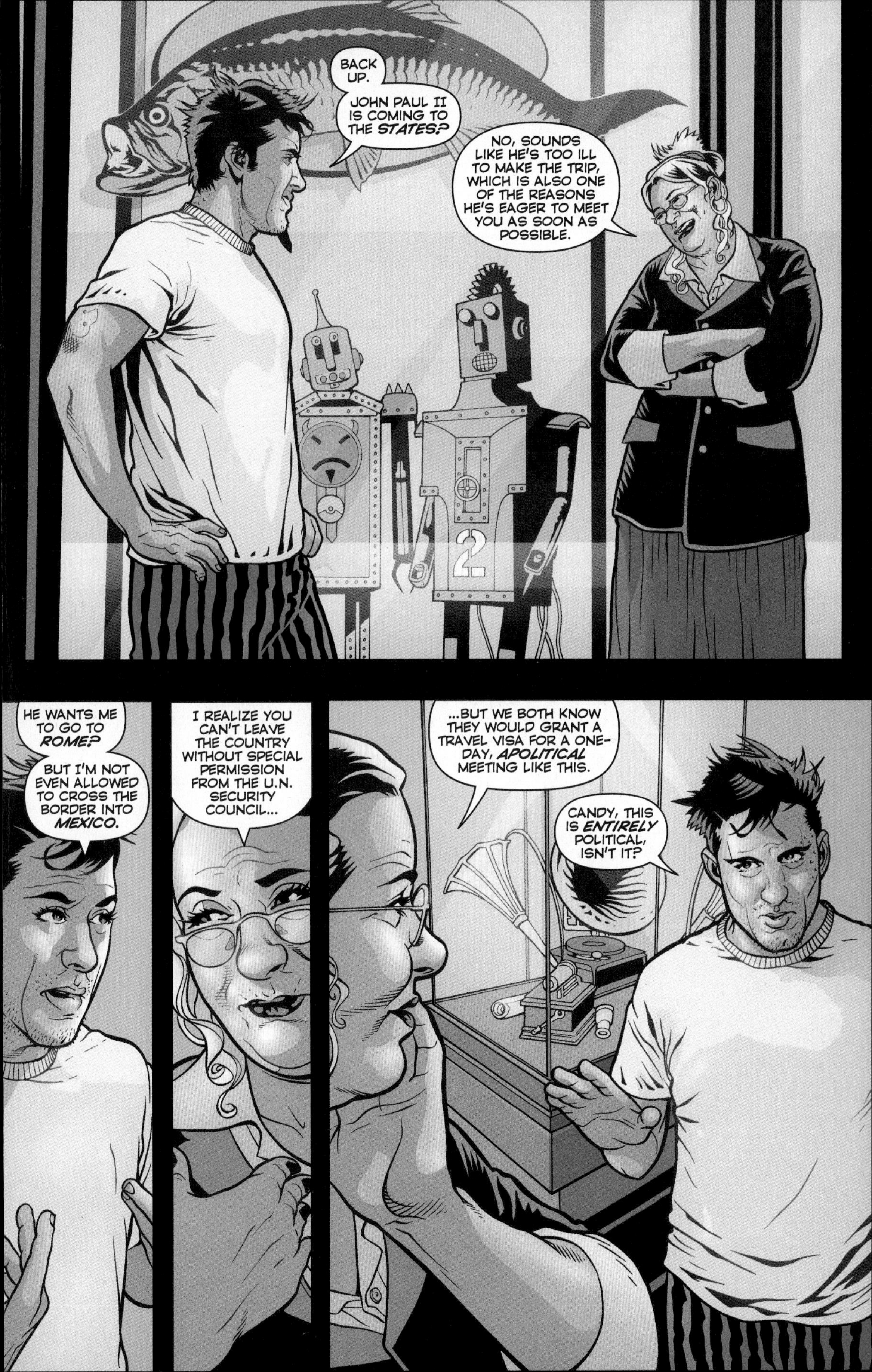
BACK UP.
JOHN PAUL II IS COMING TO THE *STATES?*
NO, SOUNDS LIKE HE'S TOO ILL TO MAKE THE TRIP, WHICH IS ALSO ONE OF THE REASONS HE'S EAGER TO MEET YOU AS SOON AS POSSIBLE.
HE WANTS ME TO GO TO *ROME?*
BUT I'M NOT EVEN ALLOWED TO CROSS THE BORDER INTO *MEXICO*.
I REALIZE YOU CAN'T LEAVE THE COUNTRY WITHOUT SPECIAL PERMISSION FROM THE U.N. SECURITY COUNCIL...
...BUT WE BOTH KNOW THEY WOULD GRANT A TRAVEL VISA FOR A ONE-DAY, *APOLITICAL* MEETING LIKE THIS.
CANDY, THIS IS *ENTIRELY* POLITICAL, ISN'T IT?
2

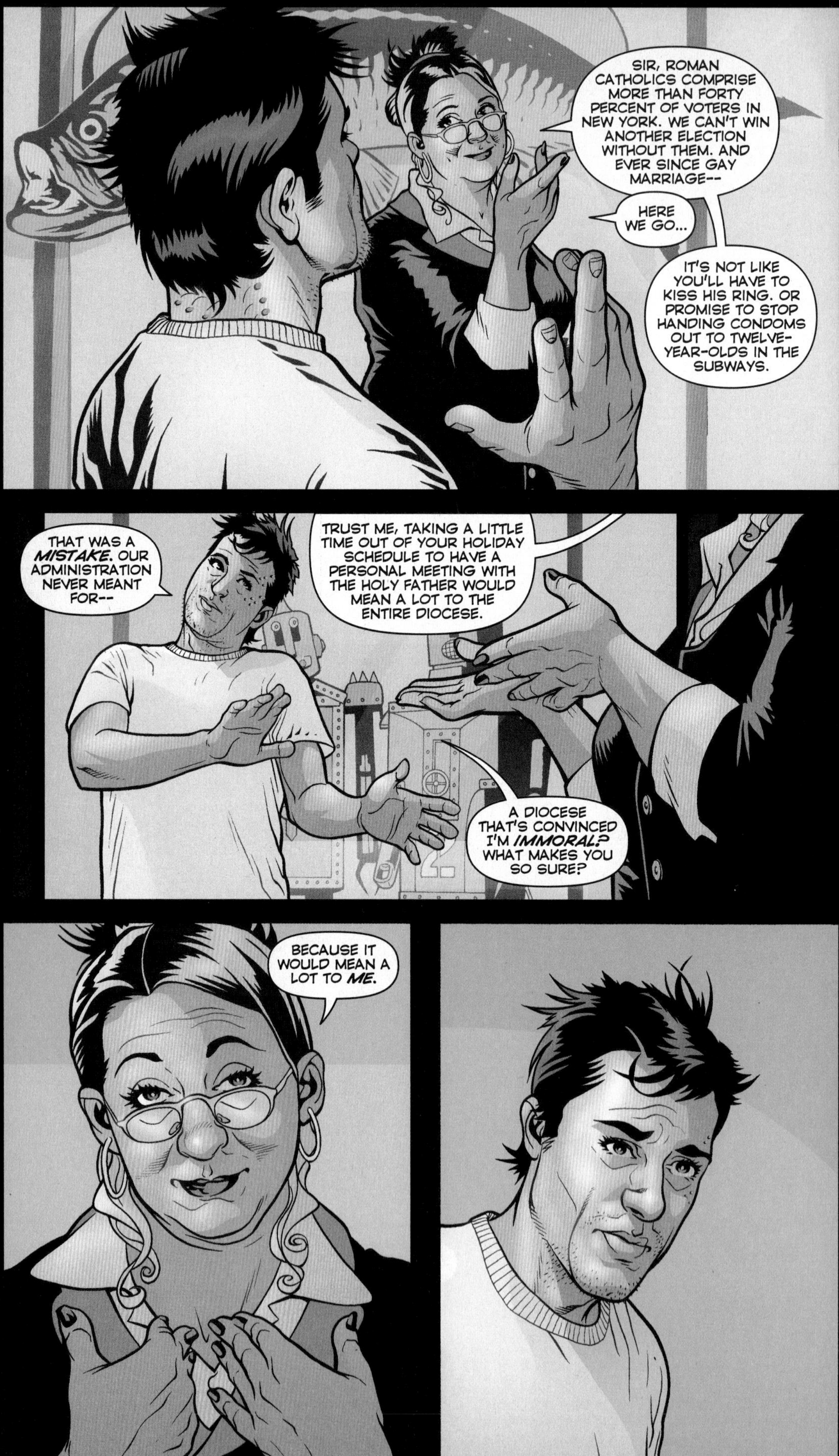
SIR, ROMAN CATHOLICS COMPRISE MORE THAN FORTY PERCENT OF VOTERS IN NEW YORK. WE CAN'T WIN ANOTHER ELECTION WITHOUT THEM. AND EVER SINCE GAY MARRIAGE--
HERE WE GO...
IT'S NOT LIKE YOU'LL HAVE TO KISS HIS RING. OR PROMISE TO STOP HANDING CONDOMS OUT TO TWELVE-YEAR-OLDS IN THE SUBWAYS.
THAT WAS A *MISTAKE*. OUR ADMINISTRATION NEVER MEANT FOR--
TRUST ME, TAKING A LITTLE TIME OUT OF YOUR HOLIDAY SCHEDULE TO HAVE A PERSONAL MEETING WITH THE HOLY FATHER WOULD MEAN A LOT TO THE ENTIRE DIOCESE.
A DIOCESE THAT'S CONVINCED I'M *IMMORAL?* WHAT MAKES YOU SO SURE?
BECAUSE IT WOULD MEAN A LOT TO *ME*.

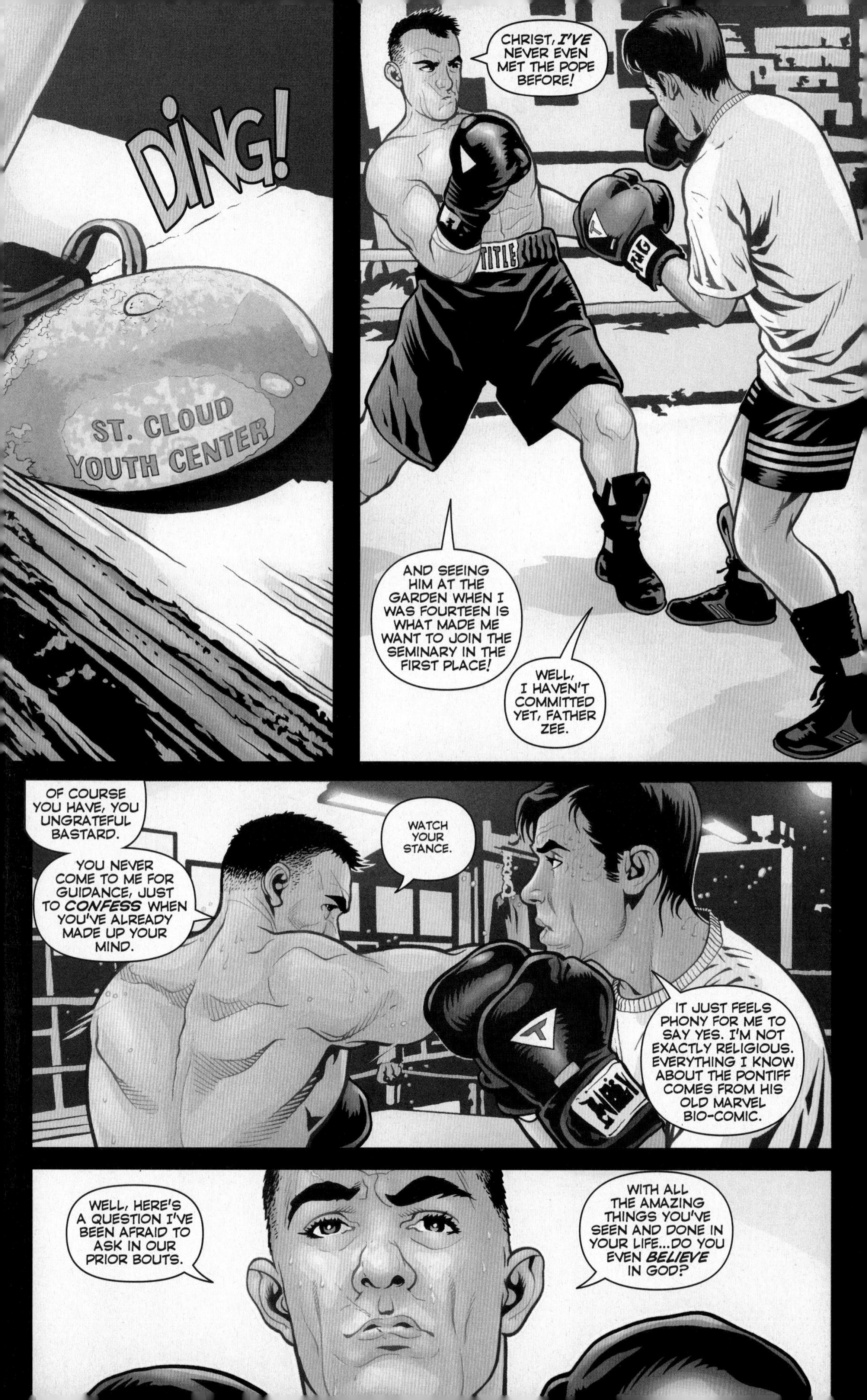
DING!
ST. CLOUD YOUTH CENTER
CHRIST, I'VE NEVER EVEN MET THE POPE BEFORE!
TITLE
AND SEEING HIM AT THE GARDEN WHEN I WAS FOURTEEN IS WHAT MADE ME WANT TO JOIN THE SEMINARY IN THE FIRST PLACE!
WELL, I HAVEN'T COMMITTED YET, FATHER ZEE.
OF COURSE YOU HAVE, YOU UNGRATEFUL BASTARD.
YOU NEVER COME TO ME FOR GUIDANCE, JUST TO CONFESS WHEN YOU'VE ALREADY MADE UP YOUR MIND.
WATCH YOUR STANCE.
IT JUST FEELS PHONY FOR ME TO SAY YES. I'M NOT EXACTLY RELIGIOUS. EVERYTHING I KNOW ABOUT THE PONTIFF COMES FROM HIS OLD MARVEL BIO-COMIC.
WELL, HERE'S A QUESTION I'VE BEEN AFRAID TO ASK IN OUR PRIOR BOUTS.
WITH ALL THE AMAZING THINGS YOU'VE SEEN AND DONE IN YOUR LIFE...DO YOU EVEN BELIEVE IN GOD?

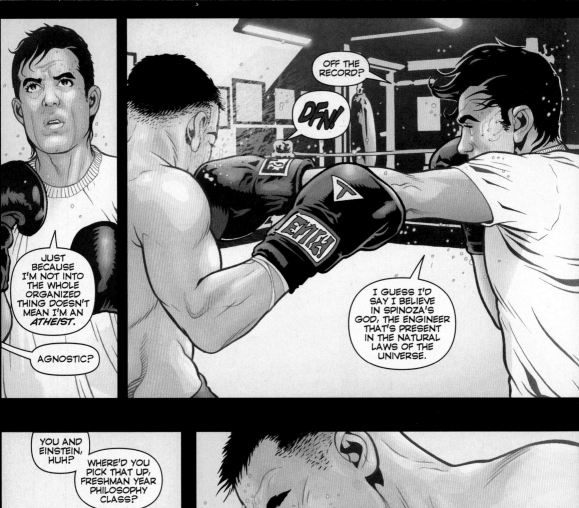

JUST BECAUSE I'M NOT INTO THE WHOLE ORGANIZED THING DOESN'T MEAN I'M AN *ATHEIST.*

AGNOSTIC?

OFF THE RECORD?

DFN!

I GUESS I'D SAY I BELIEVE IN SPINOZA'S GOD, THE ENGINEER THAT'S PRESENT IN THE NATURAL LAWS OF THE UNIVERSE.

YOU AND EINSTEIN, HUH?

WHERE'D YOU PICK THAT UP, FRESHMAN YEAR PHILOSOPHY CLASS?

WHOMP

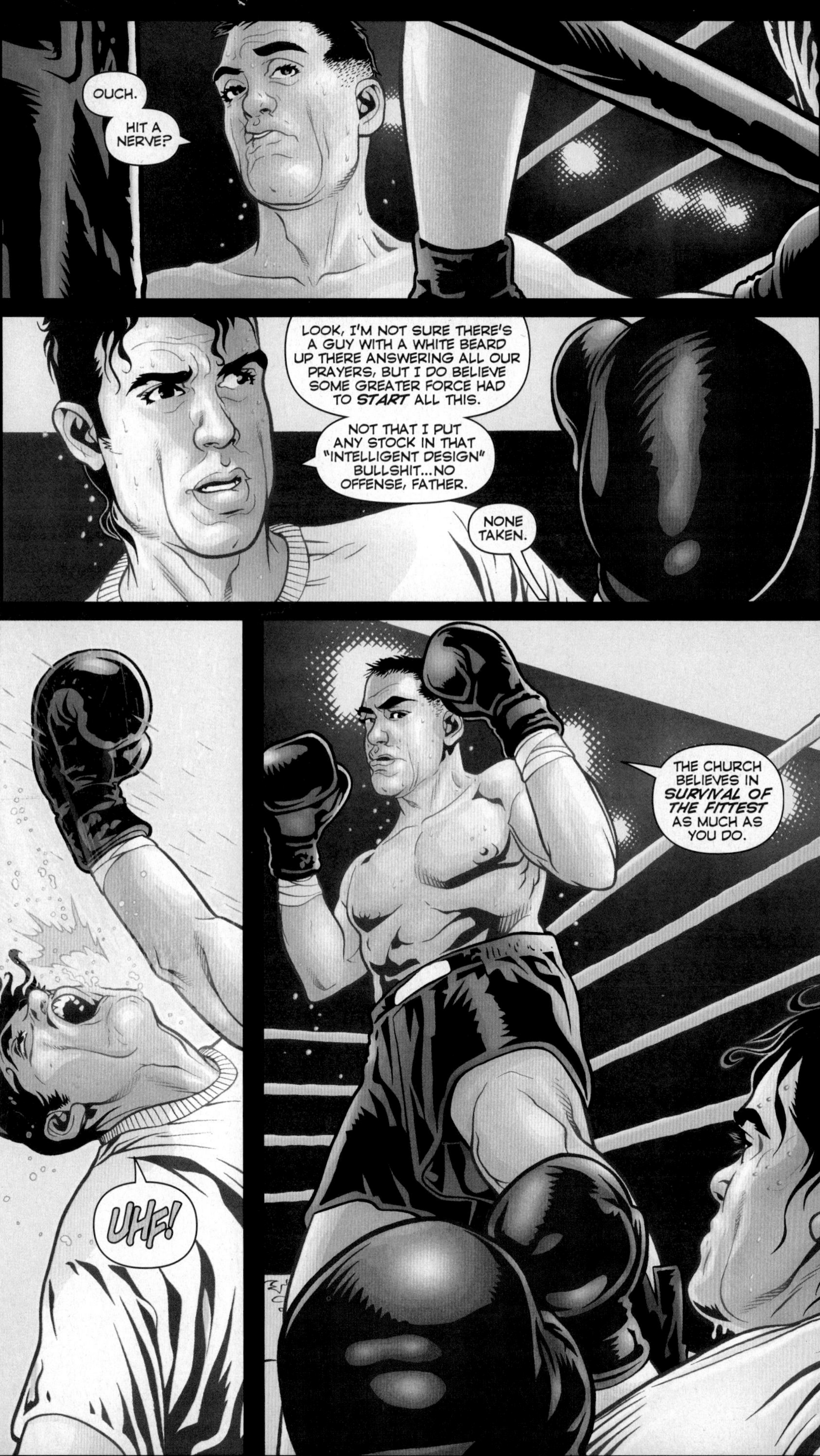
OUCH.
HIT A NERVE?
LOOK, I'M NOT SURE THERE'S A GUY WITH A WHITE BEARD UP THERE ANSWERING ALL OUR PRAYERS, BUT I DO BELIEVE SOME GREATER FORCE HAD TO *START* ALL THIS.
NOT THAT I PUT ANY STOCK IN THAT "INTELLIGENT DESIGN" BULLSHIT...NO OFFENSE, FATHER.
NONE TAKEN.
UHF!
THE CHURCH BELIEVES IN *SURVIVAL OF THE FITTEST* AS MUCH AS YOU DO.

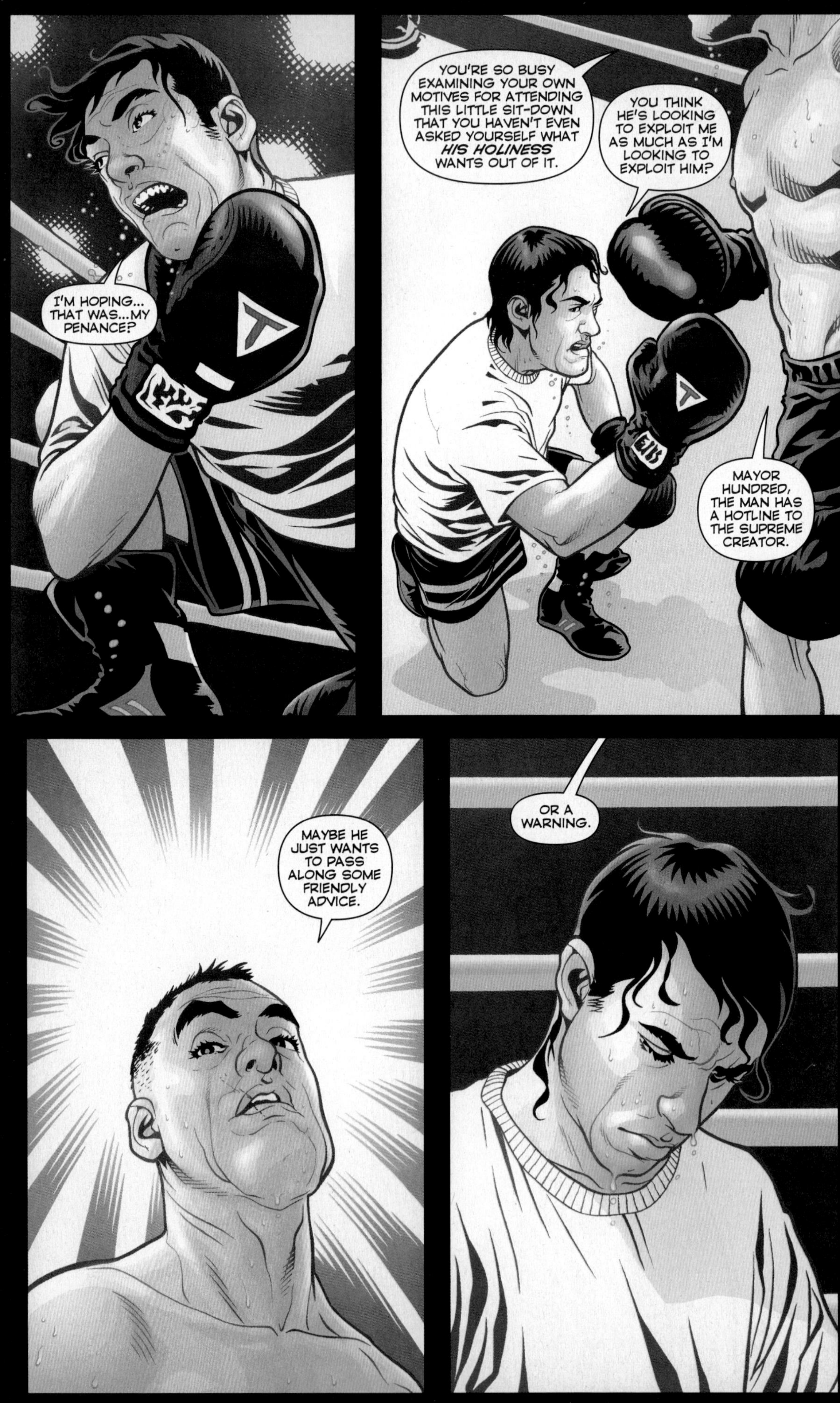
I'M HOPING... THAT WAS...MY PENANCE?
YOU'RE SO BUSY EXAMINING YOUR OWN MOTIVES FOR ATTENDING THIS LITTLE SIT-DOWN THAT YOU HAVEN'T EVEN ASKED YOURSELF WHAT HIS HOLINESS WANTS OUT OF IT.
YOU THINK HE'S LOOKING TO EXPLOIT ME AS MUCH AS I'M LOOKING TO EXPLOIT HIM?
MAYOR HUNDRED, THE MAN HAS A HOTLINE TO THE SUPREME CREATOR.
MAYBE HE JUST WANTS TO PASS ALONG SOME FRIENDLY ADVICE.
OR A WARNING.

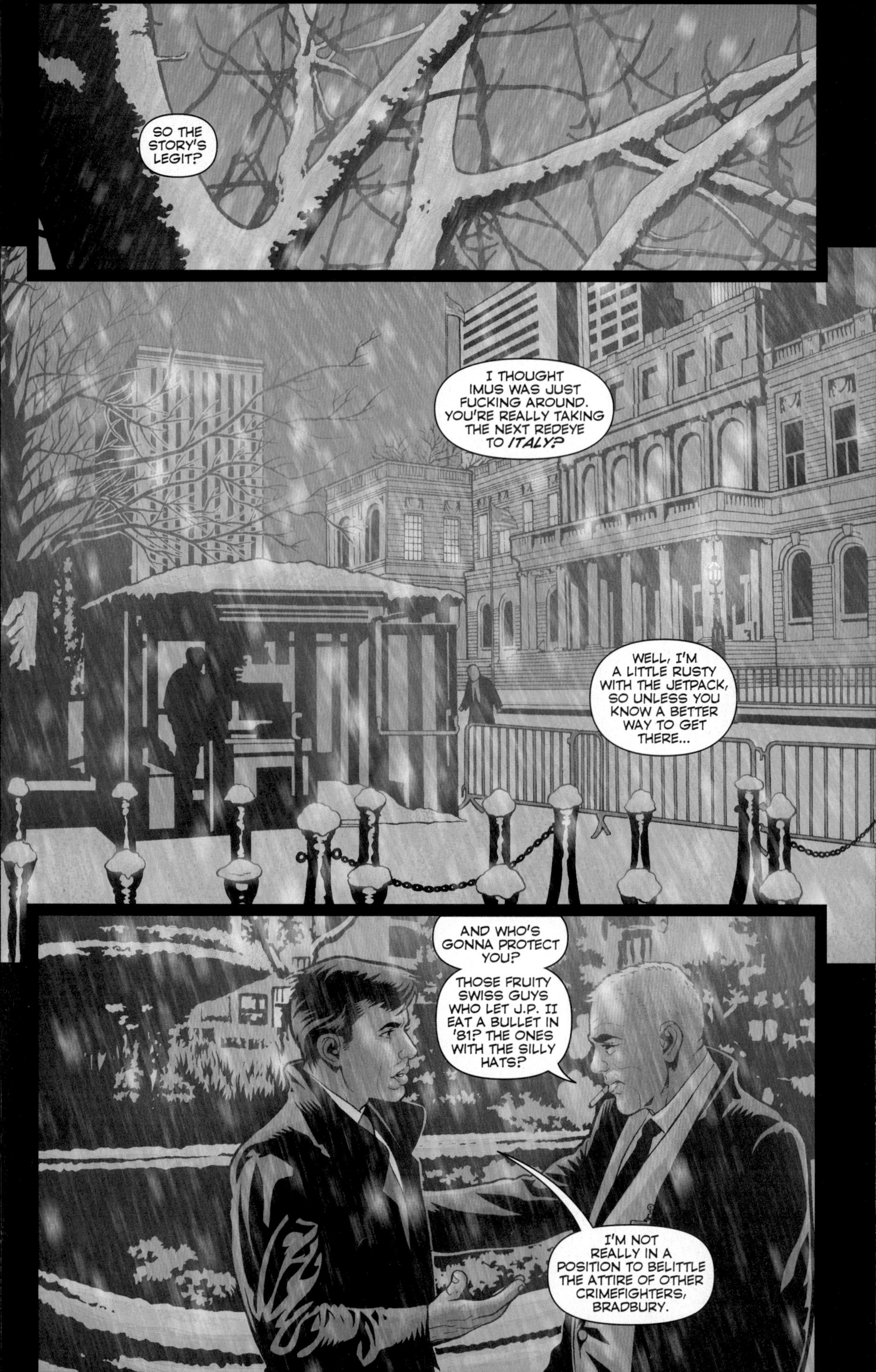
SO THE STORY'S LEGIT?
I THOUGHT IMUS WAS JUST FUCKING AROUND. YOU'RE REALLY TAKING THE NEXT REDEYE TO ITALY?
WELL, I'M A LITTLE RUSTY WITH THE JETPACK, SO UNLESS YOU KNOW A BETTER WAY TO GET THERE...
AND WHO'S GONNA PROTECT YOU?
THOSE FRUITY SWISS GUYS WHO LET J.P. II EAT A BULLET IN '81? THE ONES WITH THE SILLY HATS?
I'M NOT REALLY IN A POSITION TO BELITTLE THE ATTIRE OF OTHER CRIMEFIGHTERS, BRADBURY.

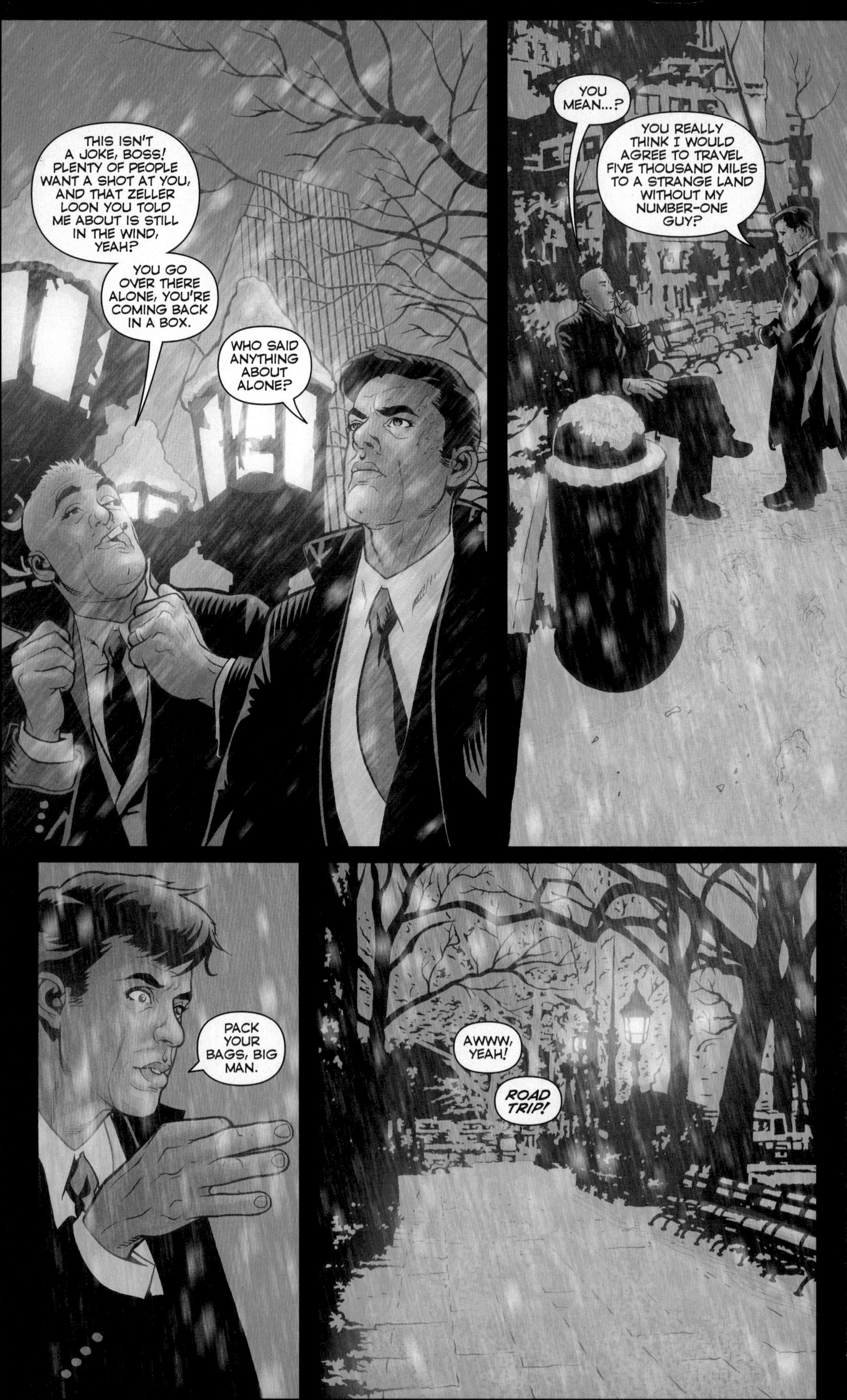
THIS ISN'T A JOKE, BOSS! PLENTY OF PEOPLE WANT A SHOT AT YOU, AND THAT ZELLER LOON YOU TOLD ME ABOUT IS STILL IN THE WIND, YEAH?
YOU GO OVER THERE ALONE, YOU'RE COMING BACK IN A BOX.
WHO SAID ANYTHING ABOUT ALONE?
YOU MEAN...?
YOU REALLY THINK I WOULD AGREE TO TRAVEL FIVE THOUSAND MILES TO A STRANGE LAND WITHOUT MY NUMBER-ONE GUY?
PACK YOUR BAGS, BIG MAN.
AWWW, YEAH!
ROAD TRIP!

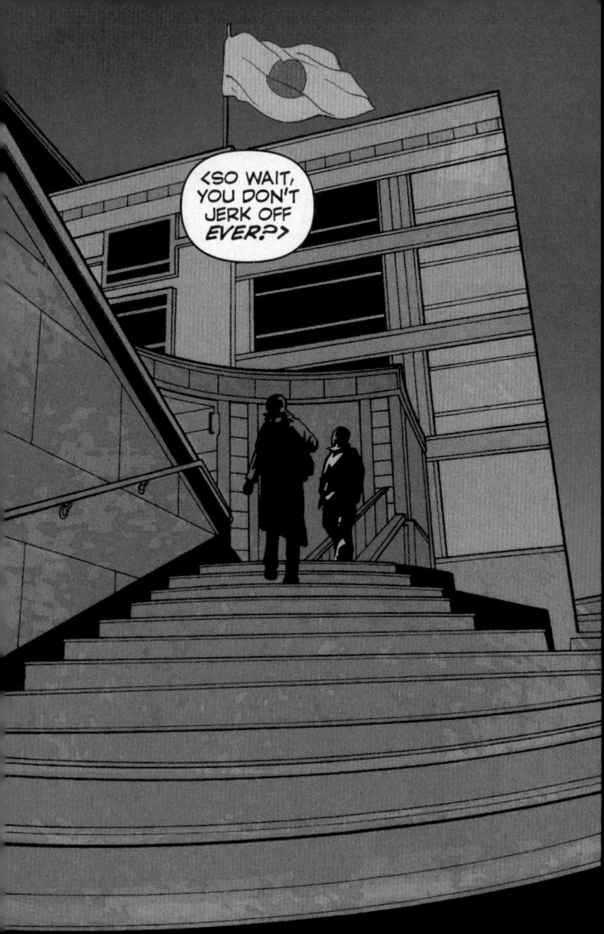
<SO WAIT, YOU DON'T JERK OFF *EVER?*>

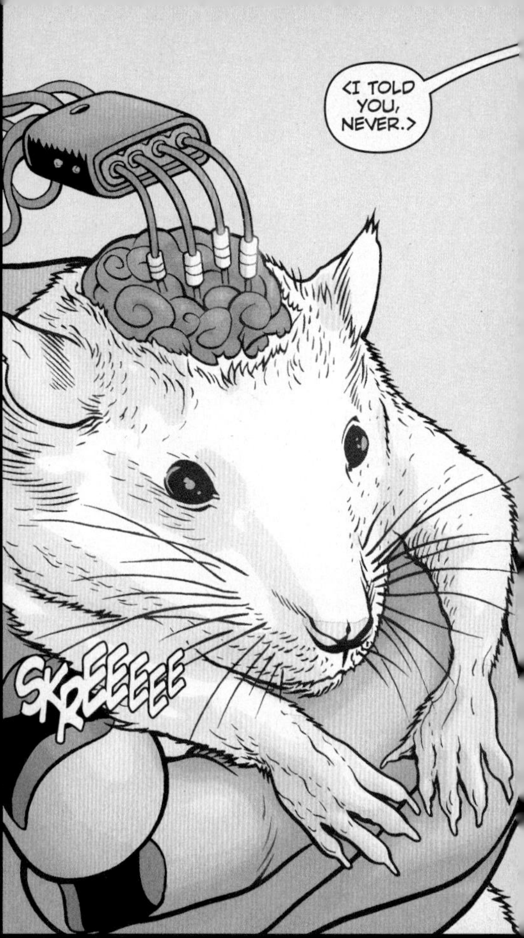
<I TOLD YOU, NEVER.>
SKREEEEEE

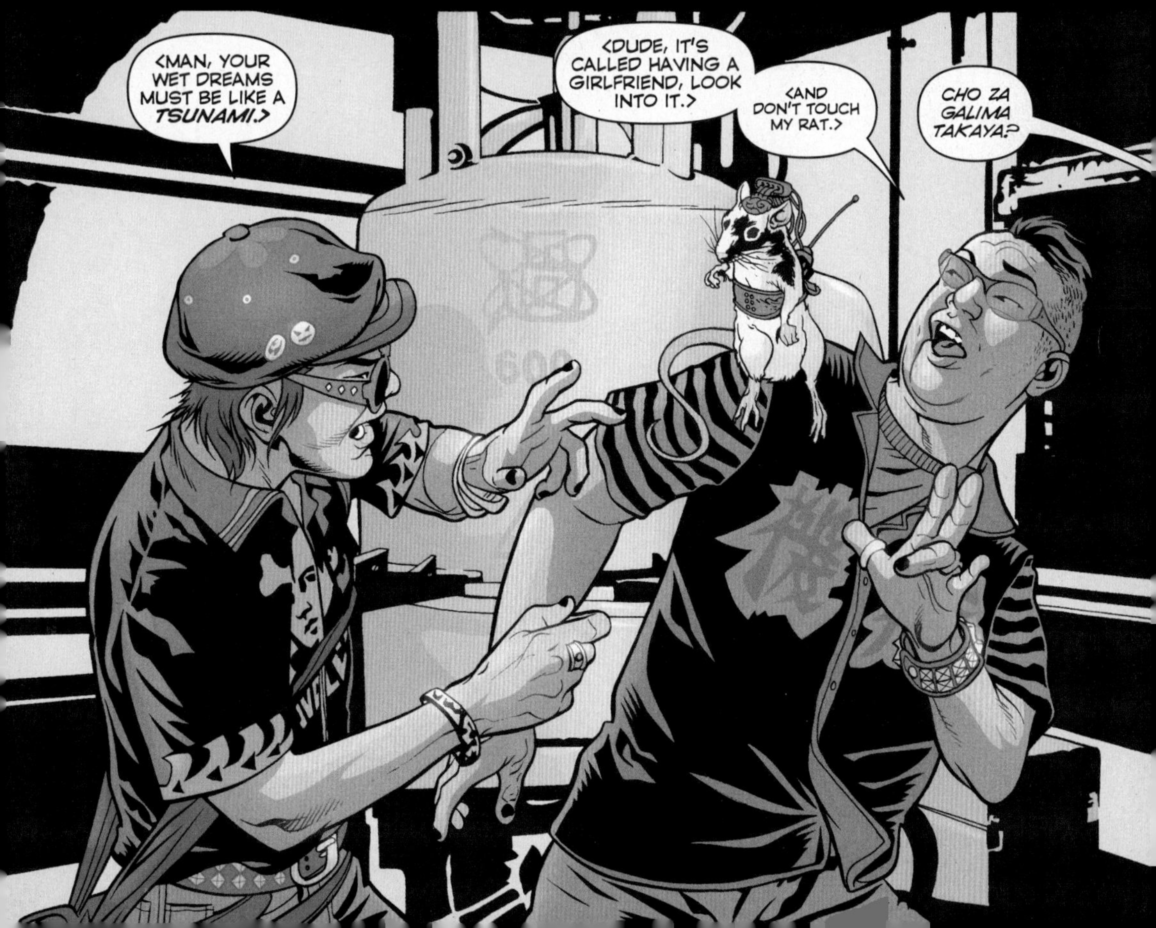
<MAN, YOUR WET DREAMS MUST BE LIKE A *TSUNAMI.*>
<DUDE, IT'S CALLED HAVING A GIRLFRIEND, LOOK INTO IT.>
<AND DON'T TOUCH MY RAT.>
CHO ZA GALIMA TAKAYA?

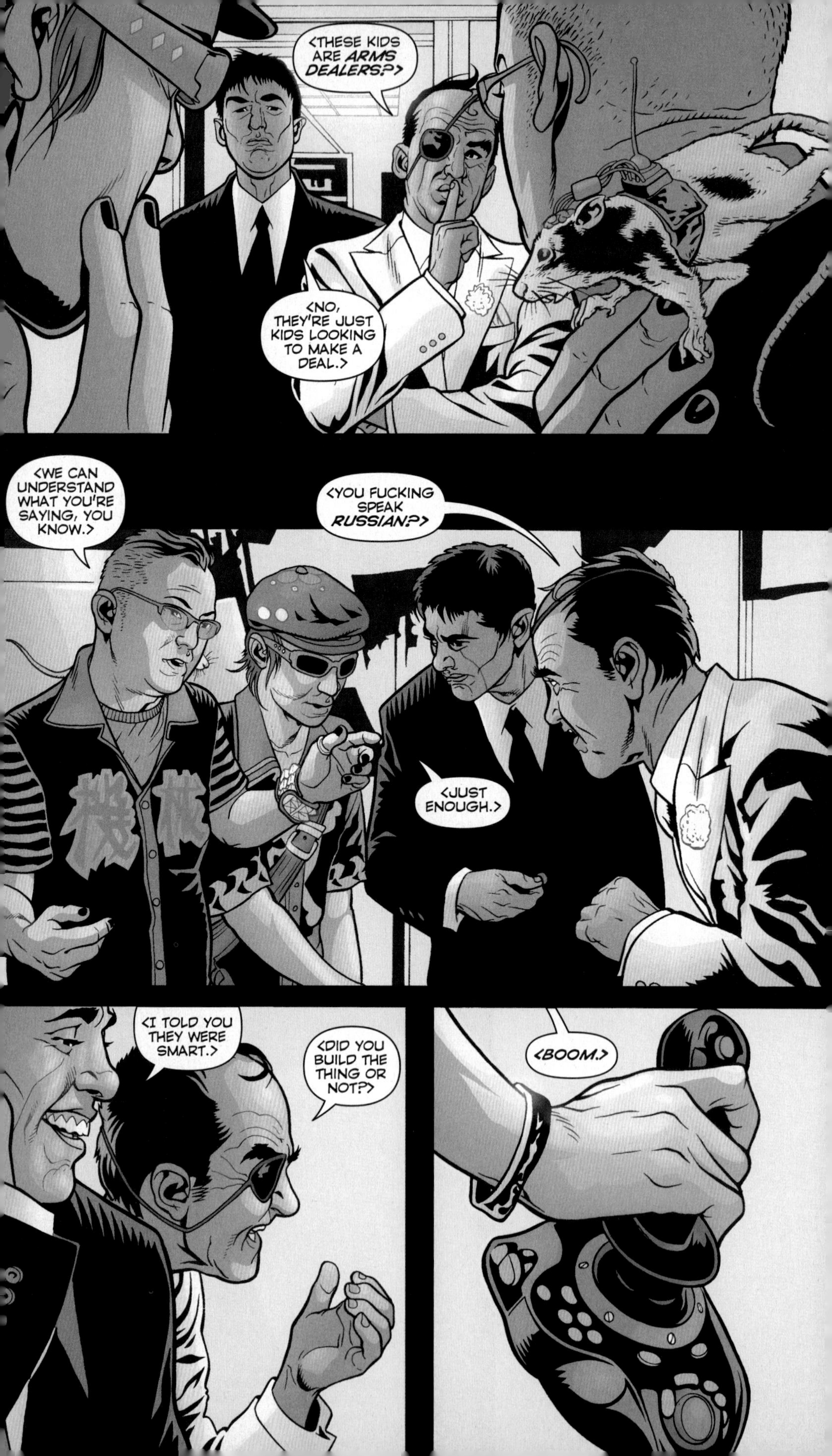

<THESE KIDS ARE ARMS DEALERS?>
<NO, THEY'RE JUST KIDS LOOKING TO MAKE A DEAL.>
<WE CAN UNDERSTAND WHAT YOU'RE SAYING, YOU KNOW.>
<YOU FUCKING SPEAK RUSSIAN?>
<JUST ENOUGH.>
<I TOLD YOU THEY WERE SMART.>
<DID YOU BUILD THE THING OR NOT?>
<BOOM.>

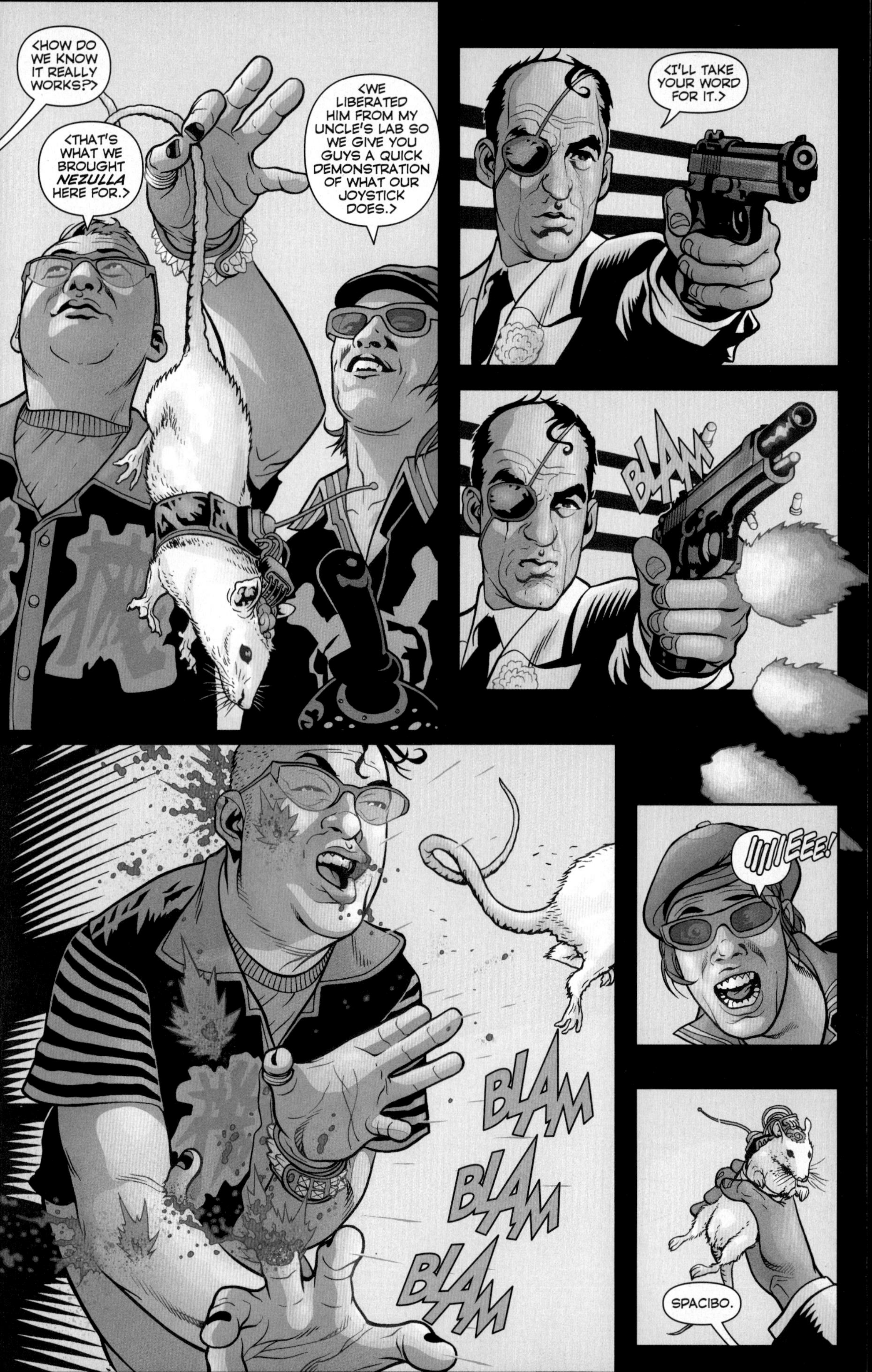
<HOW DO WE KNOW IT REALLY WORKS?>
<THAT'S WHAT WE BROUGHT NEZULLA HERE FOR.>
<WE LIBERATED HIM FROM MY UNCLE'S LAB SO WE GIVE YOU GUYS A QUICK DEMONSTRATION OF WHAT OUR JOYSTICK DOES.>
<I'LL TAKE YOUR WORD FOR IT.>
BLAM
BLAM
BLAM
BLAM
IIIIIEEE!
SPACIBO.

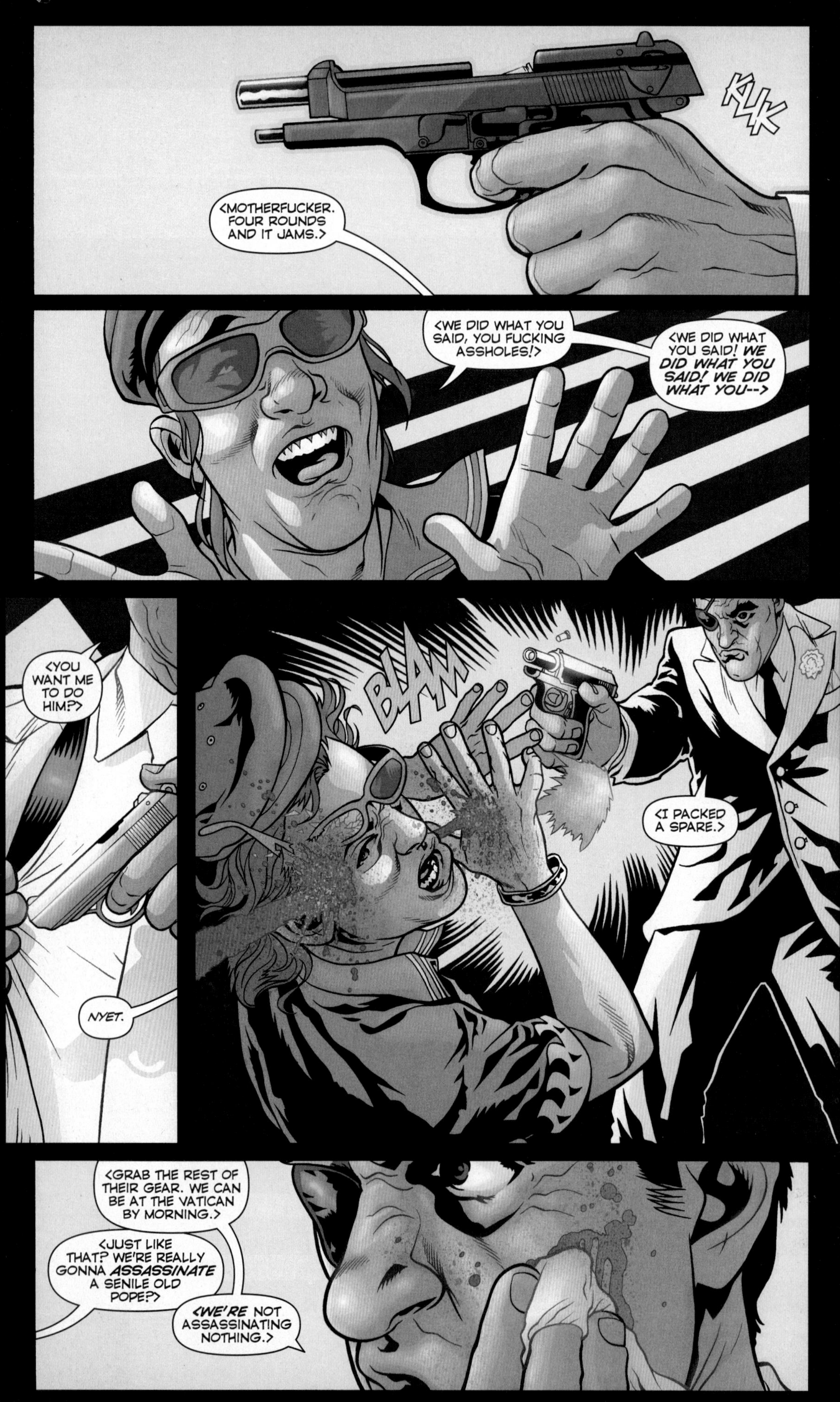
KLIK
<MOTHERFUCKER. FOUR ROUNDS AND IT JAMS.>
<WE DID WHAT YOU SAID, YOU FUCKING ASSHOLES!>
<WE DID WHAT YOU SAID! *WE DID WHAT YOU SAID! WE DID WHAT YOU--*>
<YOU WANT ME TO DO HIM?>
NYET.
BLAM
<I PACKED A SPARE.>
<GRAB THE REST OF THEIR GEAR. WE CAN BE AT THE VATICAN BY MORNING.>
<JUST LIKE THAT? WE'RE REALLY GONNA *ASSASSINATE* A SENILE OLD POPE?>
<*WE'RE* NOT ASSASSINATING NOTHING.>

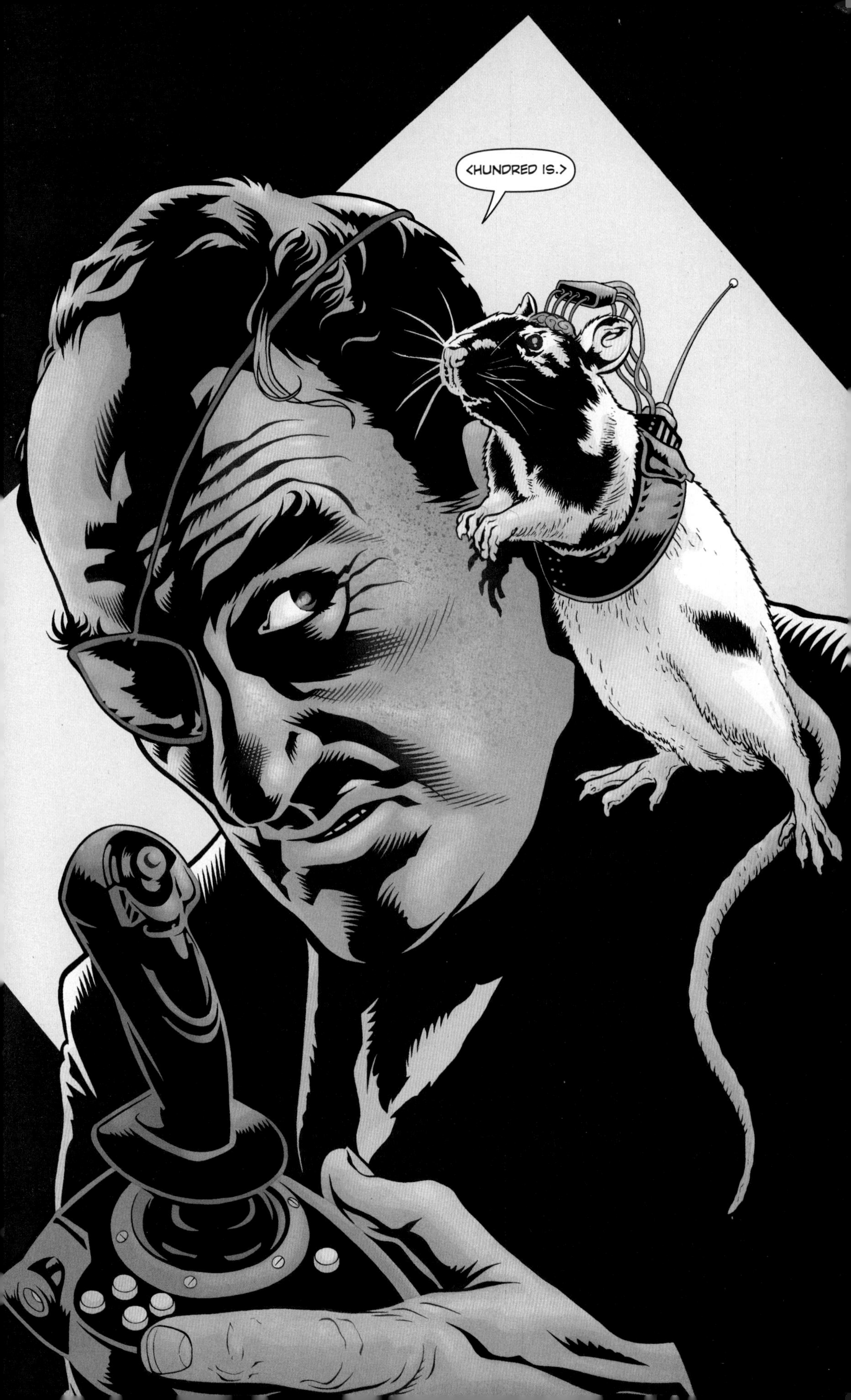
<HUNDRED IS.>

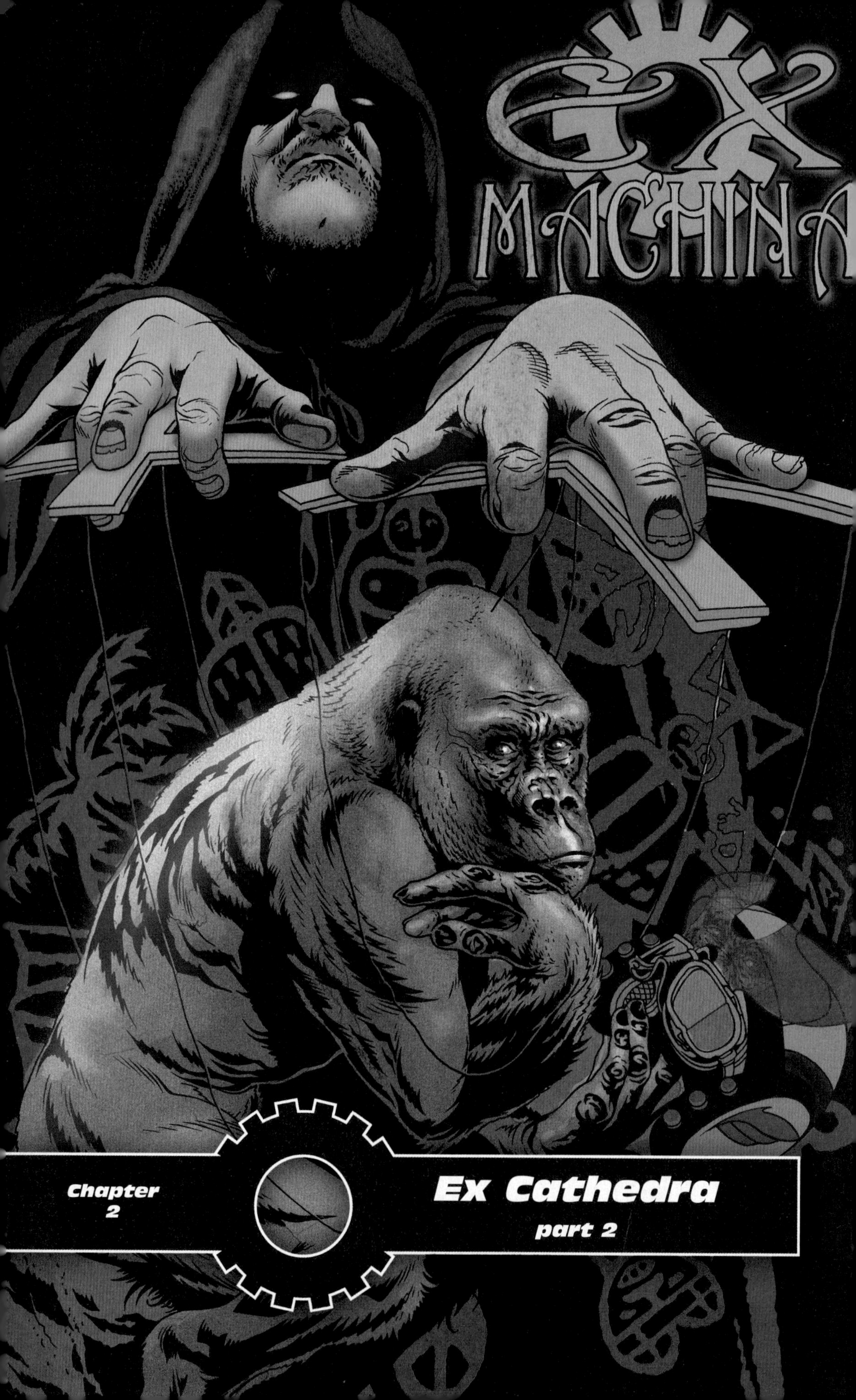
Ex
MACHINA
Chapter
2
Ex Cathedra
part 2

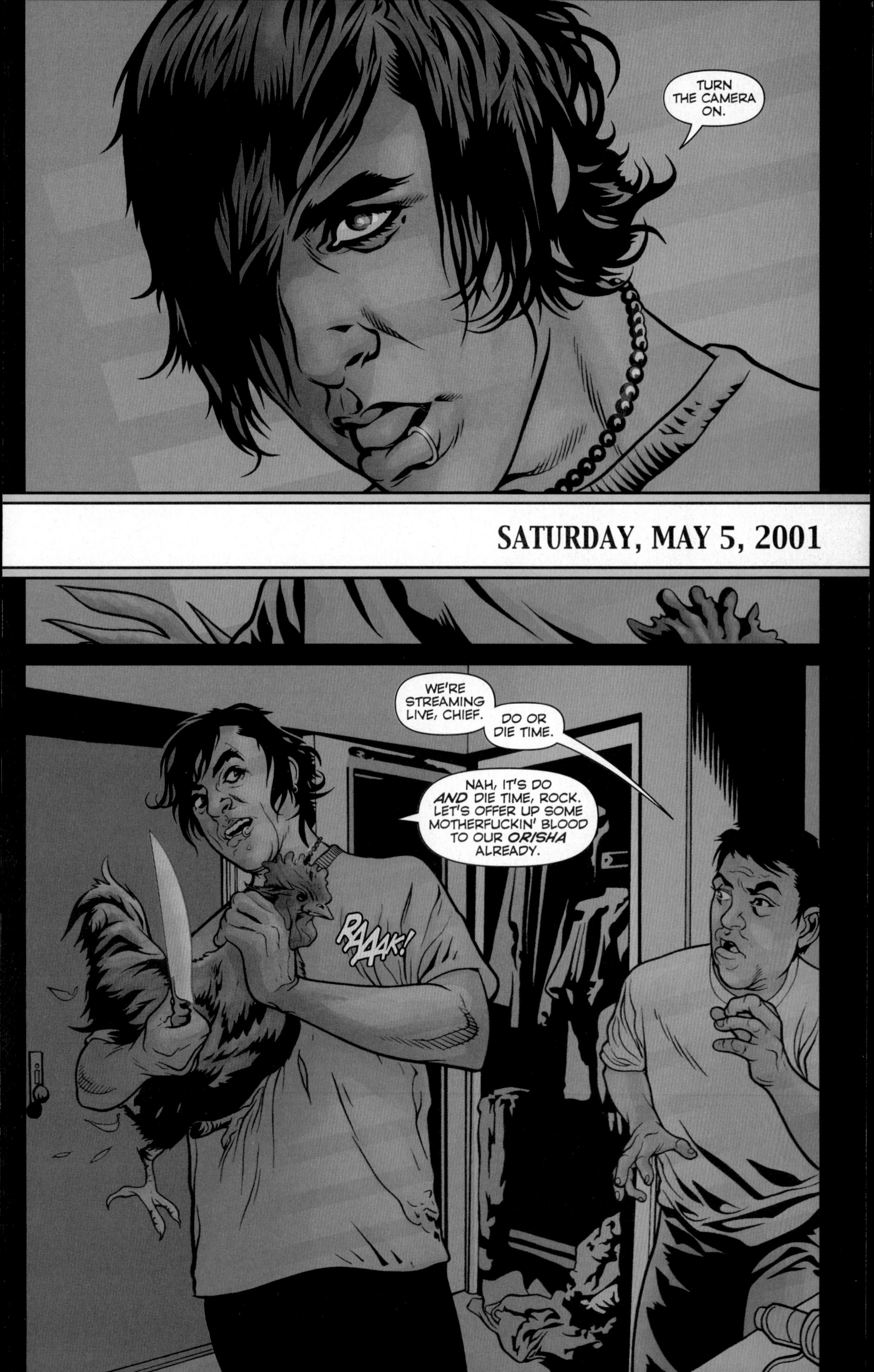
TURN THE CAMERA ON.
SATURDAY, MAY 5, 2001
WE'RE STREAMING LIVE, CHIEF.
DO OR DIE TIME.
NAH, IT'S DO *AND* DIE TIME, ROCK. LET'S OFFER UP SOME MOTHERFUCKIN' BLOOD TO OUR *ORISHA* ALREADY.
RAAAK!

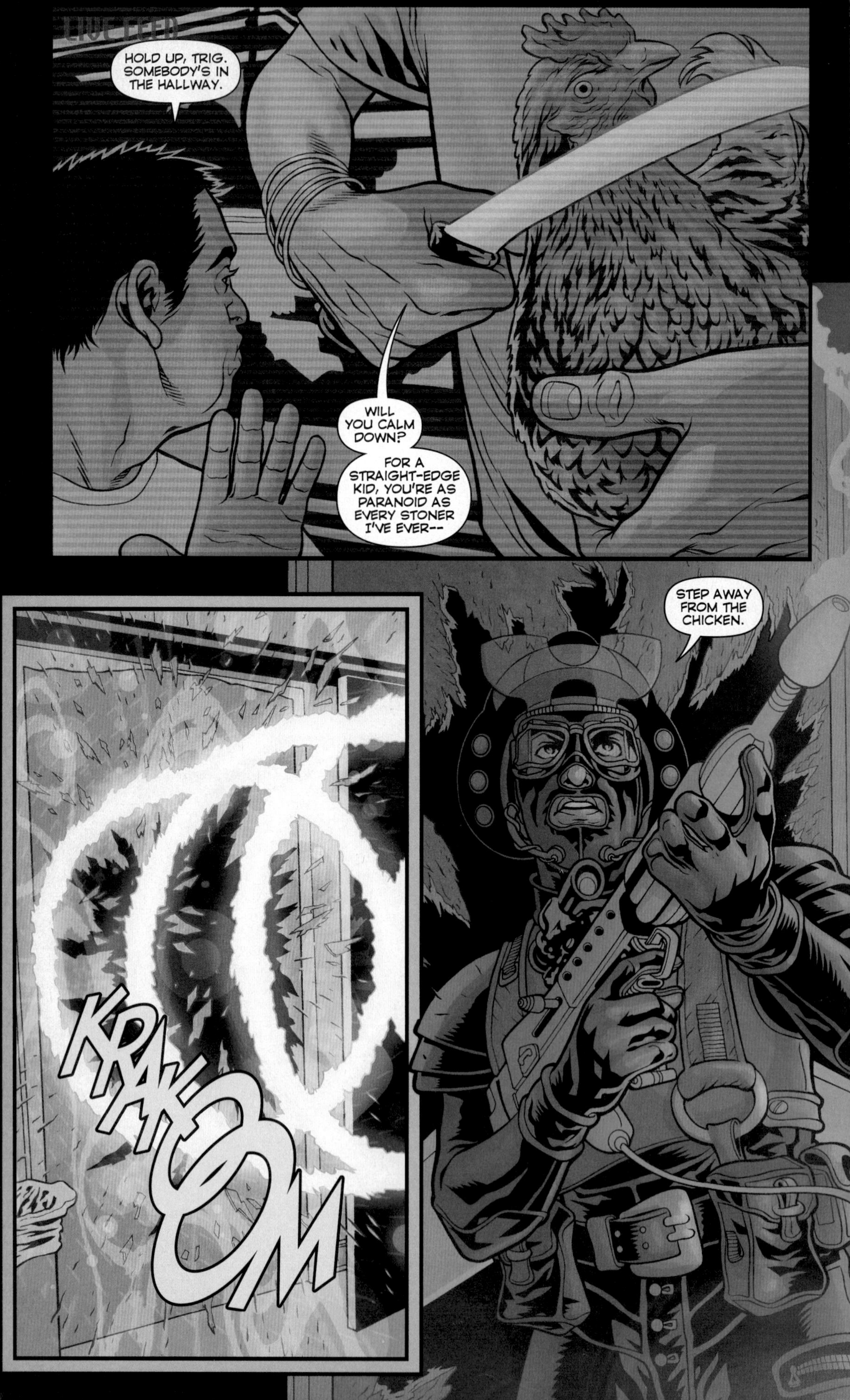

LIVE FEED
HOLD UP, TRIG. SOMEBODY'S IN THE HALLWAY.
WILL YOU CALM DOWN?
FOR A STRAIGHT-EDGE KID, YOU'RE AS PARANOID AS EVERY STONER I'VE EVER--
KRAKOOM
STEP AWAY FROM THE CHICKEN.

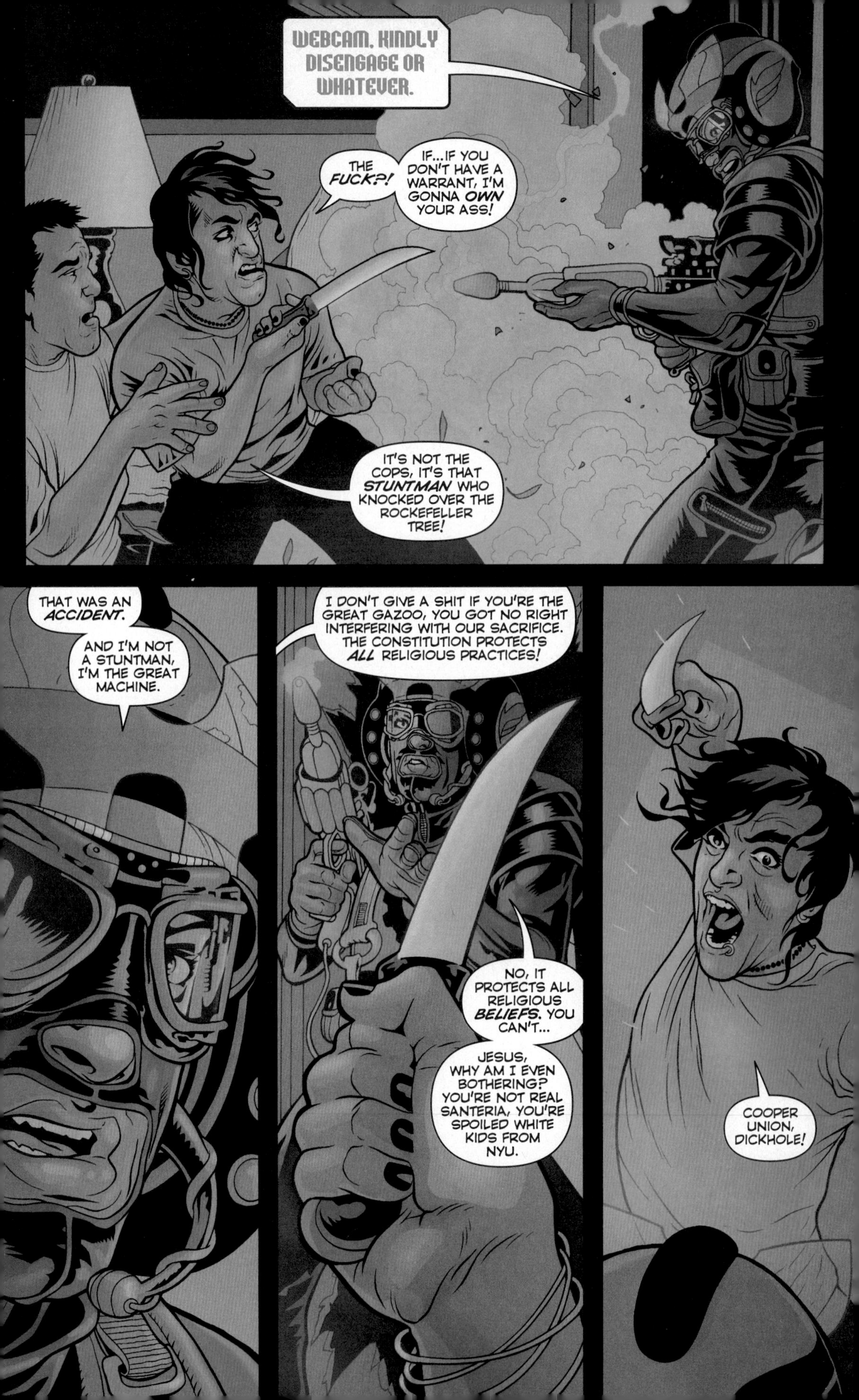
WEBCAM, KINDLY DISENGAGE OR WHATEVER.
THE FUCK?!
IF...IF YOU DON'T HAVE A WARRANT, I'M GONNA OWN YOUR ASS!
IT'S NOT THE COPS, IT'S THAT STUNTMAN WHO KNOCKED OVER THE ROCKEFELLER TREE!
THAT WAS AN ACCIDENT.
AND I'M NOT A STUNTMAN, I'M THE GREAT MACHINE.
I DON'T GIVE A SHIT IF YOU'RE THE GREAT GAZOO, YOU GOT NO RIGHT INTERFERING WITH OUR SACRIFICE. THE CONSTITUTION PROTECTS ALL RELIGIOUS PRACTICES!
NO, IT PROTECTS ALL RELIGIOUS BELIEFS. YOU CAN'T...
JESUS, WHY AM I EVEN BOTHERING? YOU'RE NOT REAL SANTERIA, YOU'RE SPOILED WHITE KIDS FROM NYU.
COOPER UNION, DICKHOLE!

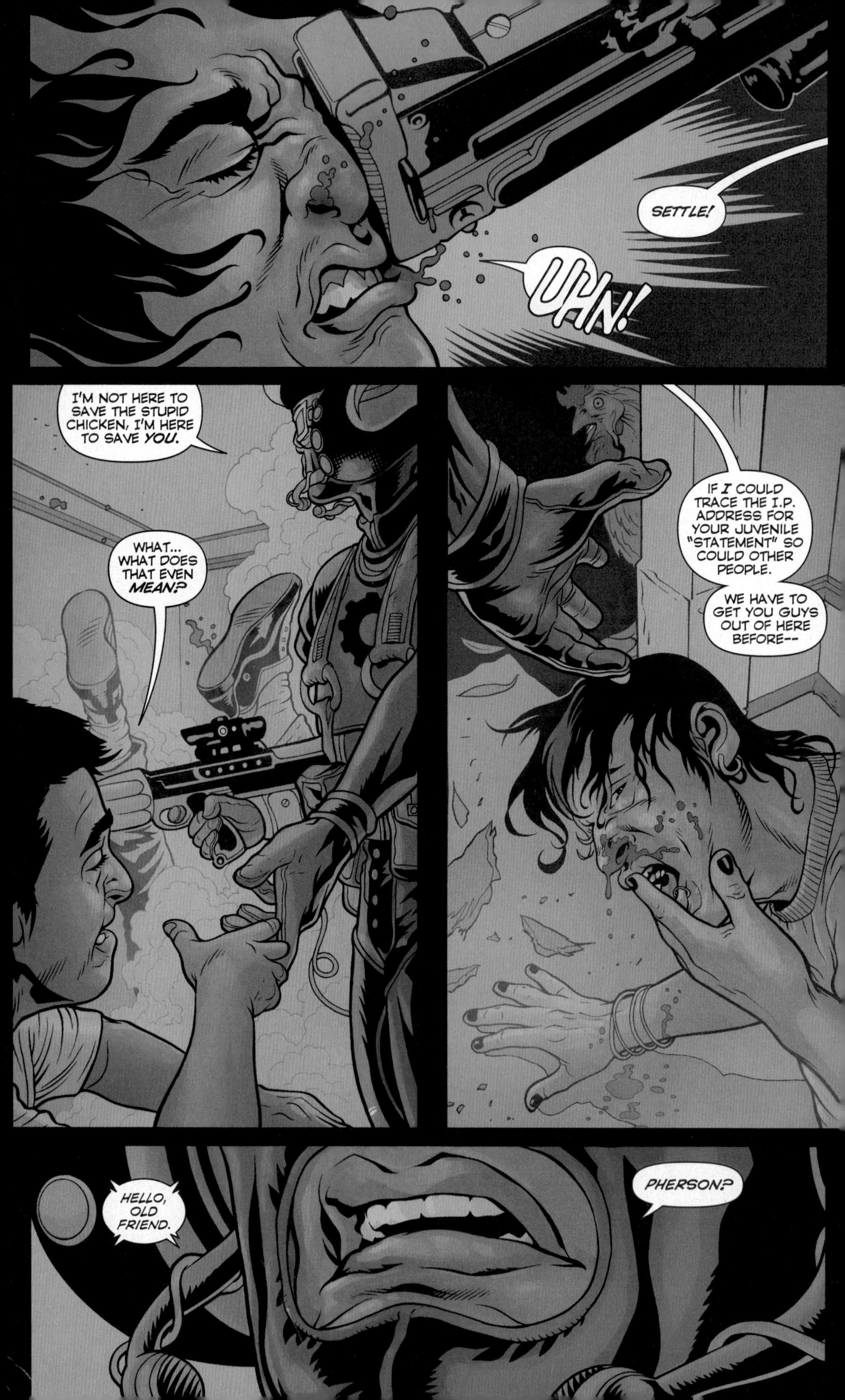
SETTLE!
UHN!
I'M NOT HERE TO SAVE THE STUPID CHICKEN, I'M HERE TO SAVE *YOU*.
WHAT... WHAT DOES THAT EVEN *MEAN?*
IF *I* COULD TRACE THE I.P. ADDRESS FOR YOUR JUVENILE "STATEMENT" SO COULD OTHER PEOPLE.
WE HAVE TO GET YOU GUYS OUT OF HERE BEFORE--
HELLO, OLD FRIEND.
PHERSON?

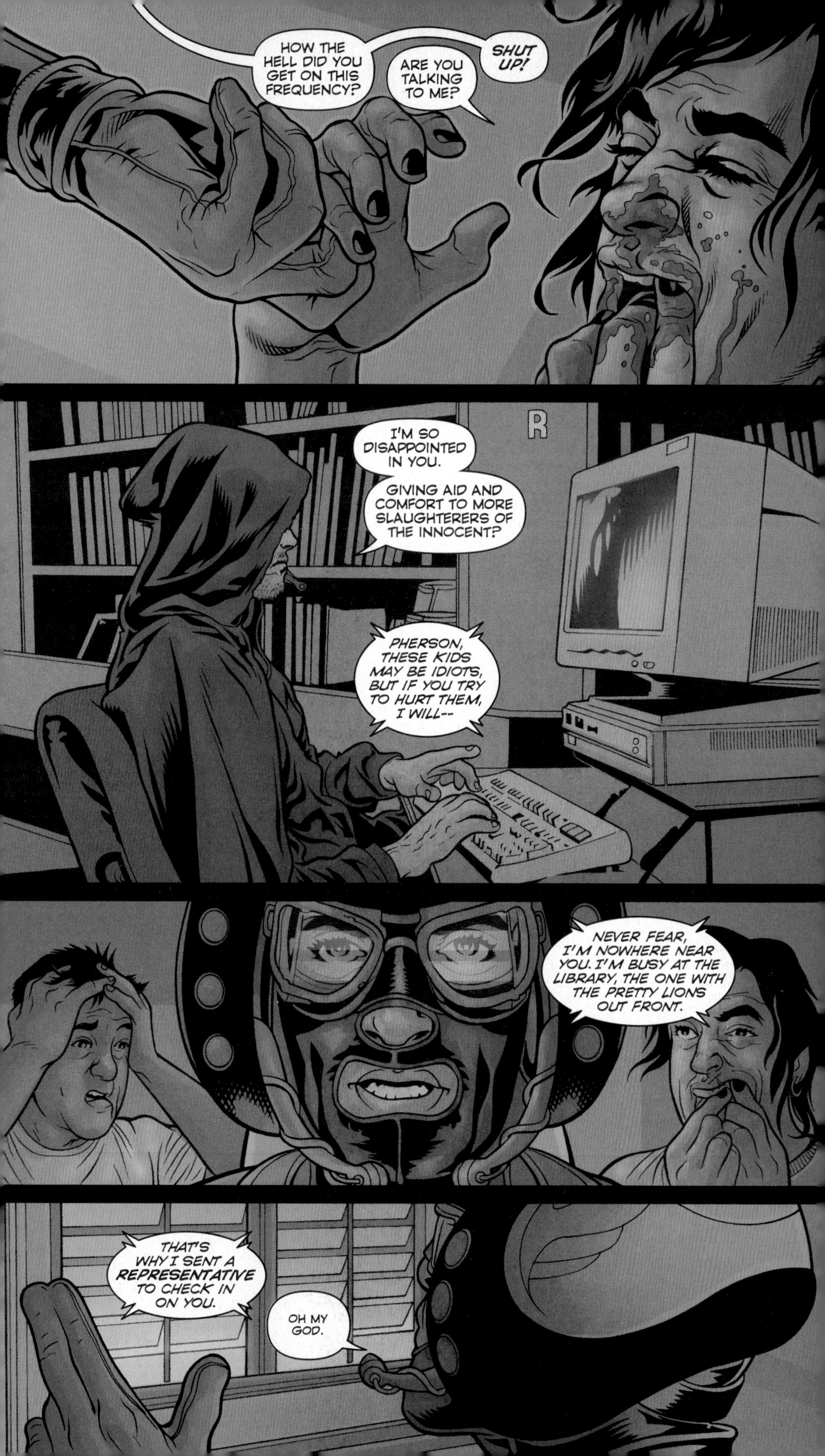
HOW THE HELL DID YOU GET ON THIS FREQUENCY?
ARE YOU TALKING TO ME?
SHUT UP!
I'M SO DISAPPOINTED IN YOU.
GIVING AID AND COMFORT TO MORE SLAUGHTERERS OF THE INNOCENT?
PHERSON, THESE KIDS MAY BE IDIOTS, BUT IF YOU TRY TO HURT THEM, I WILL--
NEVER FEAR, I'M NOWHERE NEAR YOU. I'M BUSY AT THE LIBRARY, THE ONE WITH THE PRETTY LIONS OUT FRONT.
THAT'S WHY I SENT A REPRESENTATIVE TO CHECK IN ON YOU.
OH MY GOD.

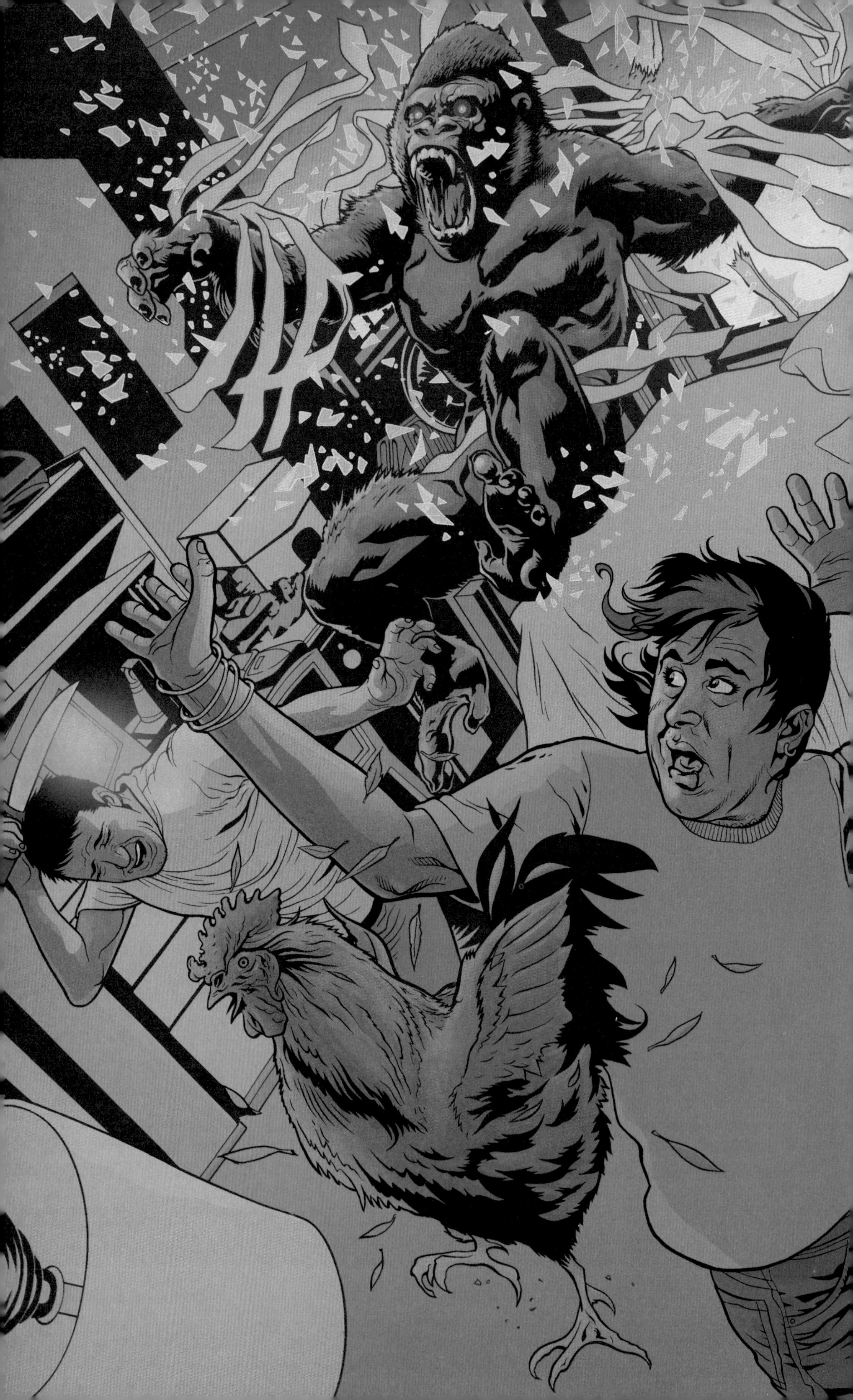

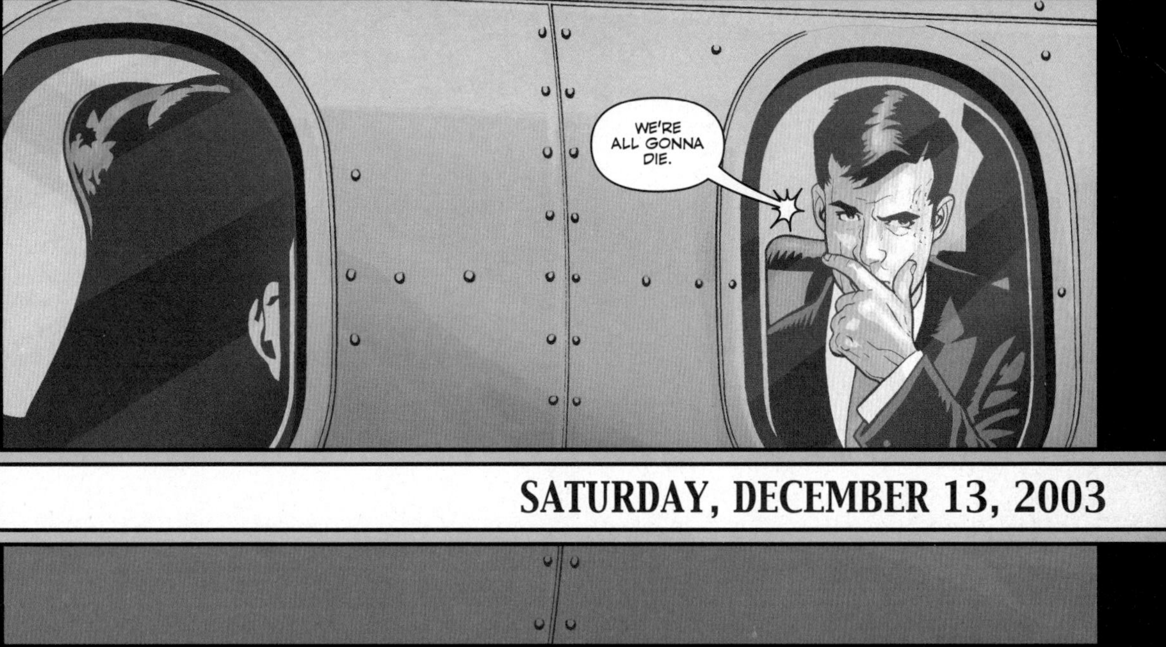
WE'RE ALL GONNA DIE.
SATURDAY, DECEMBER 13, 2003

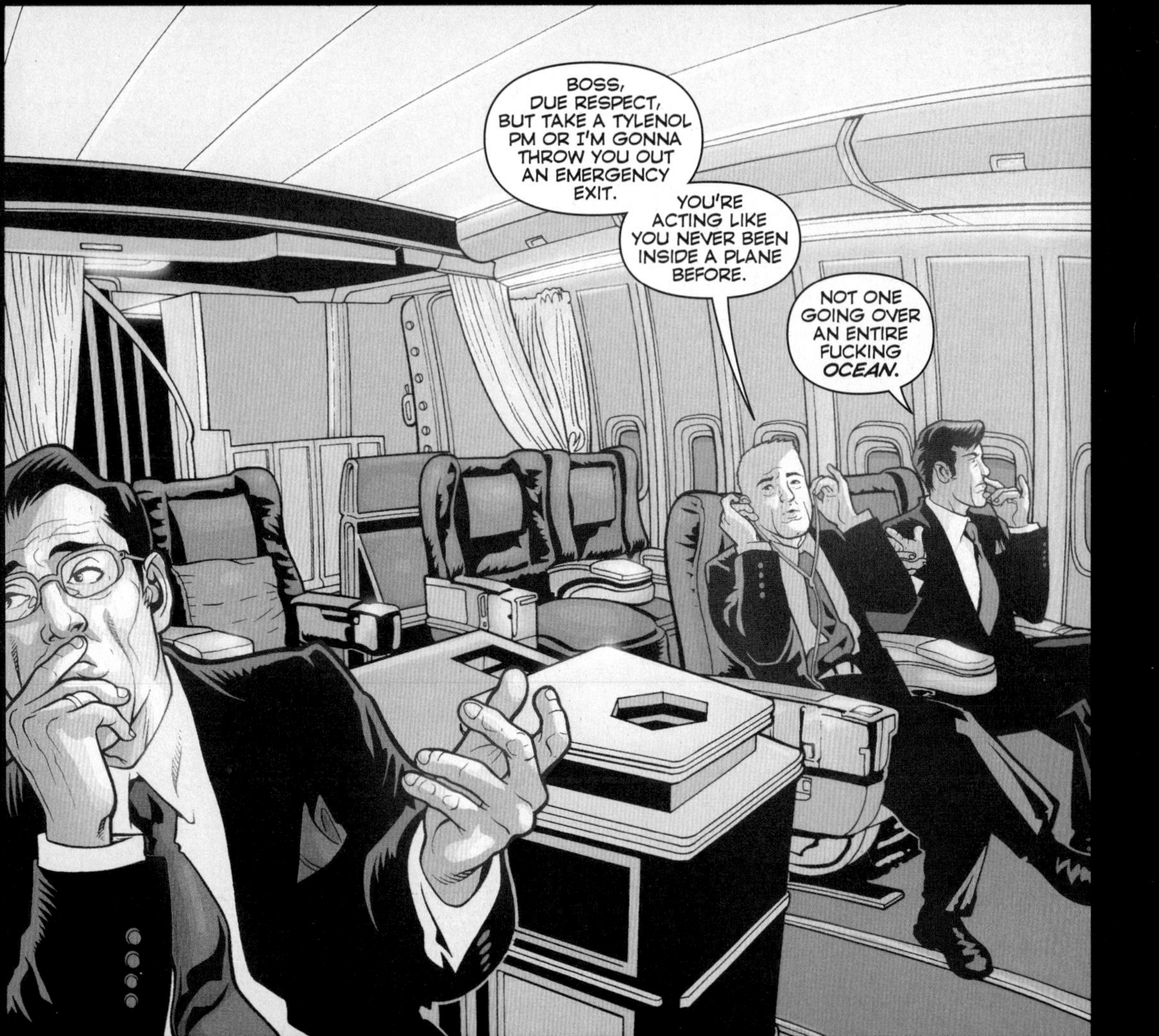
BOSS, DUE RESPECT, BUT TAKE A TYLENOL PM OR I'M GONNA THROW YOU OUT AN EMERGENCY EXIT.
YOU'RE ACTING LIKE YOU NEVER BEEN INSIDE A PLANE BEFORE.
NOT ONE GOING OVER AN ENTIRE FUCKING *OCEAN.*

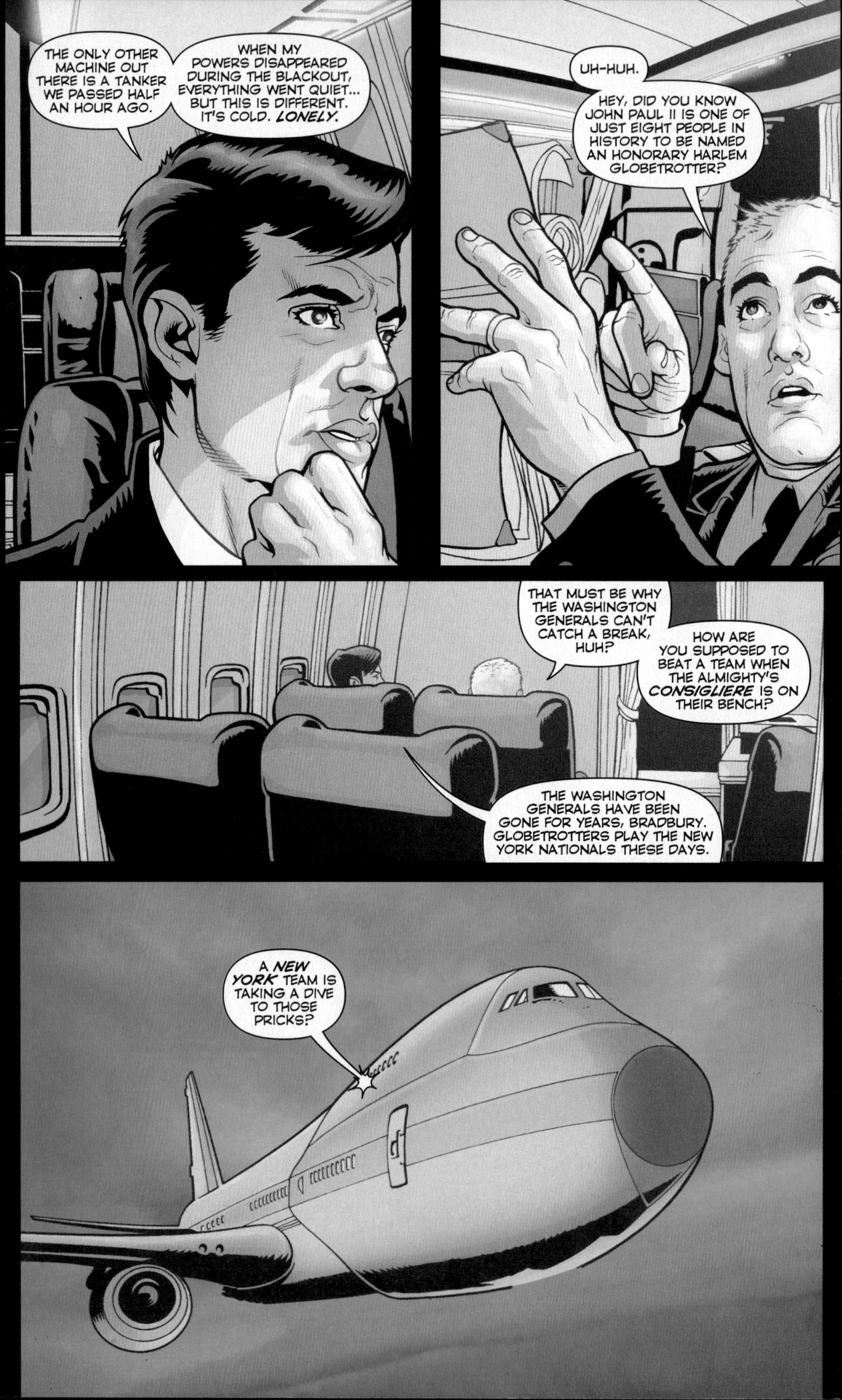
THE ONLY OTHER MACHINE OUT THERE IS A TANKER WE PASSED HALF AN HOUR AGO.
WHEN MY POWERS DISAPPEARED DURING THE BLACKOUT, EVERYTHING WENT QUIET... BUT THIS IS DIFFERENT. IT'S COLD. *LONELY.*
UH-HUH.
HEY, DID YOU KNOW JOHN PAUL II IS ONE OF JUST EIGHT PEOPLE IN HISTORY TO BE NAMED AN HONORARY HARLEM GLOBETROTTER?
THAT MUST BE WHY THE WASHINGTON GENERALS CAN'T CATCH A BREAK, HUH?
HOW ARE YOU SUPPOSED TO BEAT A TEAM WHEN THE ALMIGHTY'S *CONSIGLIERE* IS ON THEIR BENCH?
THE WASHINGTON GENERALS HAVE BEEN GONE FOR YEARS, BRADBURY. GLOBETROTTERS PLAY THE NEW YORK NATIONALS THESE DAYS.
A *NEW YORK* TEAM IS TAKING A DIVE TO THOSE PRICKS?

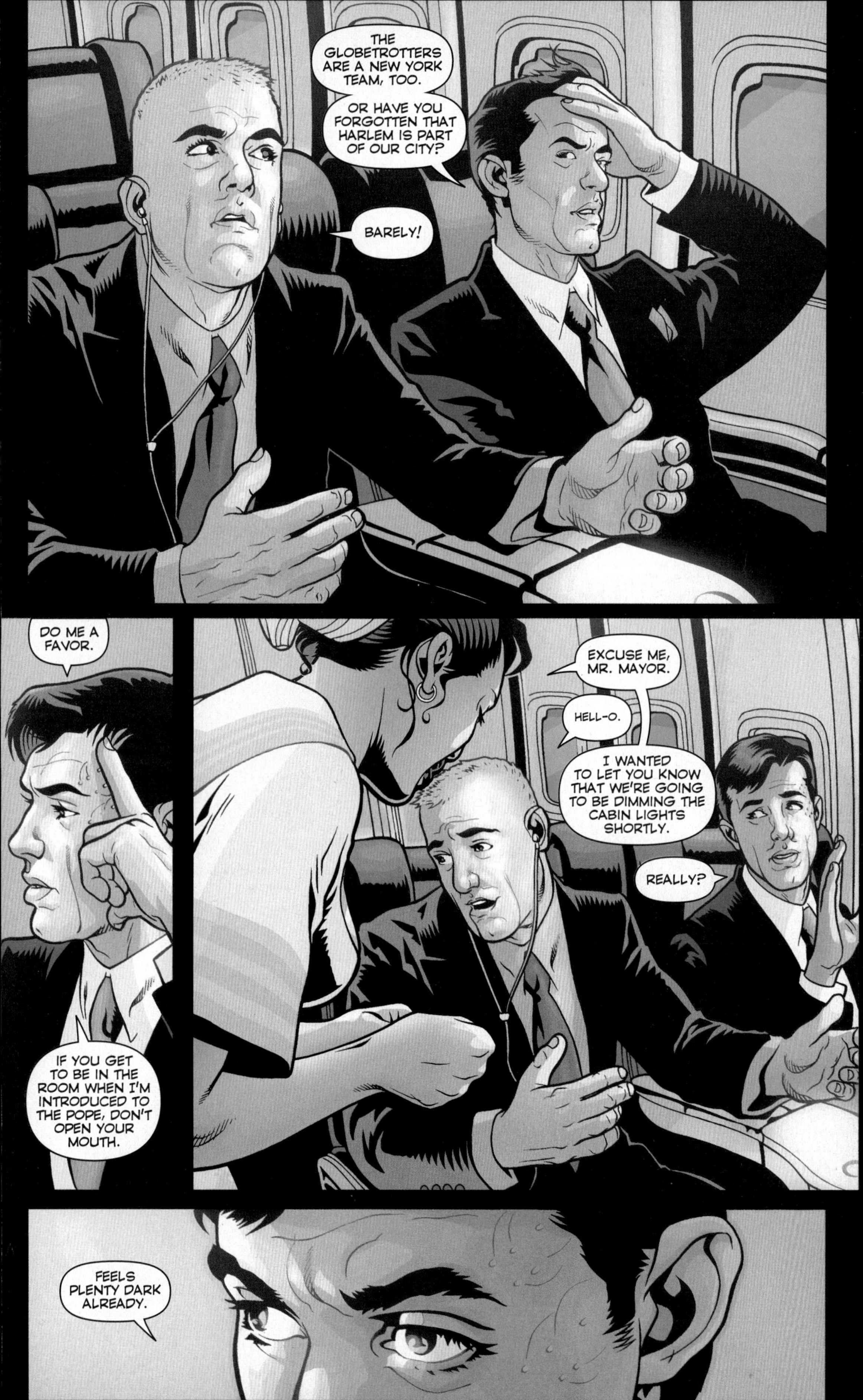
THE GLOBETROTTERS ARE A NEW YORK TEAM, TOO.
OR HAVE YOU FORGOTTEN THAT HARLEM IS PART OF OUR CITY?
BARELY!
DO ME A FAVOR.
IF YOU GET TO BE IN THE ROOM WHEN I'M INTRODUCED TO THE POPE, DON'T OPEN YOUR MOUTH.
EXCUSE ME, MR. MAYOR.
HELL-O.
I WANTED TO LET YOU KNOW THAT WE'RE GOING TO BE DIMMING THE CABIN LIGHTS SHORTLY.
REALLY?
FEELS PLENTY DARK ALREADY.

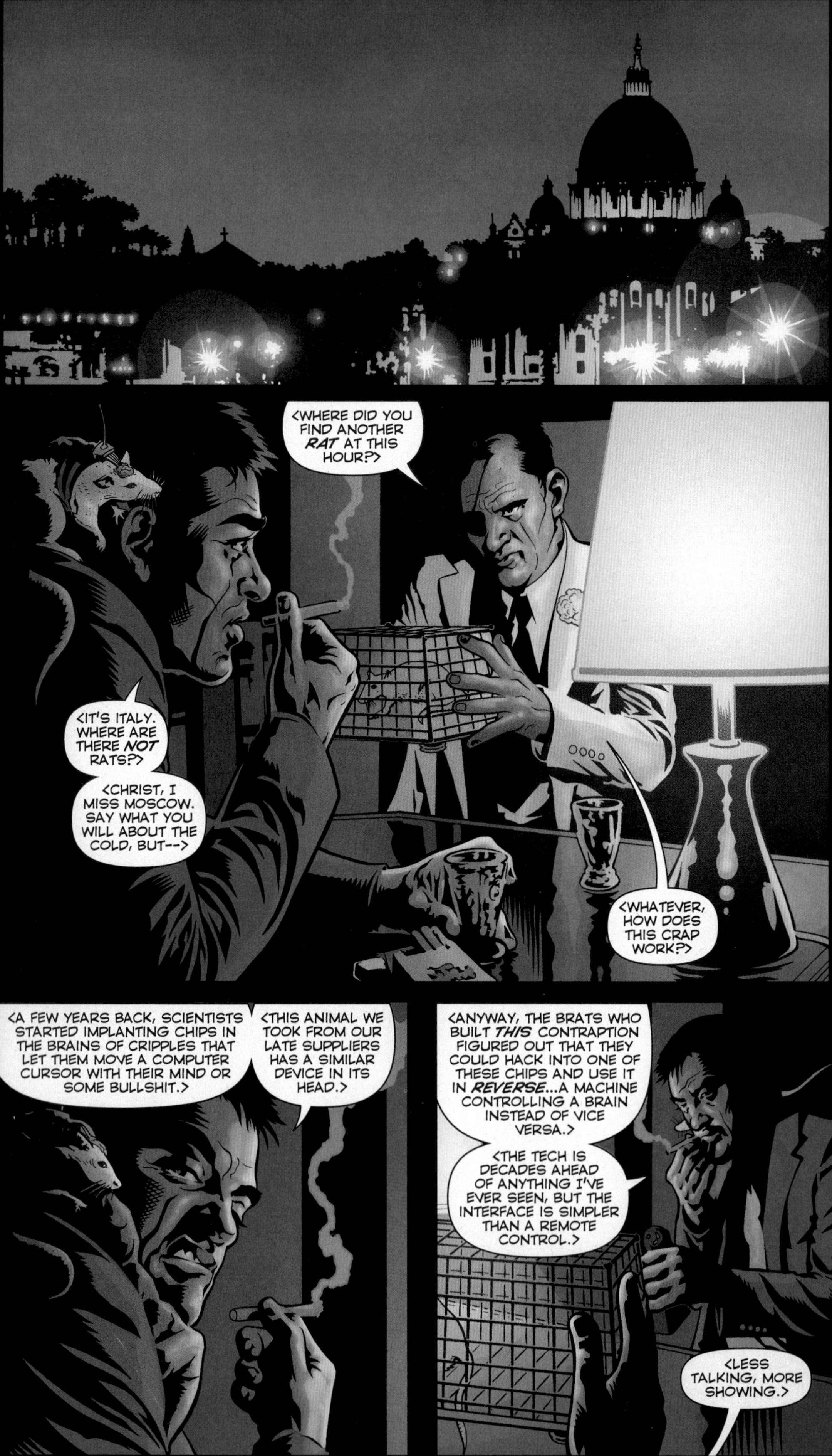
<WHERE DID YOU FIND ANOTHER *RAT* AT THIS HOUR?>
<IT'S ITALY. WHERE ARE THERE *NOT* RATS?>
<CHRIST, I MISS MOSCOW. SAY WHAT YOU WILL ABOUT THE COLD, BUT-->
<WHATEVER, HOW DOES THIS CRAP WORK?>
<A FEW YEARS BACK, SCIENTISTS STARTED IMPLANTING CHIPS IN THE BRAINS OF CRIPPLES THAT LET THEM MOVE A COMPUTER CURSOR WITH THEIR MIND OR SOME BULLSHIT.>
<THIS ANIMAL WE TOOK FROM OUR LATE SUPPLIERS HAS A SIMILAR DEVICE IN ITS HEAD.>
<ANYWAY, THE BRATS WHO BUILT *THIS* CONTRAPTION FIGURED OUT THAT THEY COULD HACK INTO ONE OF THESE CHIPS AND USE IT IN *REVERSE*...A MACHINE CONTROLLING A BRAIN INSTEAD OF VICE VERSA.>
<THE TECH IS DECADES AHEAD OF ANYTHING I'VE EVER SEEN, BUT THE INTERFACE IS SIMPLER THAN A REMOTE CONTROL.>
<LESS TALKING, MORE SHOWING.>

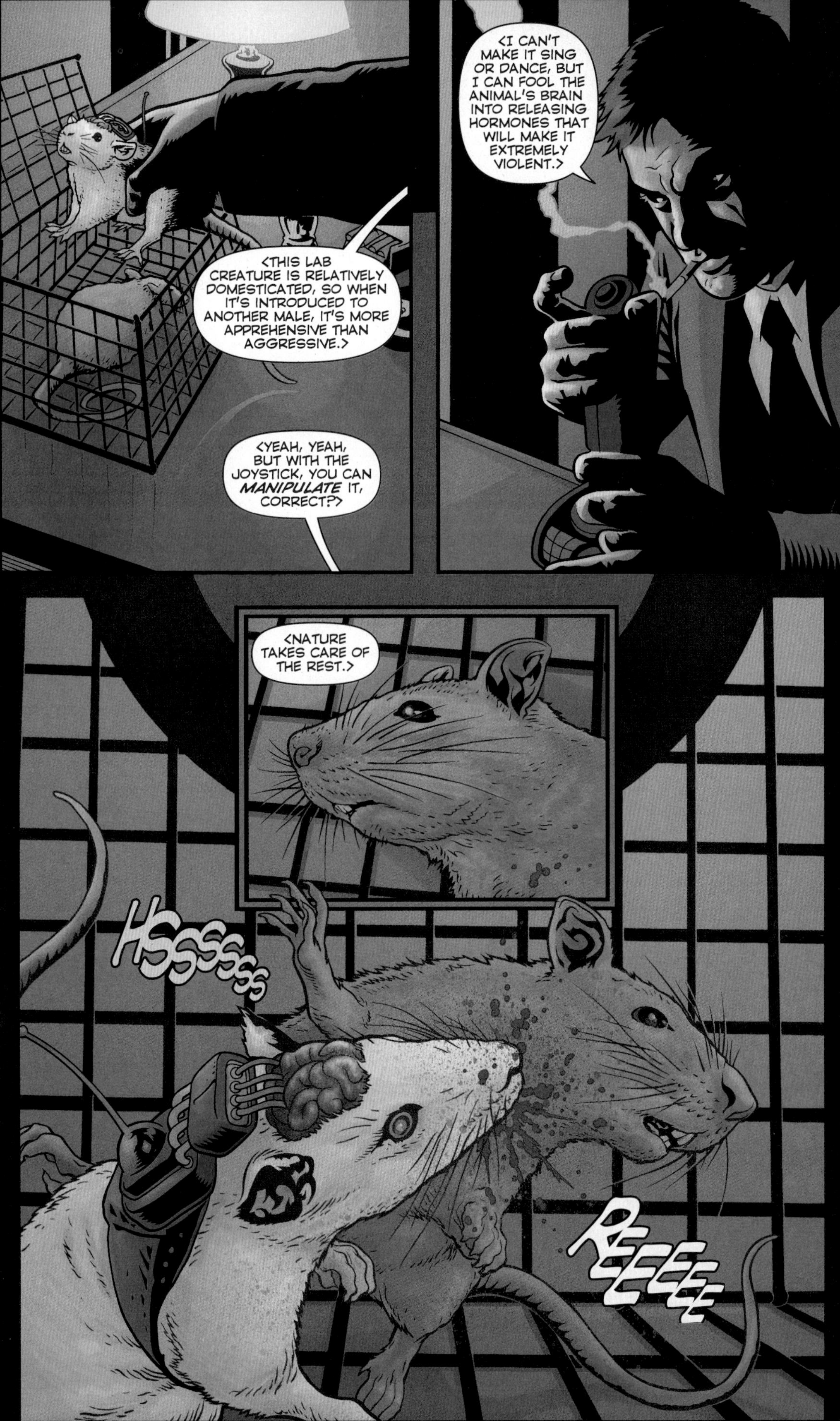
<THIS LAB CREATURE IS RELATIVELY DOMESTICATED, SO WHEN IT'S INTRODUCED TO ANOTHER MALE, IT'S MORE APPREHENSIVE THAN AGGRESSIVE.>
<YEAH, YEAH, BUT WITH THE JOYSTICK, YOU CAN *MANIPULATE* IT, CORRECT?>
<I CAN'T MAKE IT SING OR DANCE, BUT I CAN FOOL THE ANIMAL'S BRAIN INTO RELEASING HORMONES THAT WILL MAKE IT EXTREMELY VIOLENT.>
<NATURE TAKES CARE OF THE REST.>
HSSSSSS
REEEEEE

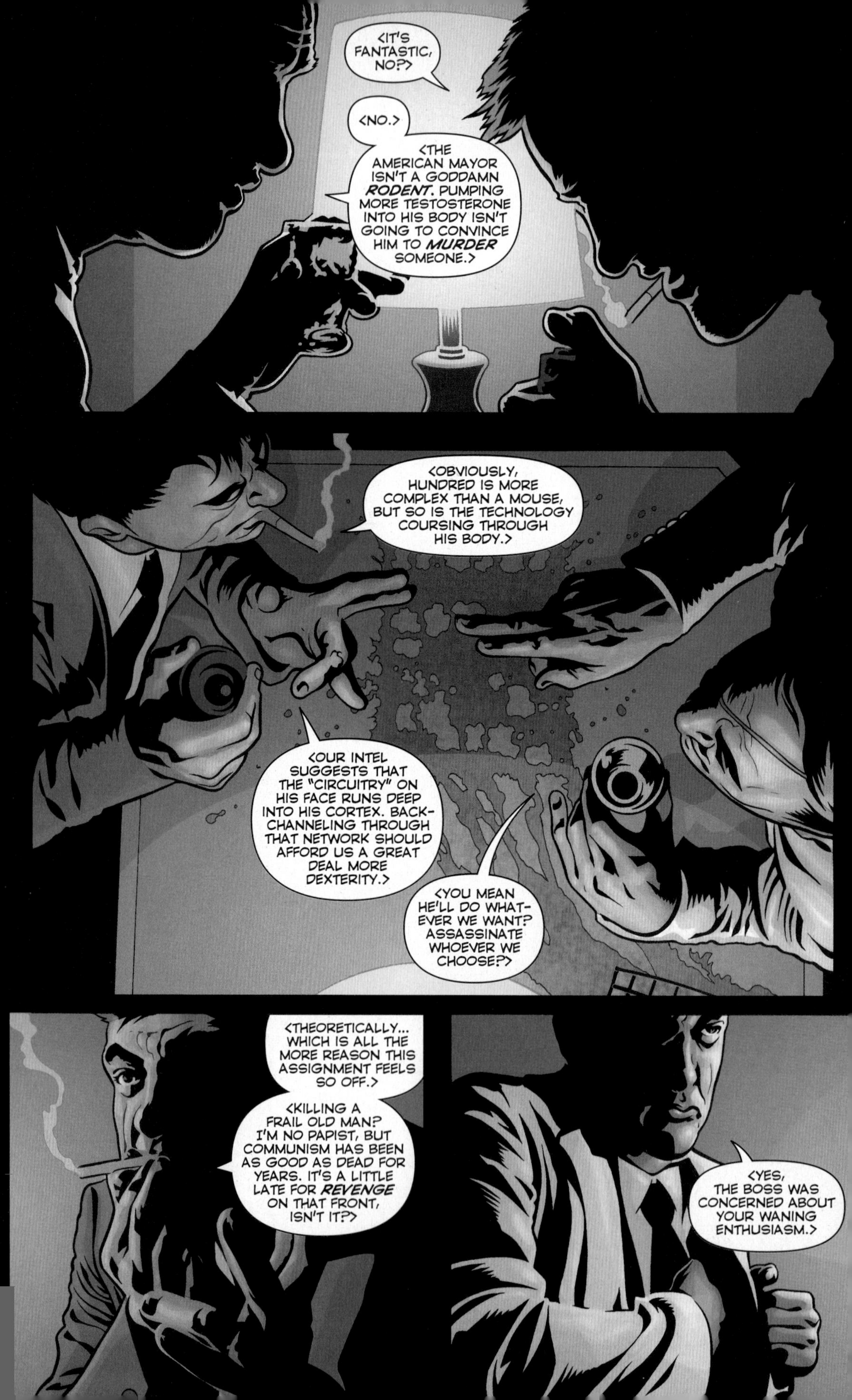

<IT'S FANTASTIC, NO?>
<NO.>
<THE AMERICAN MAYOR ISN'T A GODDAMN ***RODENT***. PUMPING MORE TESTOSTERONE INTO HIS BODY ISN'T GOING TO CONVINCE HIM TO ***MURDER*** SOMEONE.>
<OBVIOUSLY, HUNDRED IS MORE COMPLEX THAN A MOUSE, BUT SO IS THE TECHNOLOGY COURSING THROUGH HIS BODY.>
<OUR INTEL SUGGESTS THAT THE "CIRCUITRY" ON HIS FACE RUNS DEEP INTO HIS CORTEX. BACK-CHANNELING THROUGH THAT NETWORK SHOULD AFFORD US A GREAT DEAL MORE DEXTERITY.>
<YOU MEAN HE'LL DO WHATEVER WE WANT? ASSASSINATE WHOEVER WE CHOOSE?>
<THEORETICALLY... WHICH IS ALL THE MORE REASON THIS ASSIGNMENT FEELS SO OFF.>
<KILLING A FRAIL OLD MAN? I'M NO PAPIST, BUT COMMUNISM HAS BEEN AS GOOD AS DEAD FOR YEARS. IT'S A LITTLE LATE FOR ***REVENGE*** ON THAT FRONT, ISN'T IT?>
<YES, THE BOSS WAS CONCERNED ABOUT YOUR WANING ENTHUSIASM.>

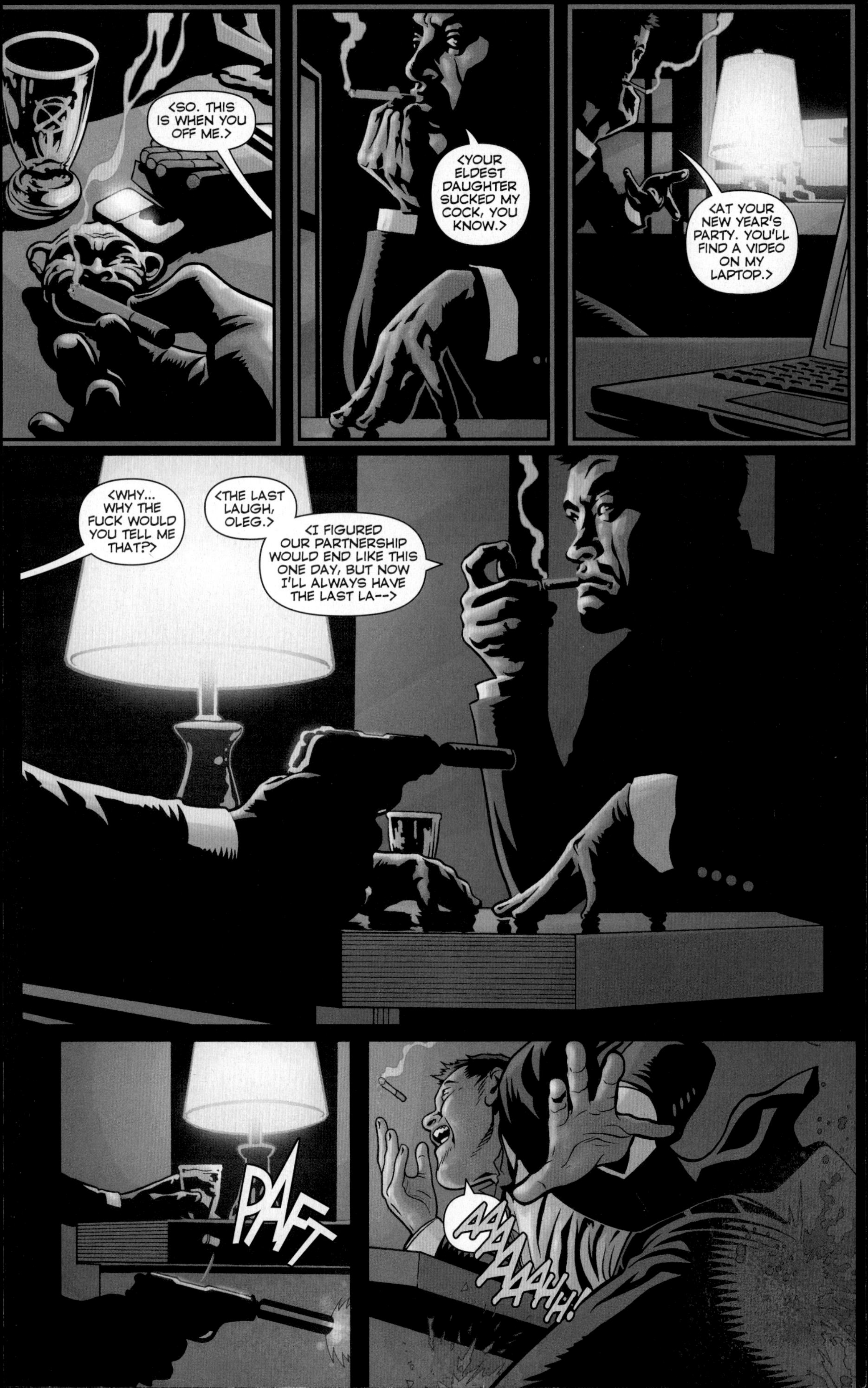
<SO. THIS IS WHEN YOU OFF ME.>
<YOUR ELDEST DAUGHTER SUCKED MY COCK, YOU KNOW.>
<AT YOUR NEW YEAR'S PARTY. YOU'LL FIND A VIDEO ON MY LAPTOP.>
<WHY... WHY THE FUCK WOULD YOU TELL ME THAT?>
<THE LAST LAUGH, OLEG.>
<I FIGURED OUR PARTNERSHIP WOULD END LIKE THIS ONE DAY, BUT NOW I'LL ALWAYS HAVE THE LAST LA-->
PAFT
AAAAAAAAHH!

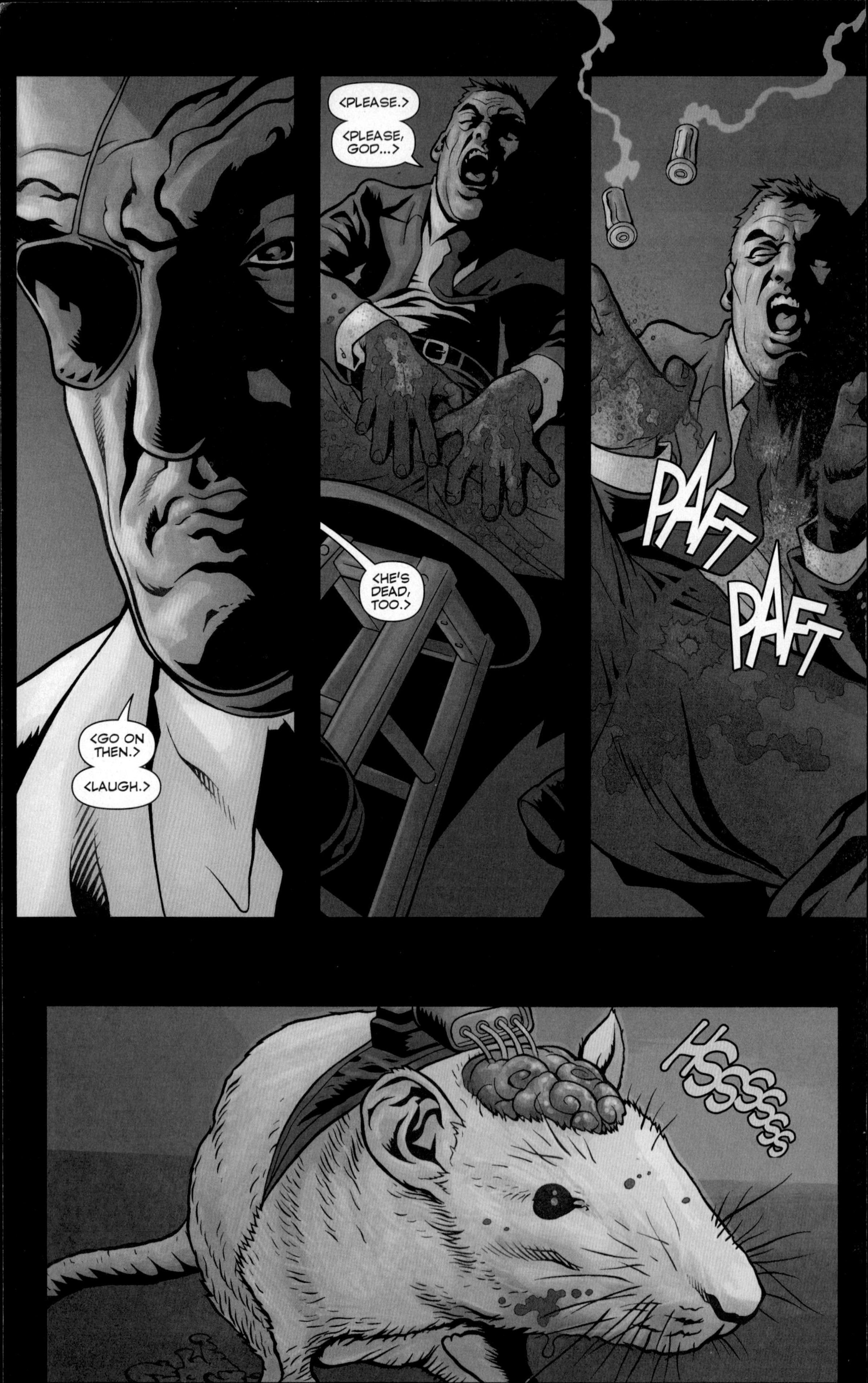

<GO ON THEN.>
<LAUGH.>
<PLEASE.>
<PLEASE, GOD...>
<HE'S DEAD, TOO.>
PAFT
PAFT
HSSSSSS

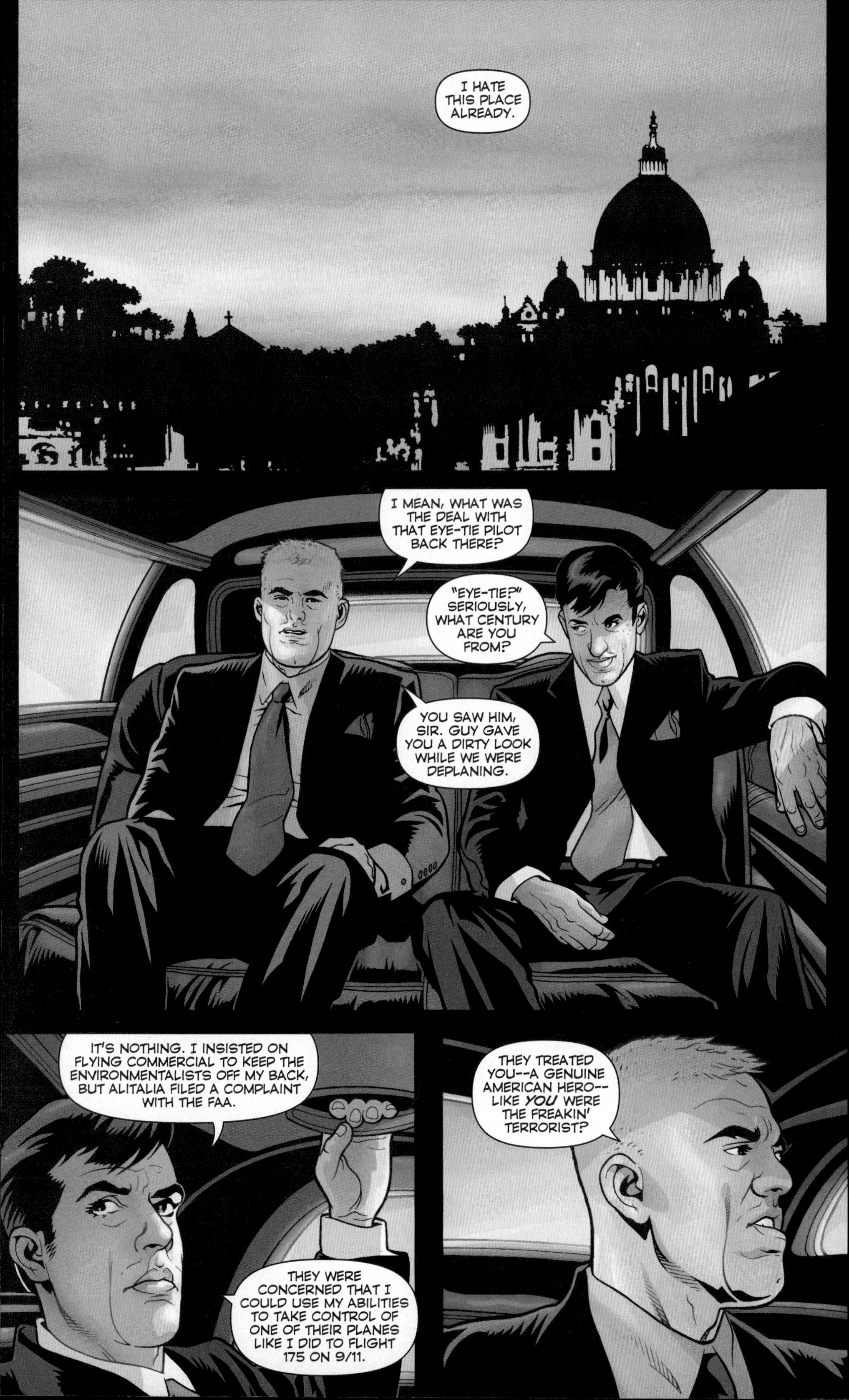
I HATE THIS PLACE ALREADY.
I MEAN, WHAT WAS THE DEAL WITH THAT EYE-TIE PILOT BACK THERE?
"EYE-TIE?" SERIOUSLY, WHAT CENTURY ARE YOU FROM?
YOU SAW HIM, SIR. GUY GAVE YOU A DIRTY LOOK WHILE WE WERE DEPLANING.
IT'S NOTHING. I INSISTED ON FLYING COMMERCIAL TO KEEP THE ENVIRONMENTALISTS OFF MY BACK, BUT ALITALIA FILED A COMPLAINT WITH THE FAA.
THEY WERE CONCERNED THAT I COULD USE MY ABILITIES TO TAKE CONTROL OF ONE OF THEIR PLANES LIKE I DID TO FLIGHT 175 ON 9/11.
THEY TREATED YOU--A GENUINE AMERICAN HERO--LIKE *YOU* WERE THE FREAKIN' TERRORIST?

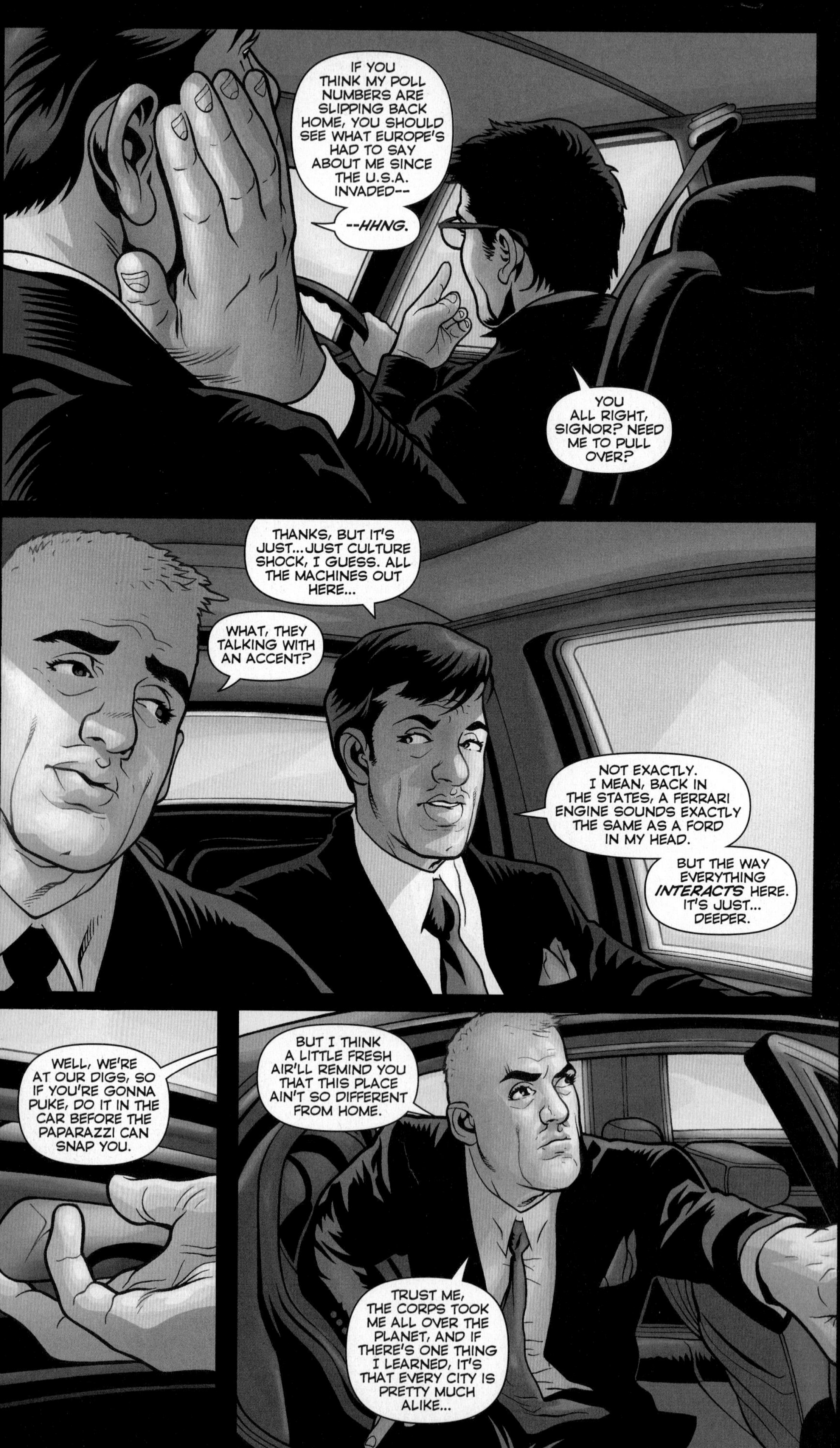
IF YOU THINK MY POLL NUMBERS ARE SLIPPING BACK HOME, YOU SHOULD SEE WHAT EUROPE'S HAD TO SAY ABOUT ME SINCE THE U.S.A. INVADED--
--HHNG.
YOU ALL RIGHT, SIGNOR? NEED ME TO PULL OVER?
THANKS, BUT IT'S JUST...JUST CULTURE SHOCK, I GUESS. ALL THE MACHINES OUT HERE...
WHAT, THEY TALKING WITH AN ACCENT?
NOT EXACTLY. I MEAN, BACK IN THE STATES, A FERRARI ENGINE SOUNDS EXACTLY THE SAME AS A FORD IN MY HEAD.
BUT THE WAY EVERYTHING INTERACTS HERE. IT'S JUST... DEEPER.
WELL, WE'RE AT OUR DIGS, SO IF YOU'RE GONNA PUKE, DO IT IN THE CAR BEFORE THE PAPARAZZI CAN SNAP YOU.
BUT I THINK A LITTLE FRESH AIR'LL REMIND YOU THAT THIS PLACE AIN'T SO DIFFERENT FROM HOME.
TRUST ME, THE CORPS TOOK ME ALL OVER THE PLANET, AND IF THERE'S ONE THING I LEARNED, IT'S THAT EVERY CITY IS PRETTY MUCH ALIKE...

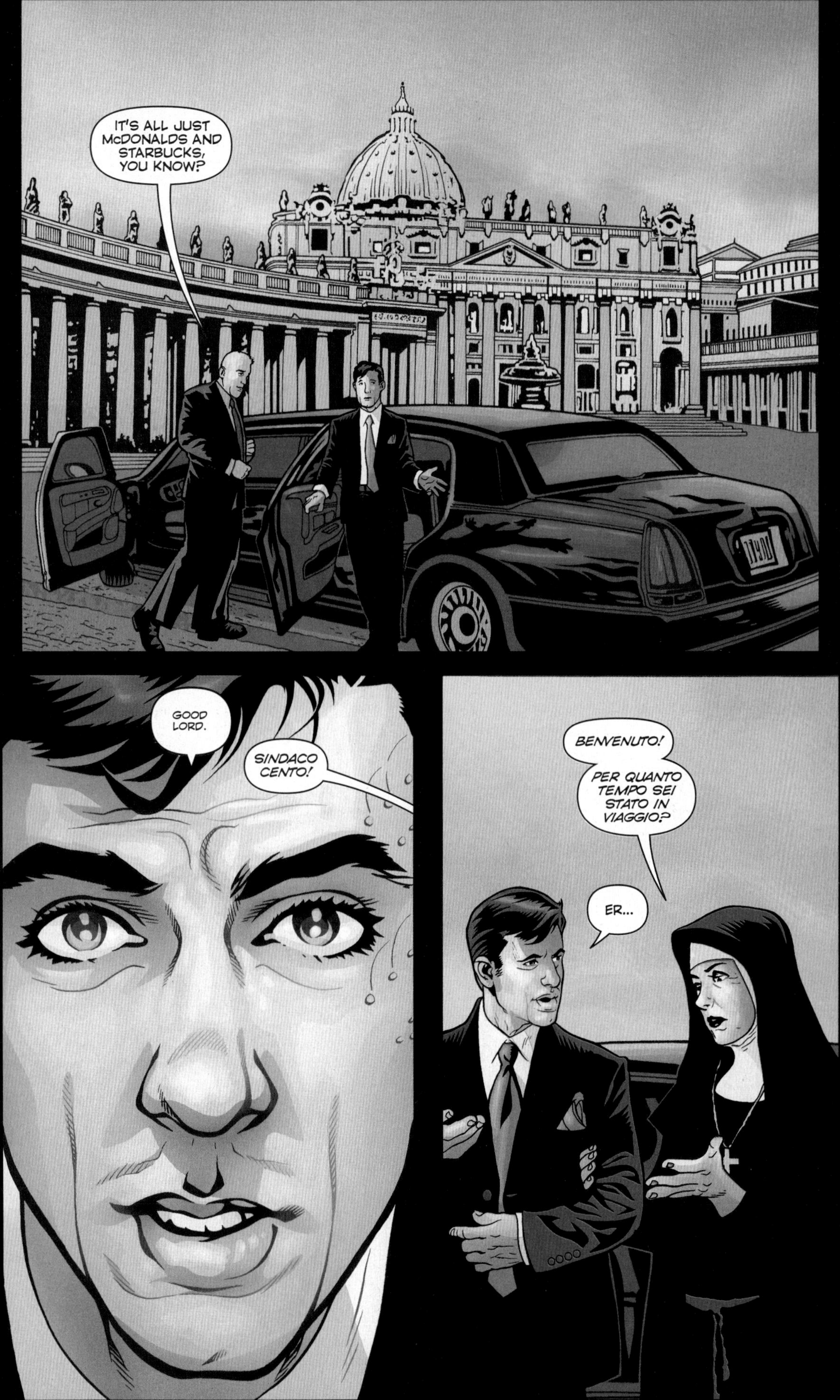
IT'S ALL JUST McDONALDS AND STARBUCKS, YOU KNOW?
GOOD LORD.
SINDACO CENTO!
BENVENUTO!
PER QUANTO TEMPO SEI STATO IN VIAGGIO?
ER...

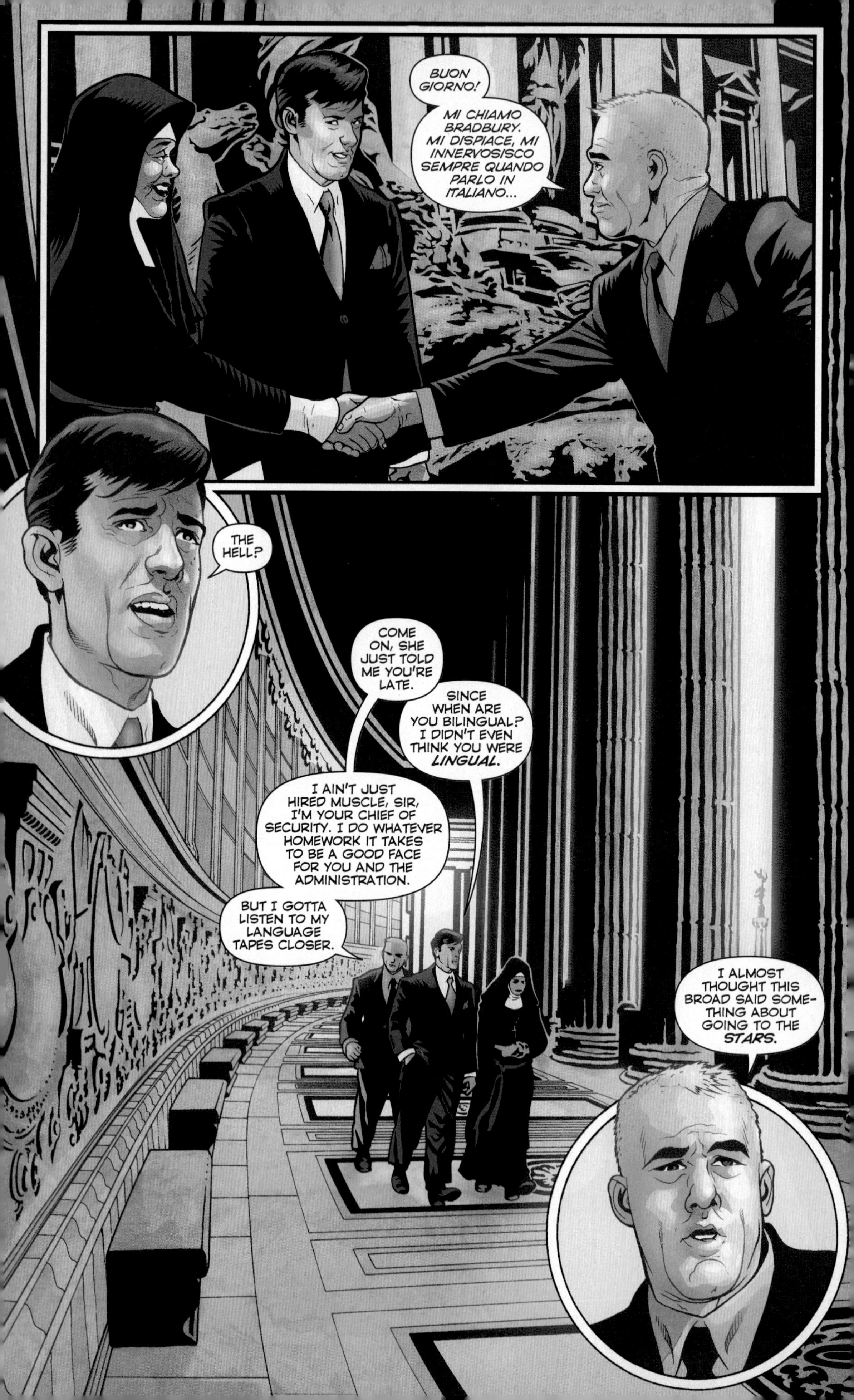
BUON GIORNO!
MI CHIAMO BRADBURY. MI DISPIACE, MI INNERVOSISCO SEMPRE QUANDO PARLO IN ITALIANO...
THE HELL?
COME ON, SHE JUST TOLD ME YOU'RE LATE.
SINCE WHEN ARE YOU BILINGUAL? I DIDN'T EVEN THINK YOU WERE LINGUAL.
I AIN'T JUST HIRED MUSCLE, SIR, I'M YOUR CHIEF OF SECURITY. I DO WHATEVER HOMEWORK IT TAKES TO BE A GOOD FACE FOR YOU AND THE ADMINISTRATION.
BUT I GOTTA LISTEN TO MY LANGUAGE TAPES CLOSER.
I ALMOST THOUGHT THIS BROAD SAID SOME-THING ABOUT GOING TO THE STARS.

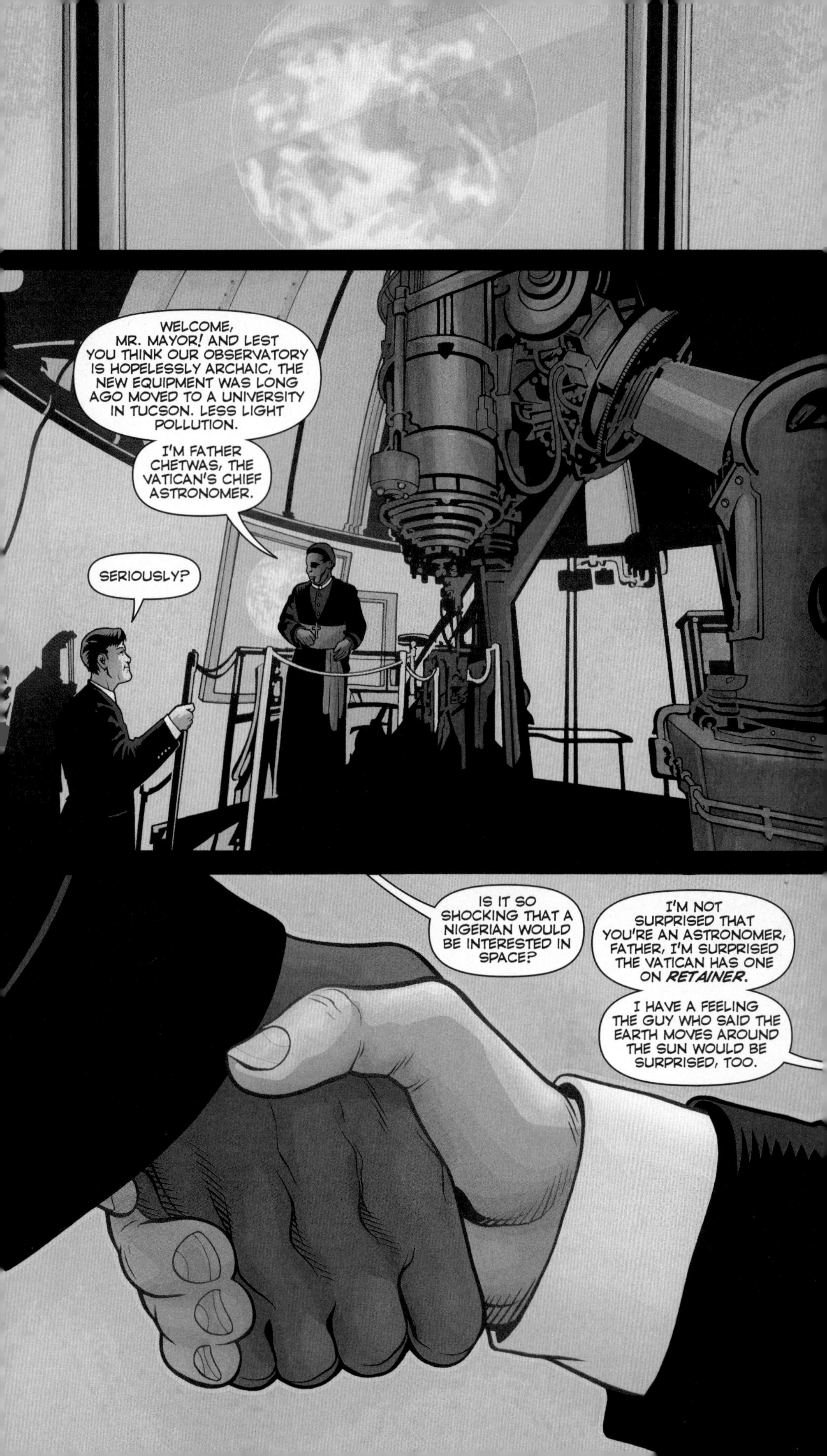
WELCOME, MR. MAYOR! AND LEST YOU THINK OUR OBSERVATORY IS HOPELESSLY ARCHAIC, THE NEW EQUIPMENT WAS LONG AGO MOVED TO A UNIVERSITY IN TUCSON. LESS LIGHT POLLUTION.
I'M FATHER CHETWAS, THE VATICAN'S CHIEF ASTRONOMER.
SERIOUSLY?
IS IT SO SHOCKING THAT A NIGERIAN WOULD BE INTERESTED IN SPACE?
I'M NOT SURPRISED THAT YOU'RE AN ASTRONOMER, FATHER, I'M SURPRISED THE VATICAN HAS ONE ON ***RETAINER***.
I HAVE A FEELING THE GUY WHO SAID THE EARTH MOVES AROUND THE SUN WOULD BE SURPRISED, TOO.

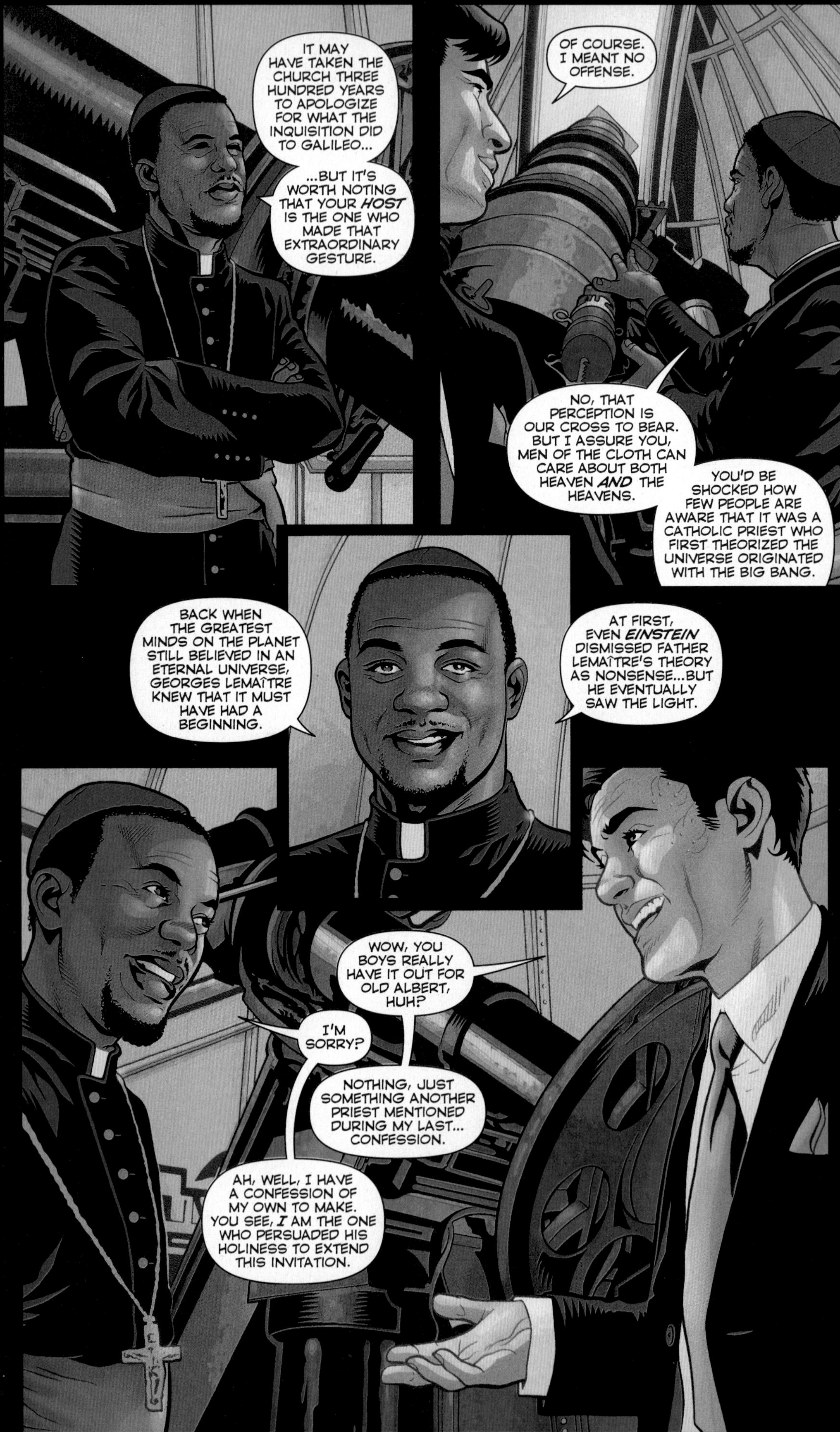
IT MAY HAVE TAKEN THE CHURCH THREE HUNDRED YEARS TO APOLOGIZE FOR WHAT THE INQUISITION DID TO GALILEO...
...BUT IT'S WORTH NOTING THAT YOUR *HOST* IS THE ONE WHO MADE THAT EXTRAORDINARY GESTURE.
OF COURSE. I MEANT NO OFFENSE.
NO, THAT PERCEPTION IS OUR CROSS TO BEAR. BUT I ASSURE YOU, MEN OF THE CLOTH CAN CARE ABOUT BOTH HEAVEN *AND* THE HEAVENS.
YOU'D BE SHOCKED HOW FEW PEOPLE ARE AWARE THAT IT WAS A CATHOLIC PRIEST WHO FIRST THEORIZED THE UNIVERSE ORIGINATED WITH THE BIG BANG.
BACK WHEN THE GREATEST MINDS ON THE PLANET STILL BELIEVED IN AN ETERNAL UNIVERSE, GEORGES LEMAÎTRE KNEW THAT IT MUST HAVE HAD A BEGINNING.
AT FIRST, EVEN *EINSTEIN* DISMISSED FATHER LEMAÎTRE'S THEORY AS NONSENSE...BUT HE EVENTUALLY SAW THE LIGHT.
WOW, YOU BOYS REALLY HAVE IT OUT FOR OLD ALBERT, HUH?
I'M SORRY?
NOTHING, JUST SOMETHING ANOTHER PRIEST MENTIONED DURING MY LAST... CONFESSION.
AH, WELL, I HAVE A CONFESSION OF MY OWN TO MAKE. YOU SEE, *I* AM THE ONE WHO PERSUADED HIS HOLINESS TO EXTEND THIS INVITATION.

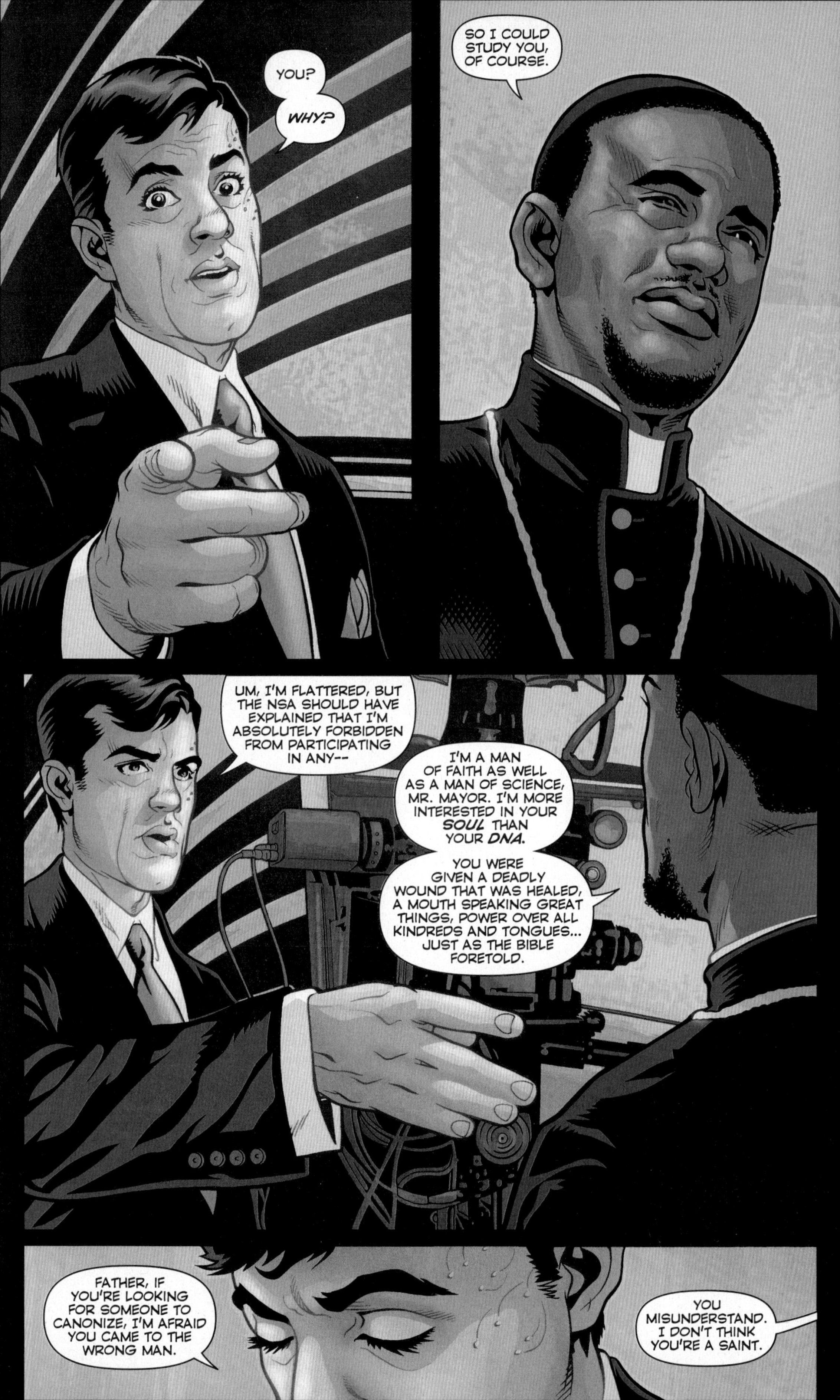
YOU?
WHY?
SO I COULD STUDY YOU, OF COURSE.
UM, I'M FLATTERED, BUT THE NSA SHOULD HAVE EXPLAINED THAT I'M ABSOLUTELY FORBIDDEN FROM PARTICIPATING IN ANY--
I'M A MAN OF FAITH AS WELL AS A MAN OF SCIENCE, MR. MAYOR. I'M MORE INTERESTED IN YOUR *SOUL* THAN YOUR *DNA*.
YOU WERE GIVEN A DEADLY WOUND THAT WAS HEALED, A MOUTH SPEAKING GREAT THINGS, POWER OVER ALL KINDREDS AND TONGUES... JUST AS THE BIBLE FORETOLD.
FATHER, IF YOU'RE LOOKING FOR SOMEONE TO CANONIZE, I'M AFRAID YOU CAME TO THE WRONG MAN.
YOU MISUNDERSTAND. I DON'T THINK YOU'RE A SAINT.

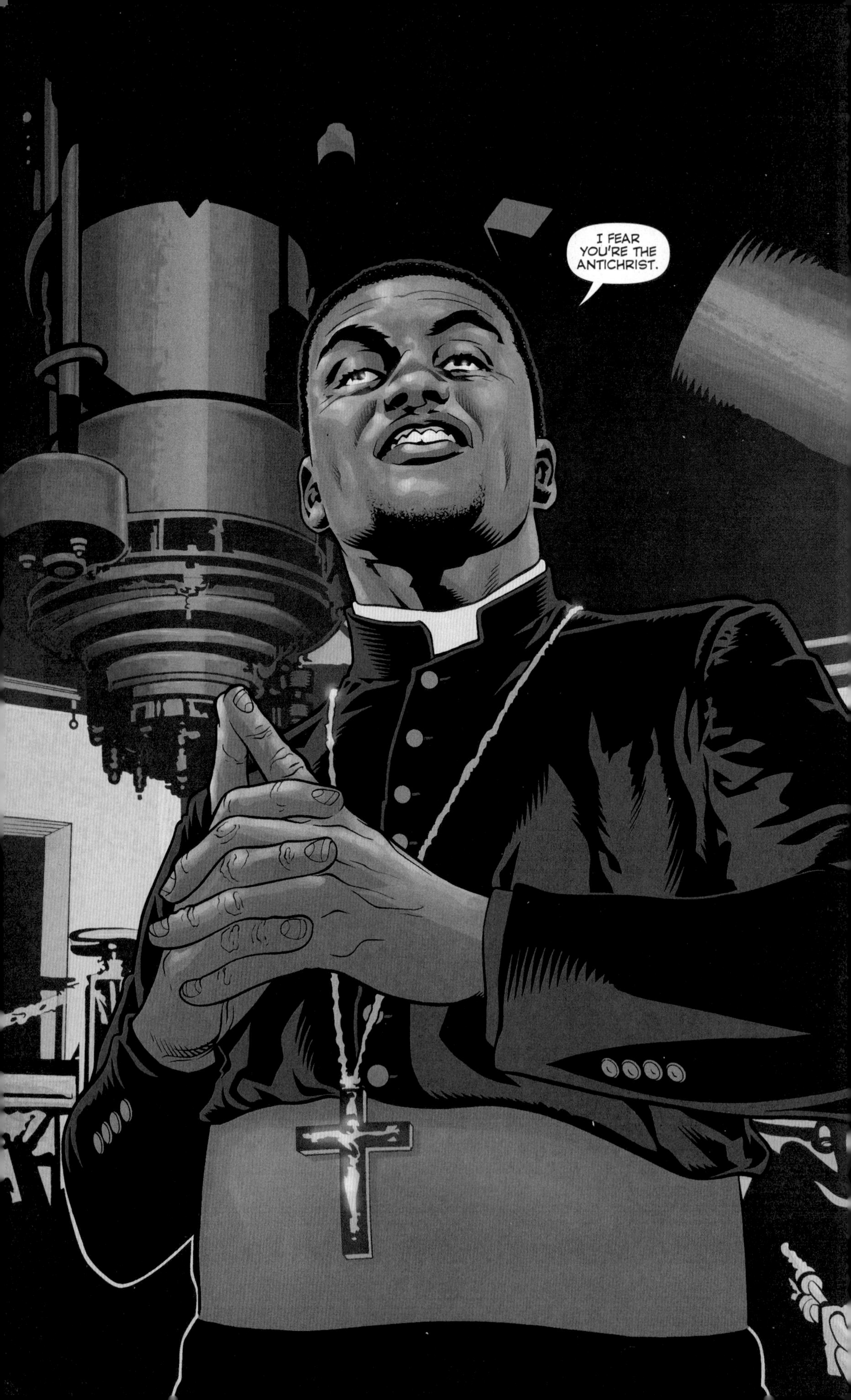
I FEAR YOU'RE THE ANTICHRIST.

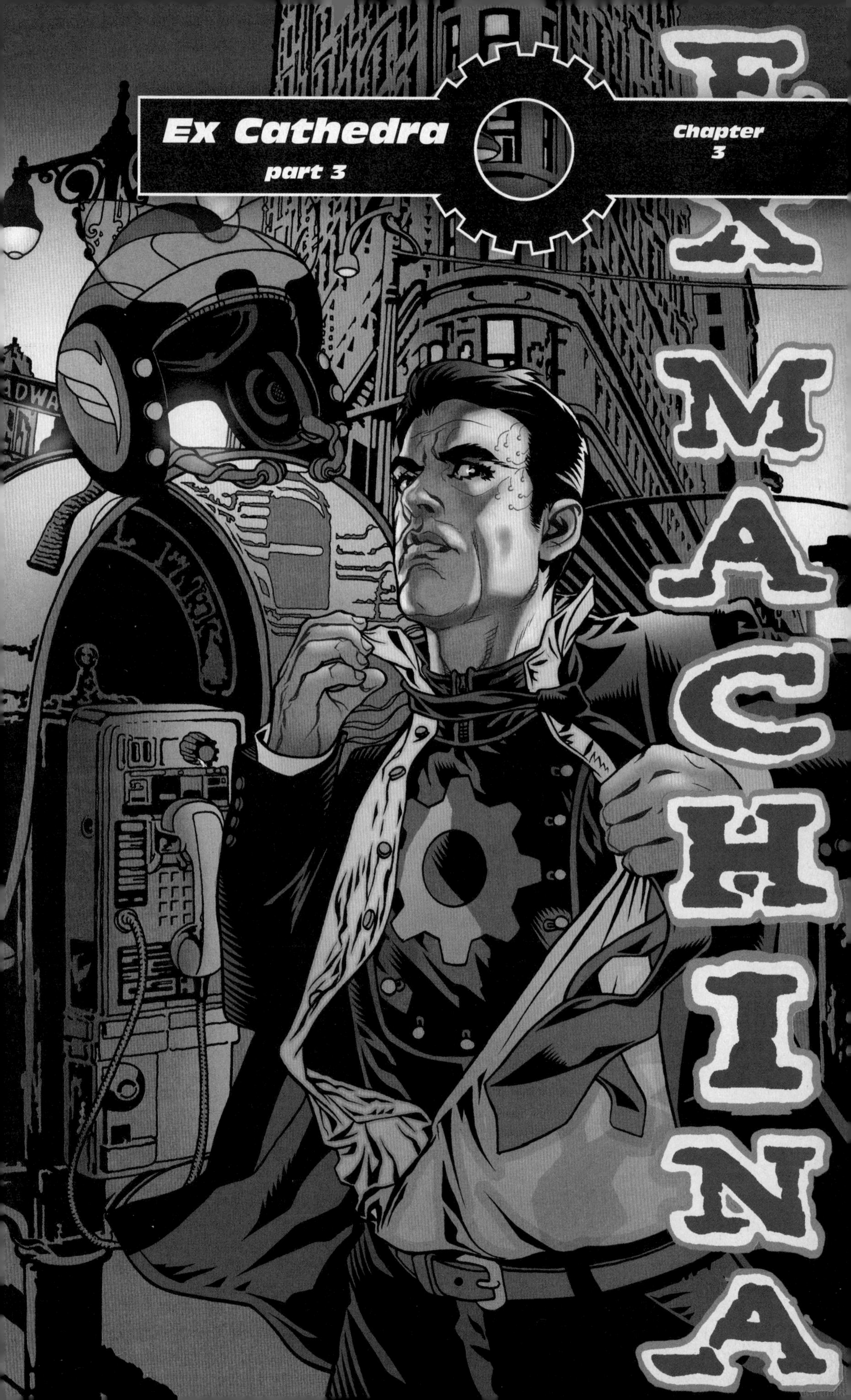
Ex Cathedra
part 3
Chapter
3
EX MACHINA

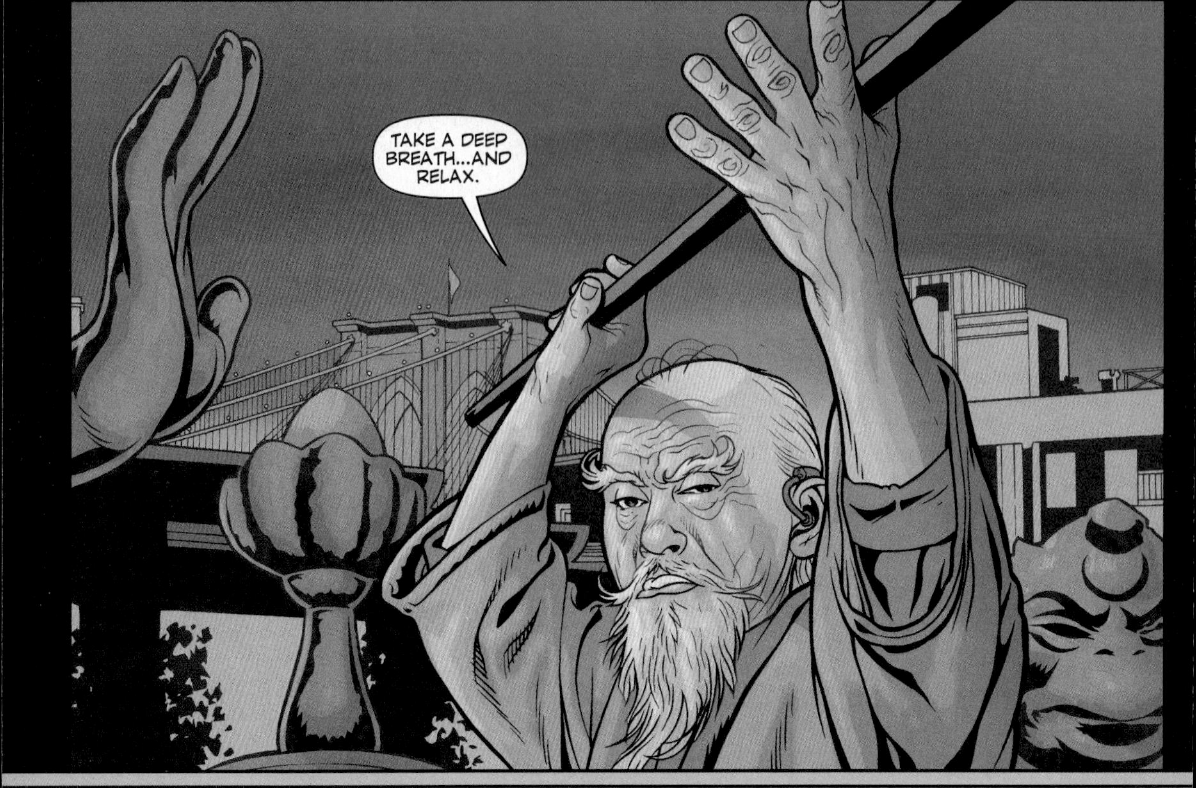
TAKE A DEEP BREATH...AND RELAX.

TUESDAY, MAY 29, 2001

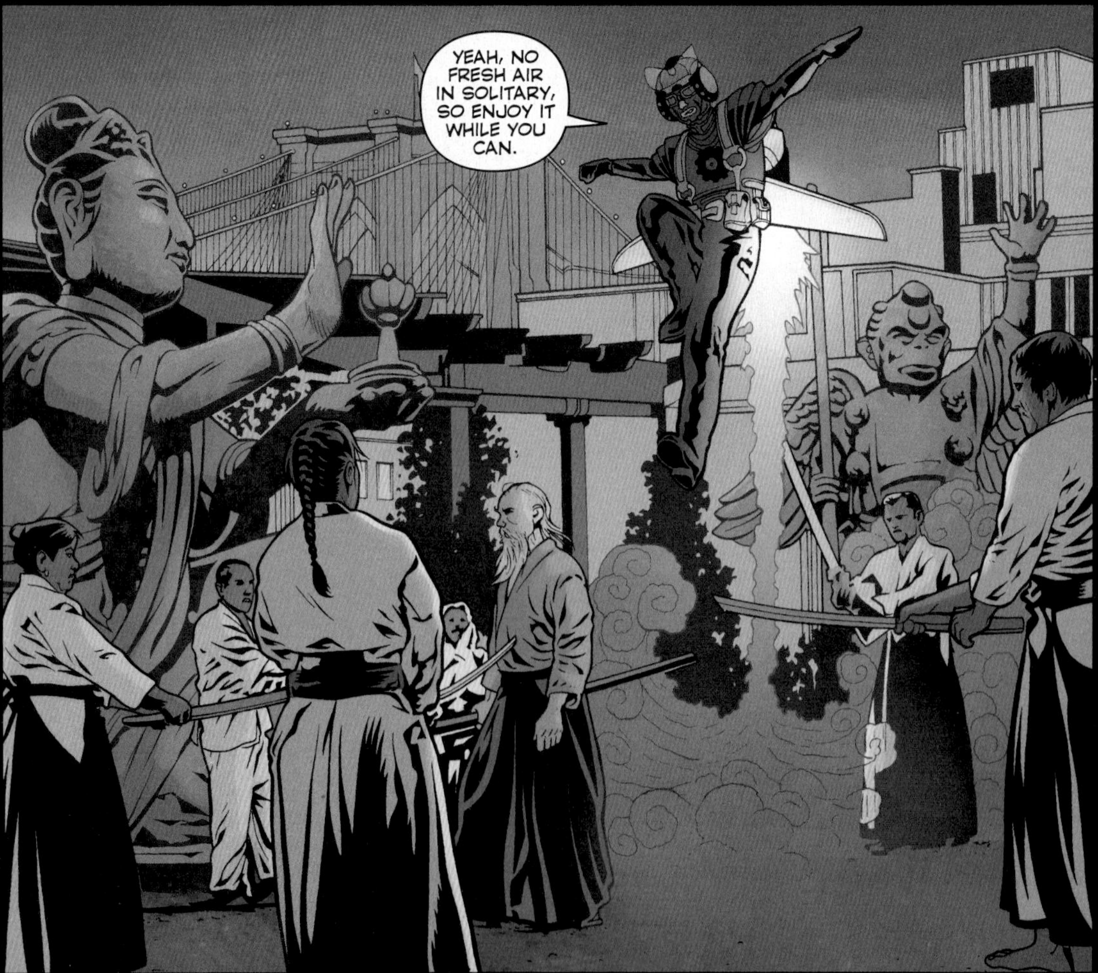
YEAH, NO FRESH AIR IN SOLITARY, SO ENJOY IT WHILE YOU CAN.

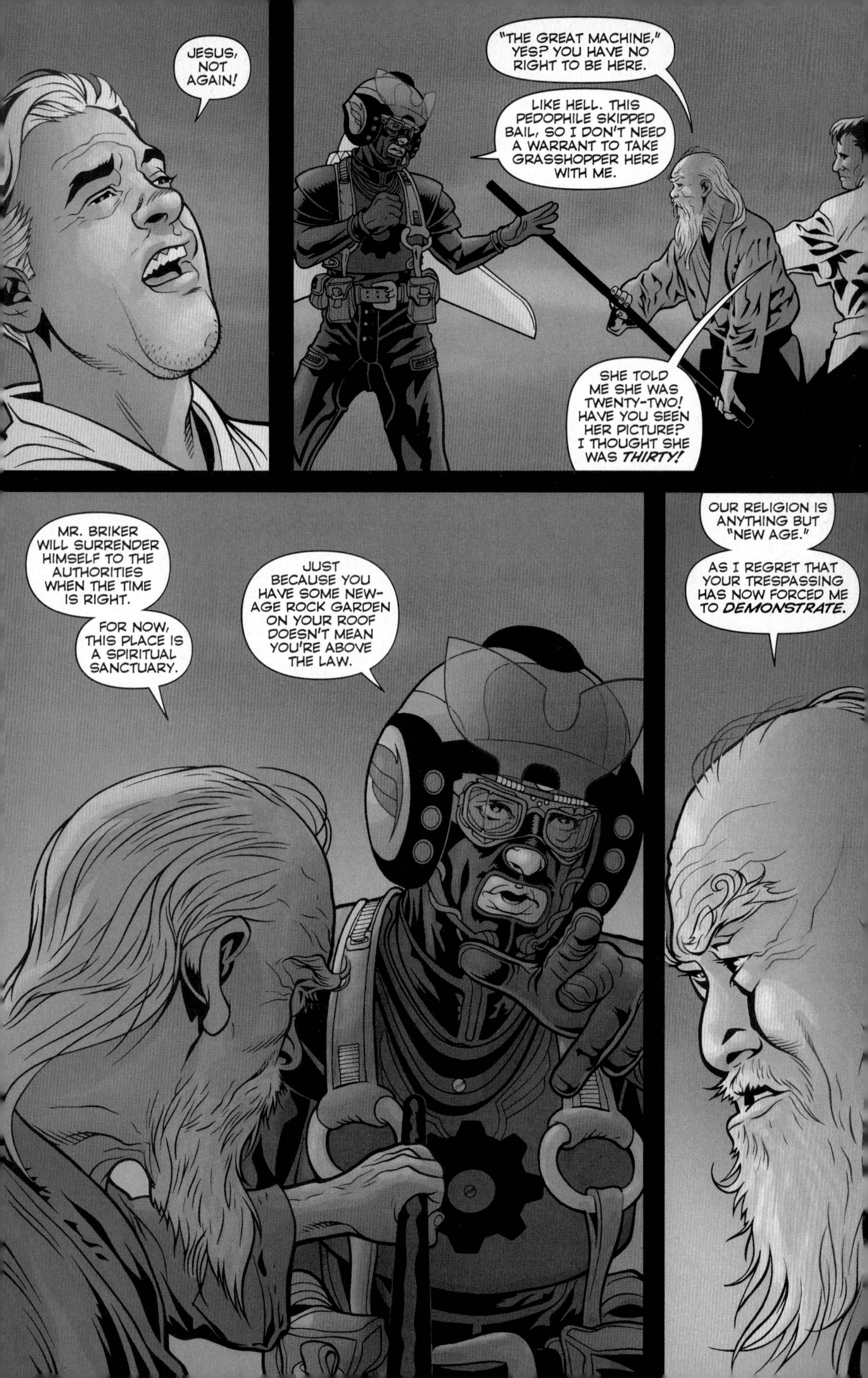
JESUS, NOT AGAIN!
"THE GREAT MACHINE," YES? YOU HAVE NO RIGHT TO BE HERE.
LIKE HELL. THIS PEDOPHILE SKIPPED BAIL, SO I DON'T NEED A WARRANT TO TAKE GRASSHOPPER HERE WITH ME.
SHE TOLD ME SHE WAS TWENTY-TWO! HAVE YOU SEEN HER PICTURE? I THOUGHT SHE WAS THIRTY!
MR. BRIKER WILL SURRENDER HIMSELF TO THE AUTHORITIES WHEN THE TIME IS RIGHT.
FOR NOW, THIS PLACE IS A SPIRITUAL SANCTUARY.
JUST BECAUSE YOU HAVE SOME NEW-AGE ROCK GARDEN ON YOUR ROOF DOESN'T MEAN YOU'RE ABOVE THE LAW.
OUR RELIGION IS ANYTHING BUT "NEW AGE."
AS I REGRET THAT YOUR TRESPASSING HAS NOW FORCED ME TO DEMONSTRATE.

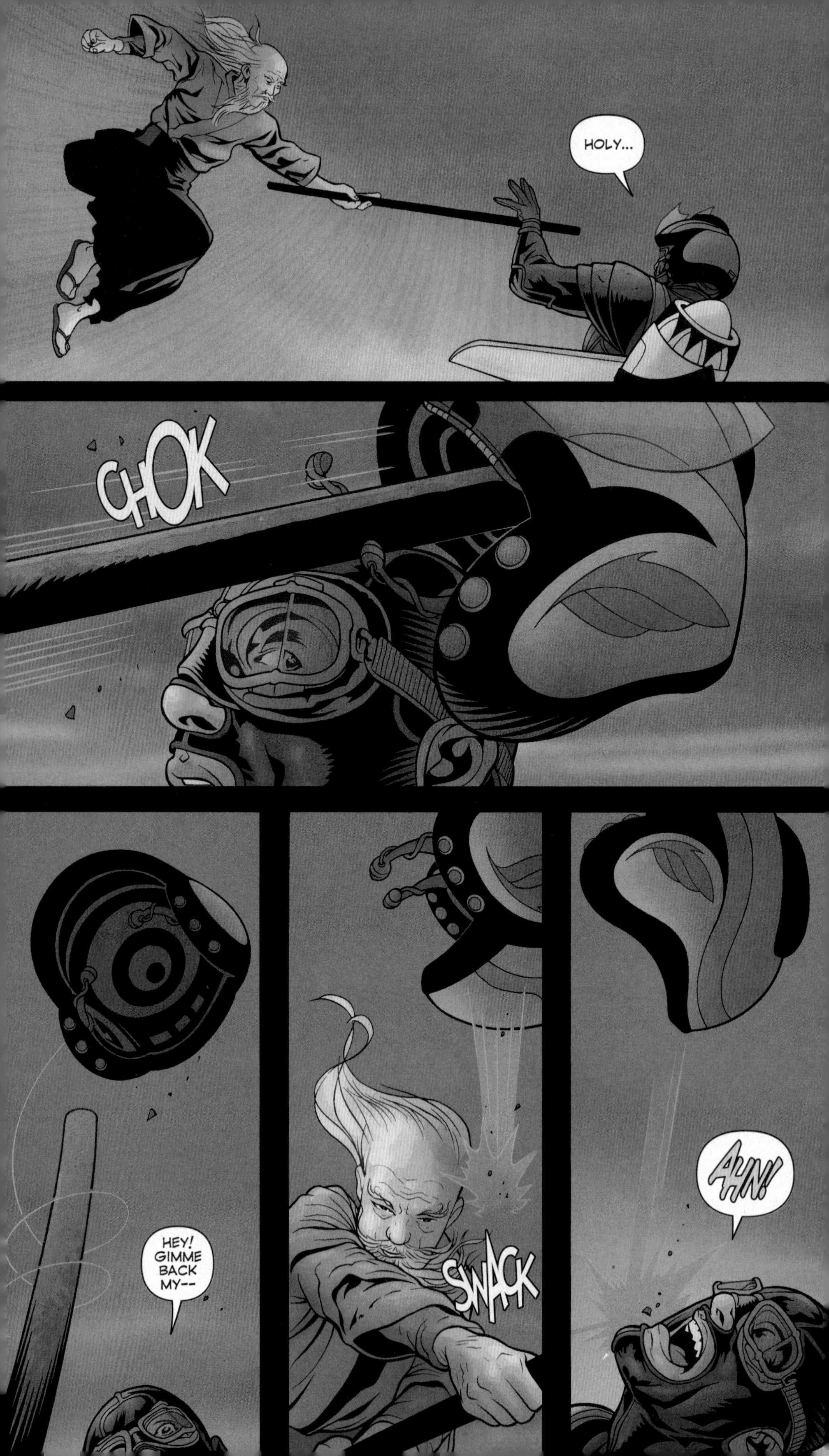
HOLY...
CHOK
HEY! GIMME BACK MY--
SWACK
AHN!

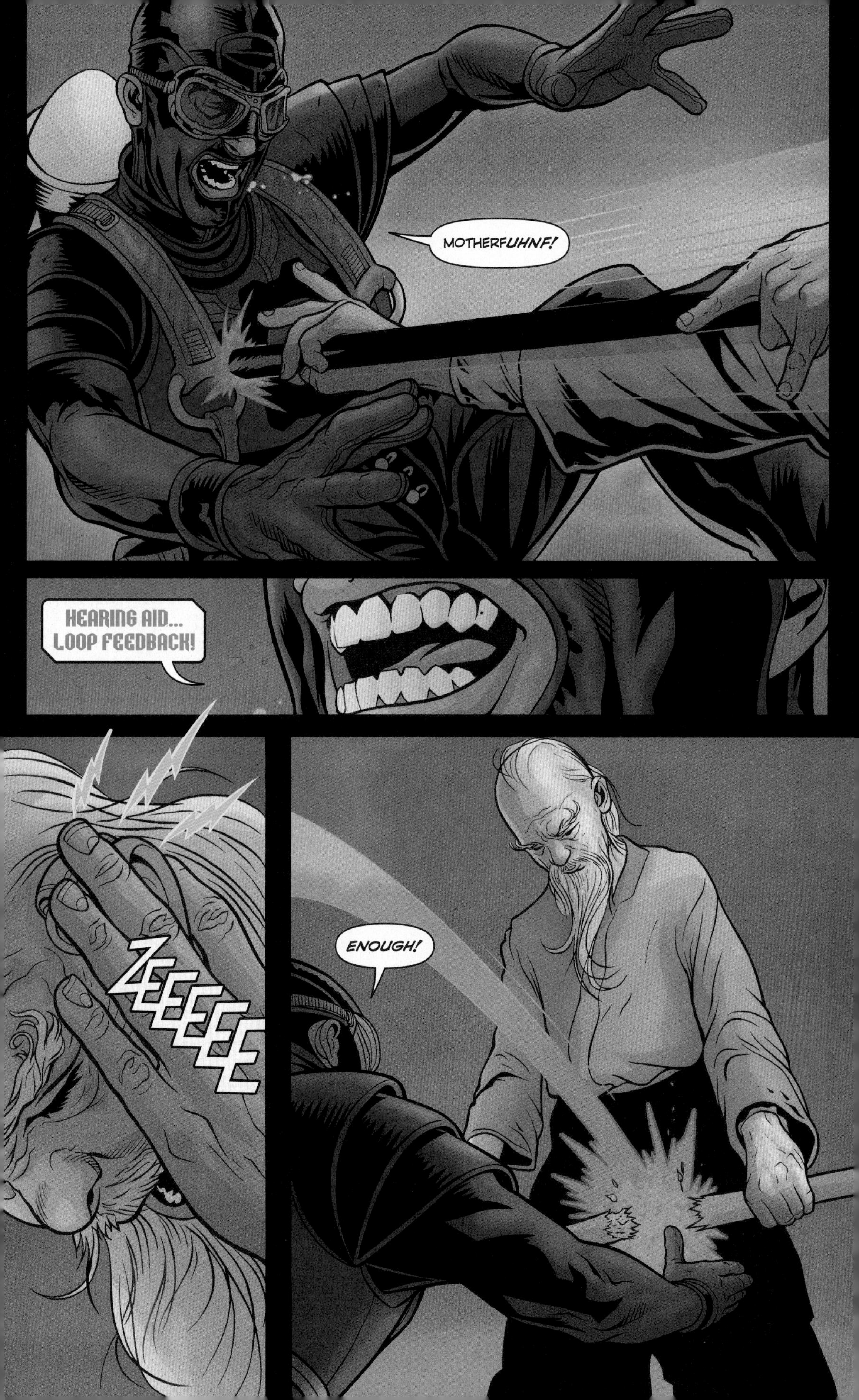
MOTHERFUHNF!
HEARING AID... LOOP FEEDBACK!
ZEEEEEE
ENOUGH!

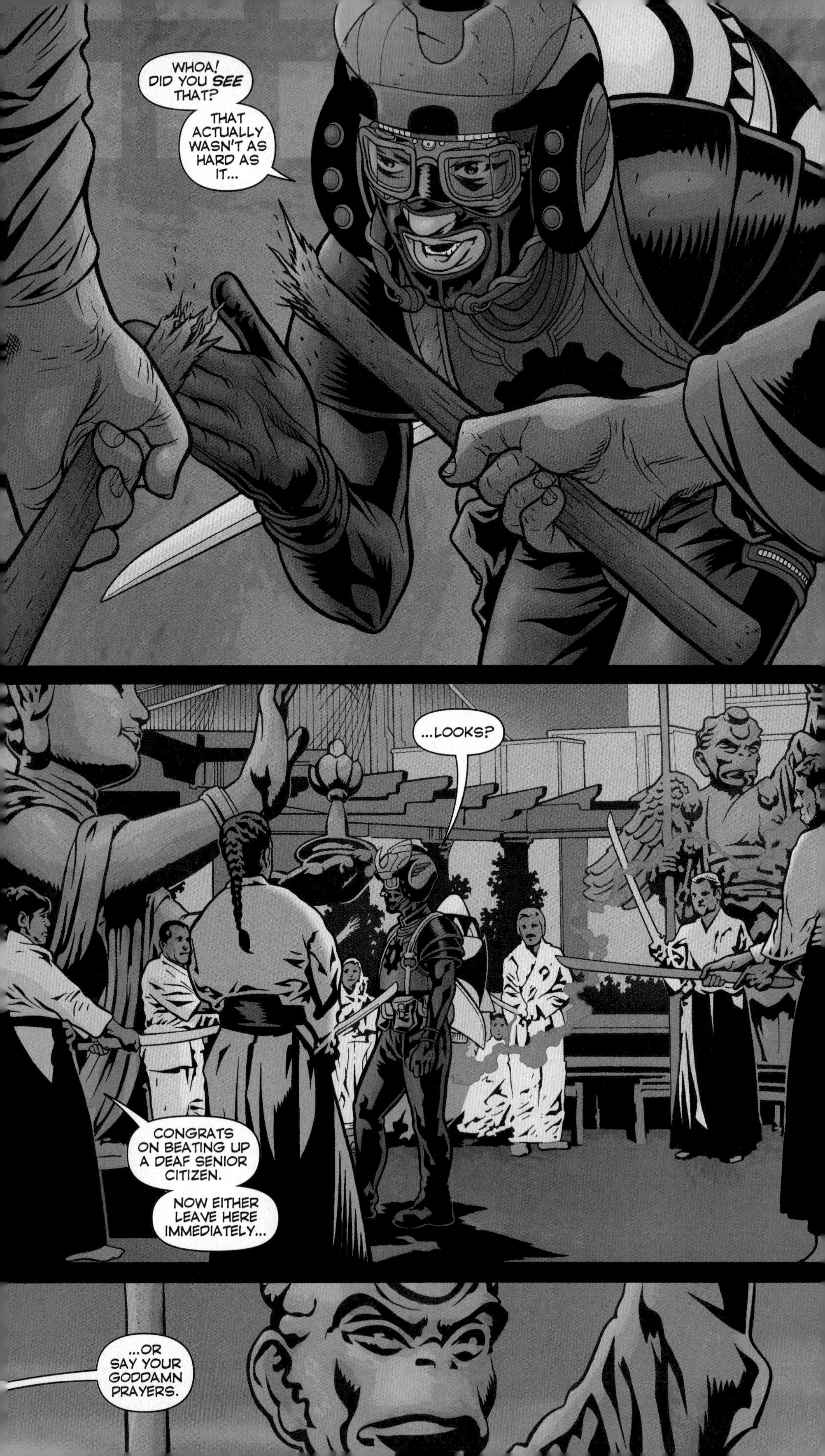
WHOA! DID YOU SEE THAT?
THAT ACTUALLY WASN'T AS HARD AS IT...
...LOOKS?
CONGRATS ON BEATING UP A DEAF SENIOR CITIZEN.
NOW EITHER LEAVE HERE IMMEDIATELY...
...OR SAY YOUR GODDAMN PRAYERS.

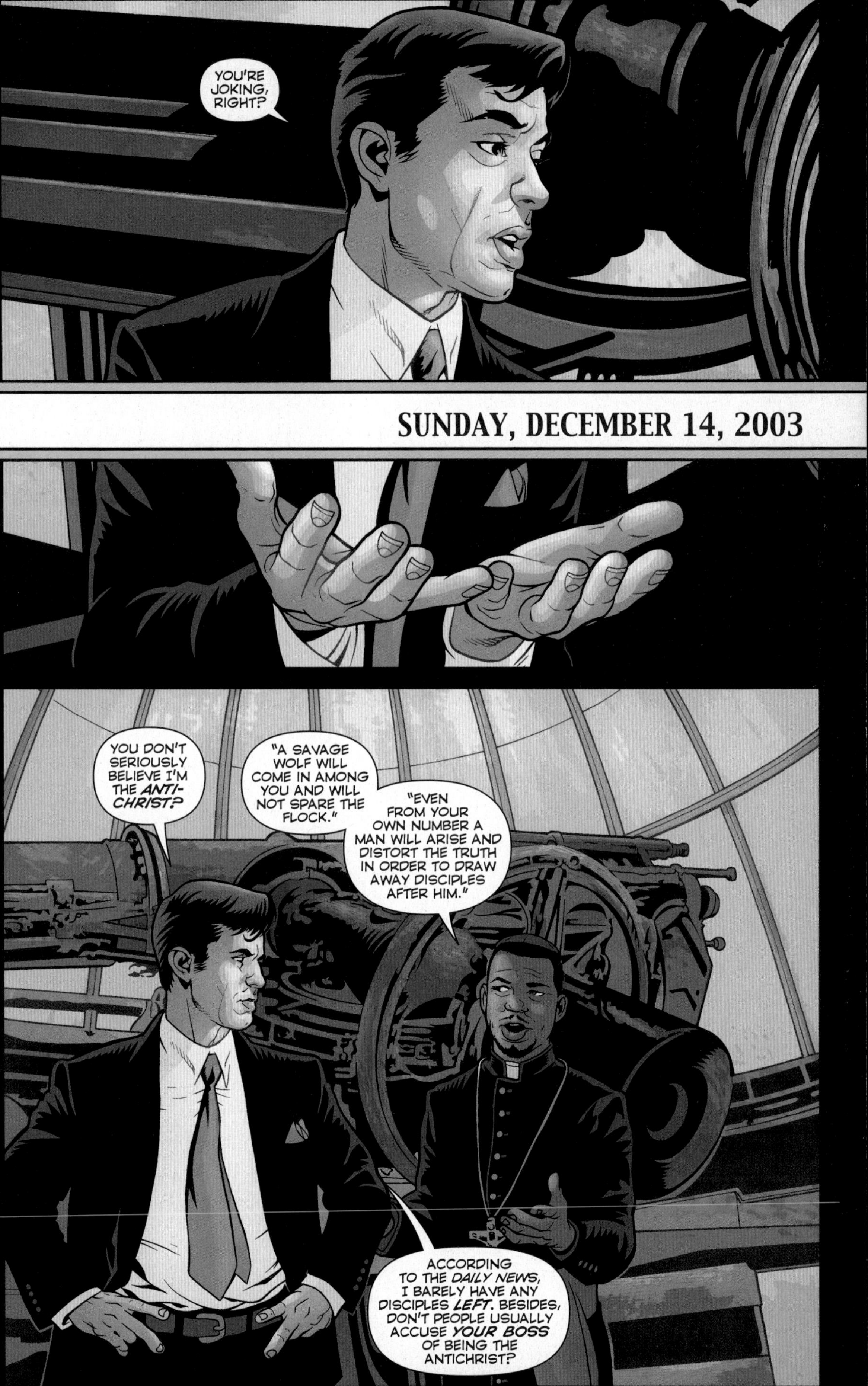
YOU'RE JOKING, RIGHT?
SUNDAY, DECEMBER 14, 2003
YOU DON'T SERIOUSLY BELIEVE I'M THE *ANTI-CHRIST?*
"A SAVAGE WOLF WILL COME IN AMONG YOU AND WILL NOT SPARE THE FLOCK."
"EVEN FROM YOUR OWN NUMBER A MAN WILL ARISE AND DISTORT THE TRUTH IN ORDER TO DRAW AWAY DISCIPLES AFTER HIM."
ACCORDING TO THE *DAILY NEWS*, I BARELY HAVE ANY DISCIPLES *LEFT*. BESIDES, DON'T PEOPLE USUALLY ACCUSE ***YOUR BOSS*** OF BEING THE ANTICHRIST?

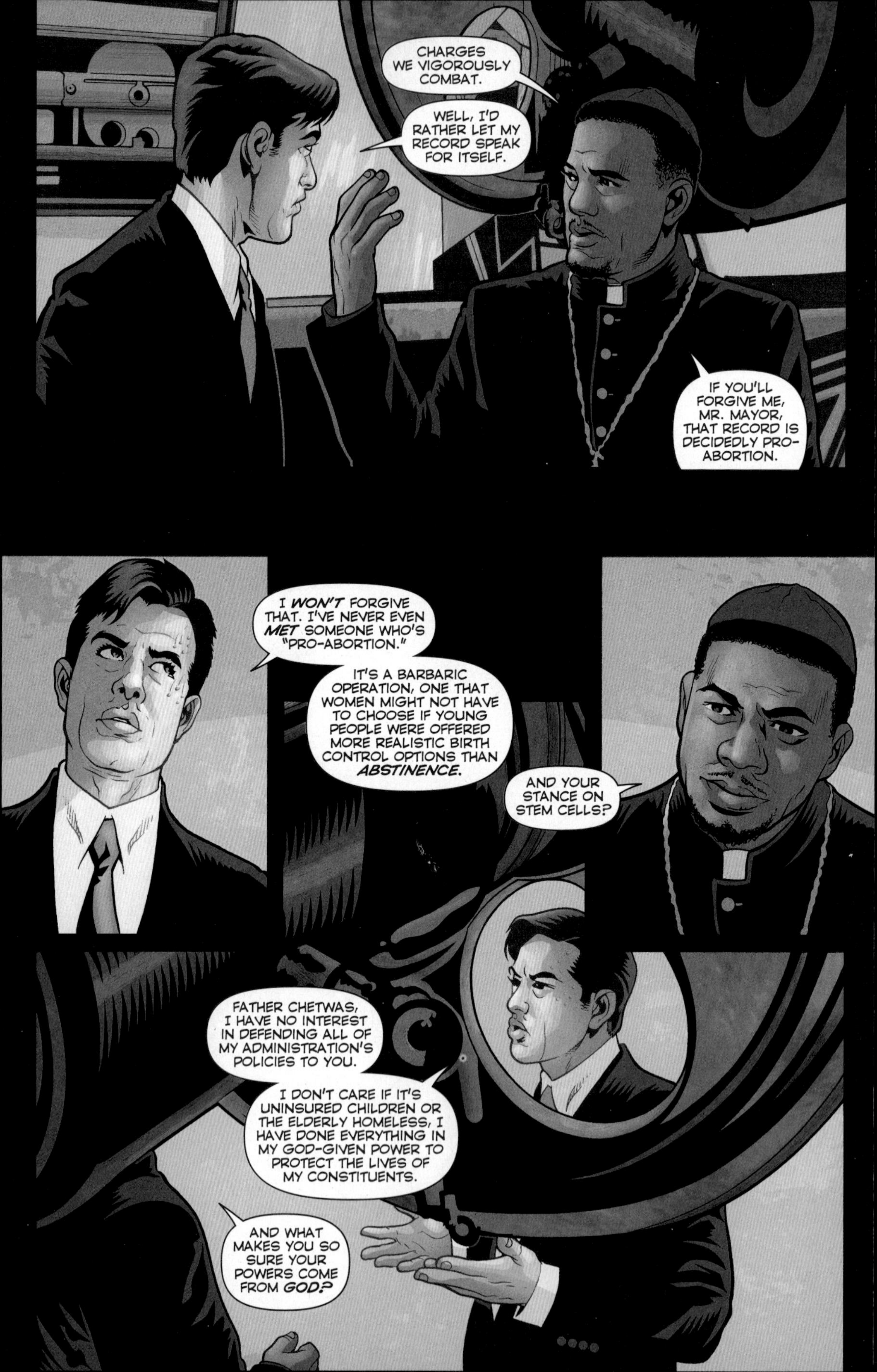
CHARGES WE VIGOROUSLY COMBAT.
WELL, I'D RATHER LET MY RECORD SPEAK FOR ITSELF.
IF YOU'LL FORGIVE ME, MR. MAYOR, THAT RECORD IS DECIDEDLY PRO-ABORTION.
I *WON'T* FORGIVE THAT. I'VE NEVER EVEN *MET* SOMEONE WHO'S "PRO-ABORTION."
IT'S A BARBARIC OPERATION, ONE THAT WOMEN MIGHT NOT HAVE TO CHOOSE IF YOUNG PEOPLE WERE OFFERED MORE REALISTIC BIRTH CONTROL OPTIONS THAN *ABSTINENCE*.
AND YOUR STANCE ON STEM CELLS?
FATHER CHETWAS, I HAVE NO INTEREST IN DEFENDING ALL OF MY ADMINISTRATION'S POLICIES TO YOU.
I DON'T CARE IF IT'S UNINSURED CHILDREN OR THE ELDERLY HOMELESS, I HAVE DONE EVERYTHING IN MY GOD-GIVEN POWER TO PROTECT THE LIVES OF MY CONSTITUENTS.
AND WHAT MAKES YOU SO SURE YOUR POWERS COME FROM *GOD?*

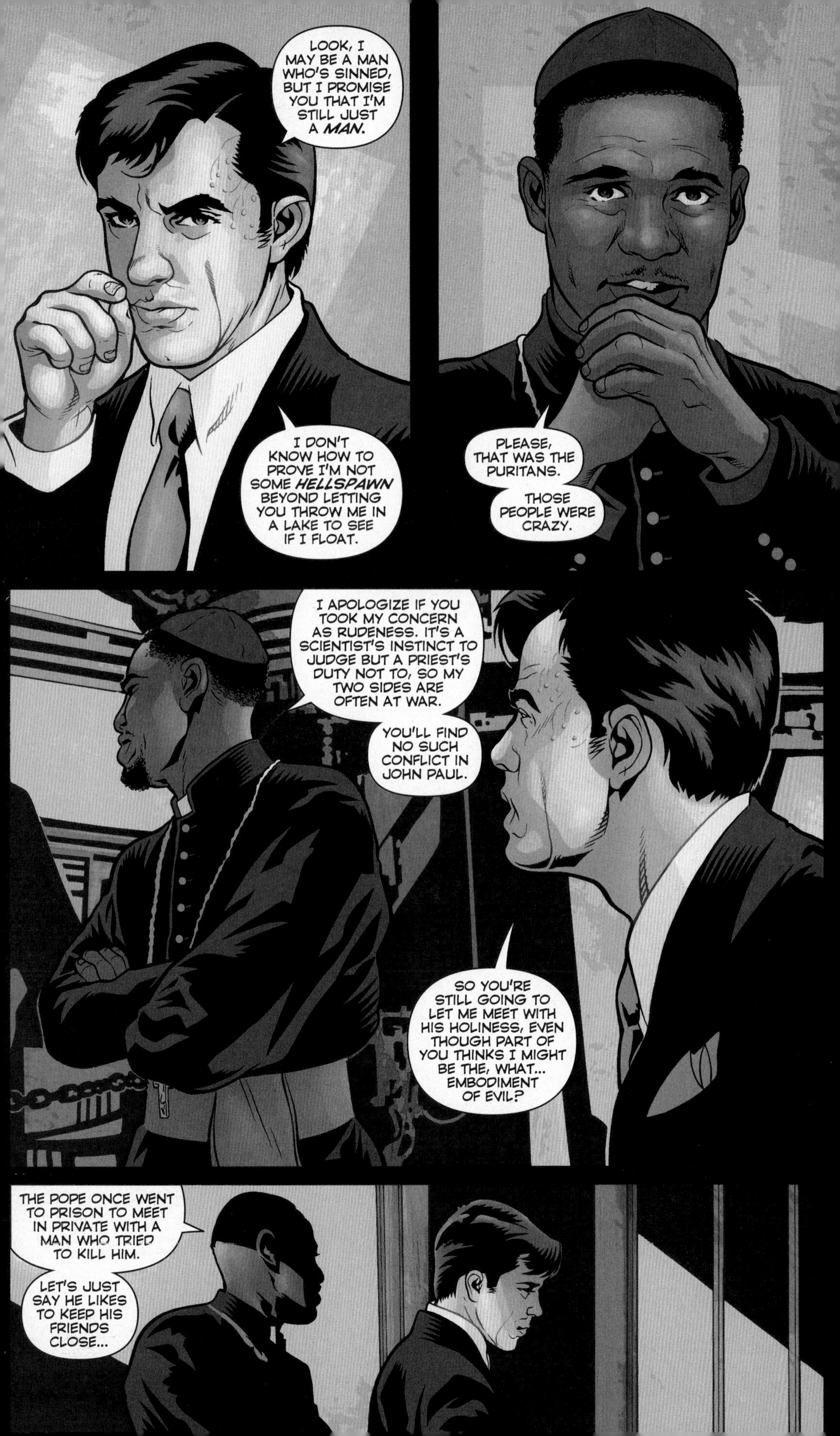
LOOK, I MAY BE A MAN WHO'S SINNED, BUT I PROMISE YOU THAT I'M STILL JUST A *MAN.*
I DON'T KNOW HOW TO PROVE I'M NOT SOME *HELLSPAWN* BEYOND LETTING YOU THROW ME IN A LAKE TO SEE IF I FLOAT.
PLEASE, THAT WAS THE PURITANS.
THOSE PEOPLE WERE CRAZY.
I APOLOGIZE IF YOU TOOK MY CONCERN AS RUDENESS. IT'S A SCIENTIST'S INSTINCT TO JUDGE BUT A PRIEST'S DUTY NOT TO, SO MY TWO SIDES ARE OFTEN AT WAR.
YOU'LL FIND NO SUCH CONFLICT IN JOHN PAUL.
SO YOU'RE STILL GOING TO LET ME MEET WITH HIS HOLINESS, EVEN THOUGH PART OF YOU THINKS I MIGHT BE THE, WHAT... EMBODIMENT OF EVIL?
THE POPE ONCE WENT TO PRISON TO MEET IN PRIVATE WITH A MAN WHO TRIED TO KILL HIM.
LET'S JUST SAY HE LIKES TO KEEP HIS FRIENDS CLOSE...

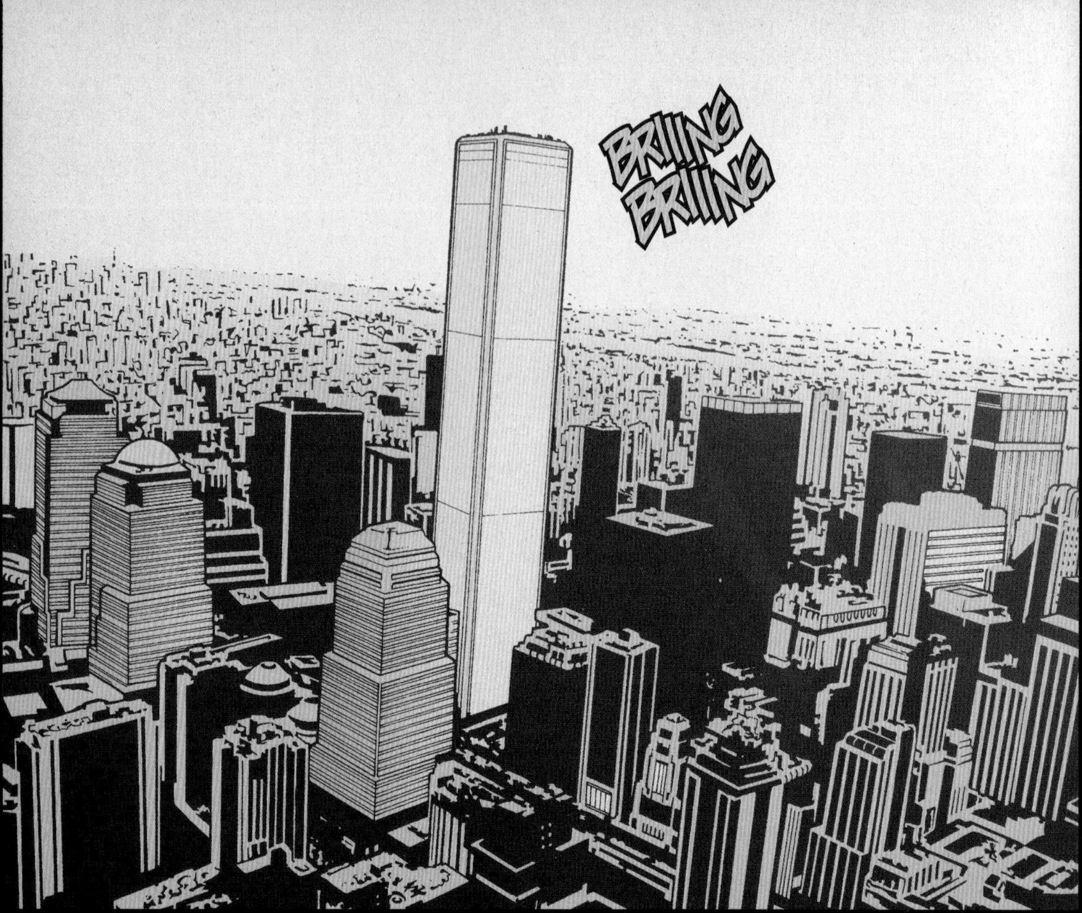
BRIIING BRIIING

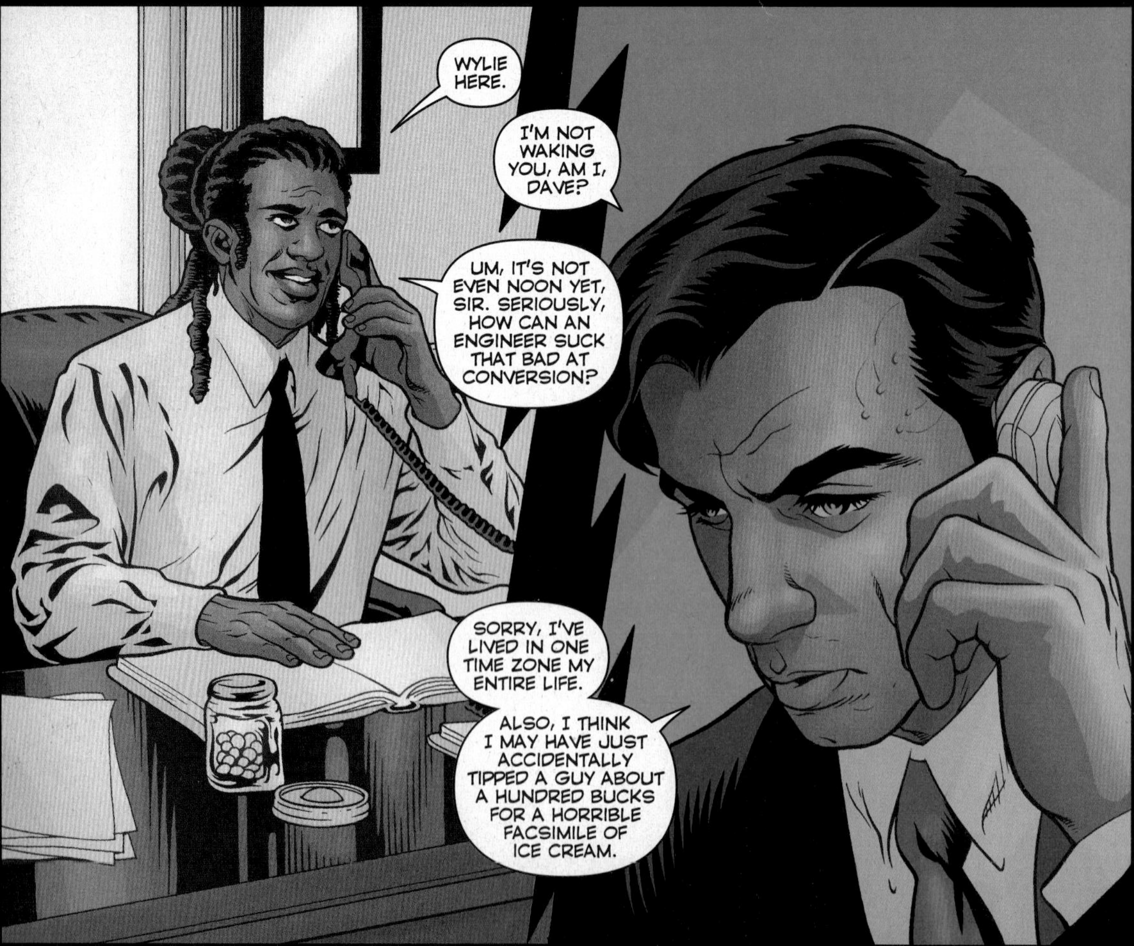
WYLIE HERE.
I'M NOT WAKING YOU, AM I, DAVE?
UM, IT'S NOT EVEN NOON YET, SIR. SERIOUSLY, HOW CAN AN ENGINEER SUCK THAT BAD AT CONVERSION?
SORRY, I'VE LIVED IN ONE TIME ZONE MY ENTIRE LIFE.
ALSO, I THINK I MAY HAVE JUST ACCIDENTALLY TIPPED A GUY ABOUT A HUNDRED BUCKS FOR A HORRIBLE FACSIMILE OF ICE CREAM.

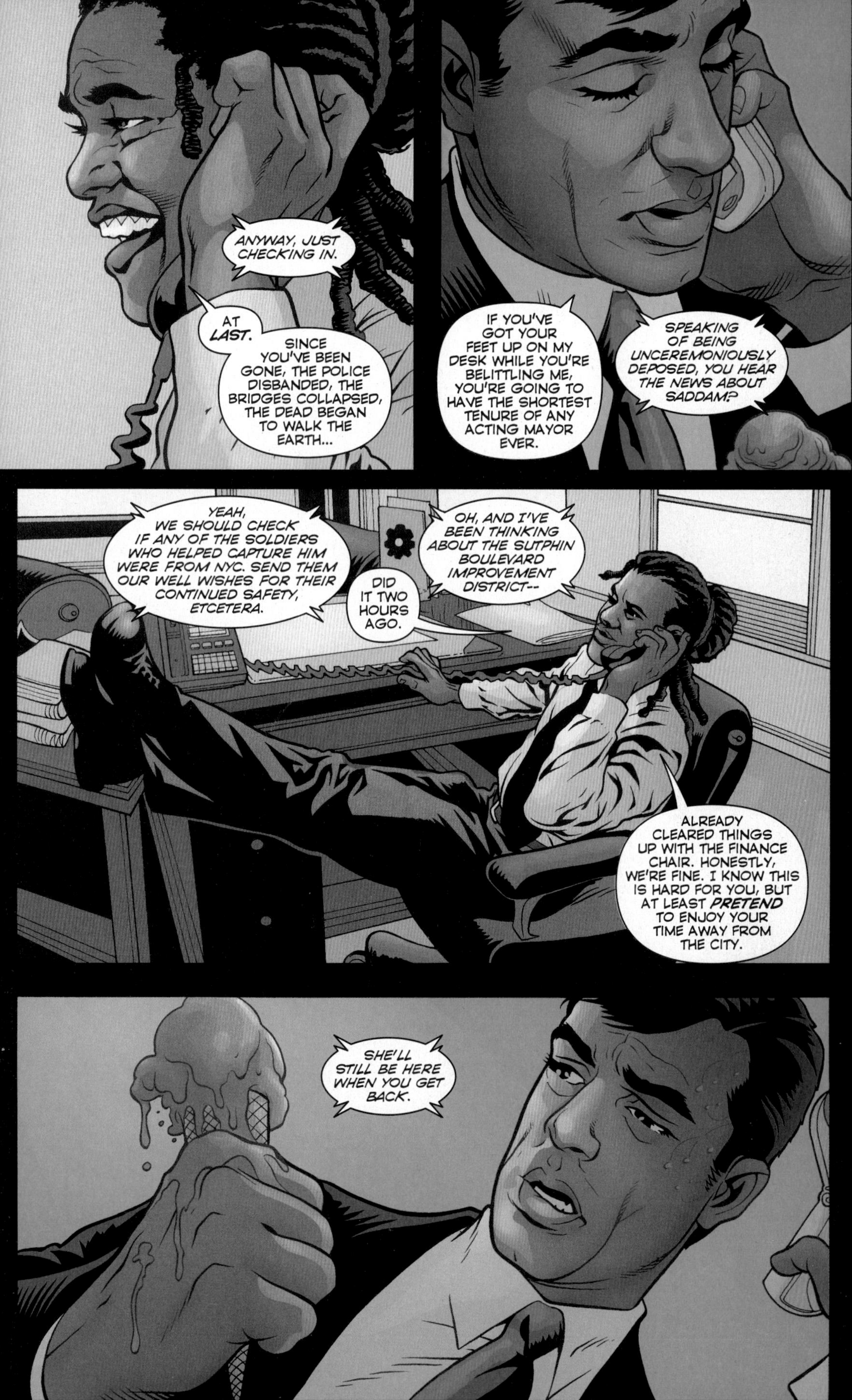

ANYWAY, JUST CHECKING IN.
AT *LAST*.
SINCE YOU'VE BEEN GONE, THE POLICE DISBANDED, THE BRIDGES COLLAPSED, THE DEAD BEGAN TO WALK THE EARTH...
IF YOU'VE GOT YOUR FEET UP ON MY DESK WHILE YOU'RE BELITTLING ME, YOU'RE GOING TO HAVE THE SHORTEST TENURE OF ANY ACTING MAYOR EVER.
SPEAKING OF BEING UNCEREMONIOUSLY DEPOSED, YOU HEAR THE NEWS ABOUT SADDAM?
YEAH, WE SHOULD CHECK IF ANY OF THE SOLDIERS WHO HELPED CAPTURE HIM WERE FROM NYC. SEND THEM OUR WELL WISHES FOR THEIR CONTINUED SAFETY, ETCETERA.
DID IT TWO HOURS AGO.
OH, AND I'VE BEEN THINKING ABOUT THE SUTPHIN BOULEVARD IMPROVEMENT DISTRICT--
ALREADY CLEARED THINGS UP WITH THE FINANCE CHAIR. HONESTLY, WE'RE FINE. I KNOW THIS IS HARD FOR YOU, BUT AT LEAST *PRETEND* TO ENJOY YOUR TIME AWAY FROM THE CITY.
SHE'LL STILL BE HERE WHEN YOU GET BACK.

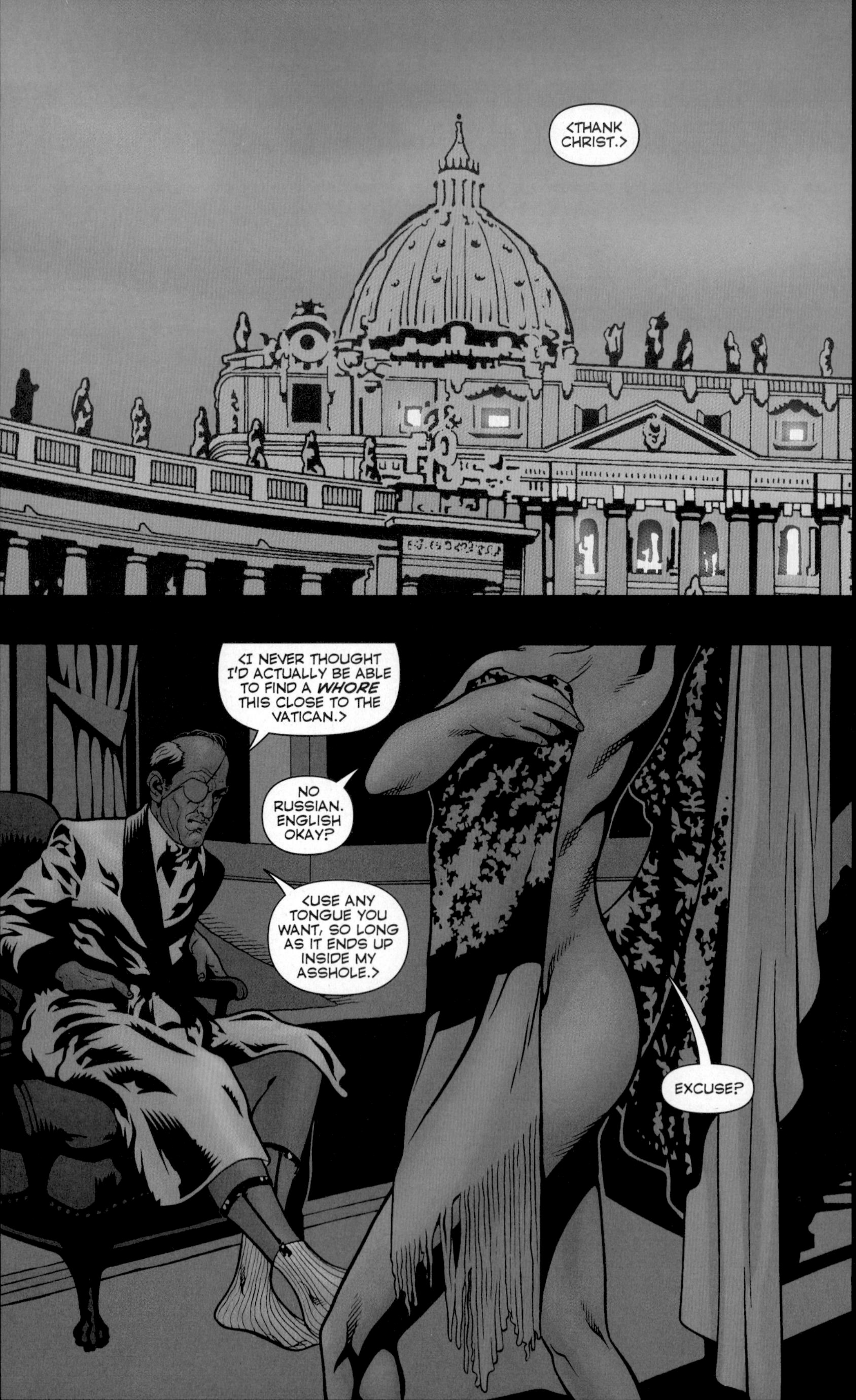
<THANK CHRIST.>
<I NEVER THOUGHT I'D ACTUALLY BE ABLE TO FIND A *WHORE* THIS CLOSE TO THE VATICAN.>
NO RUSSIAN. ENGLISH OKAY?
<USE ANY TONGUE YOU WANT, SO LONG AS IT ENDS UP INSIDE MY ASSHOLE.>
EXCUSE?

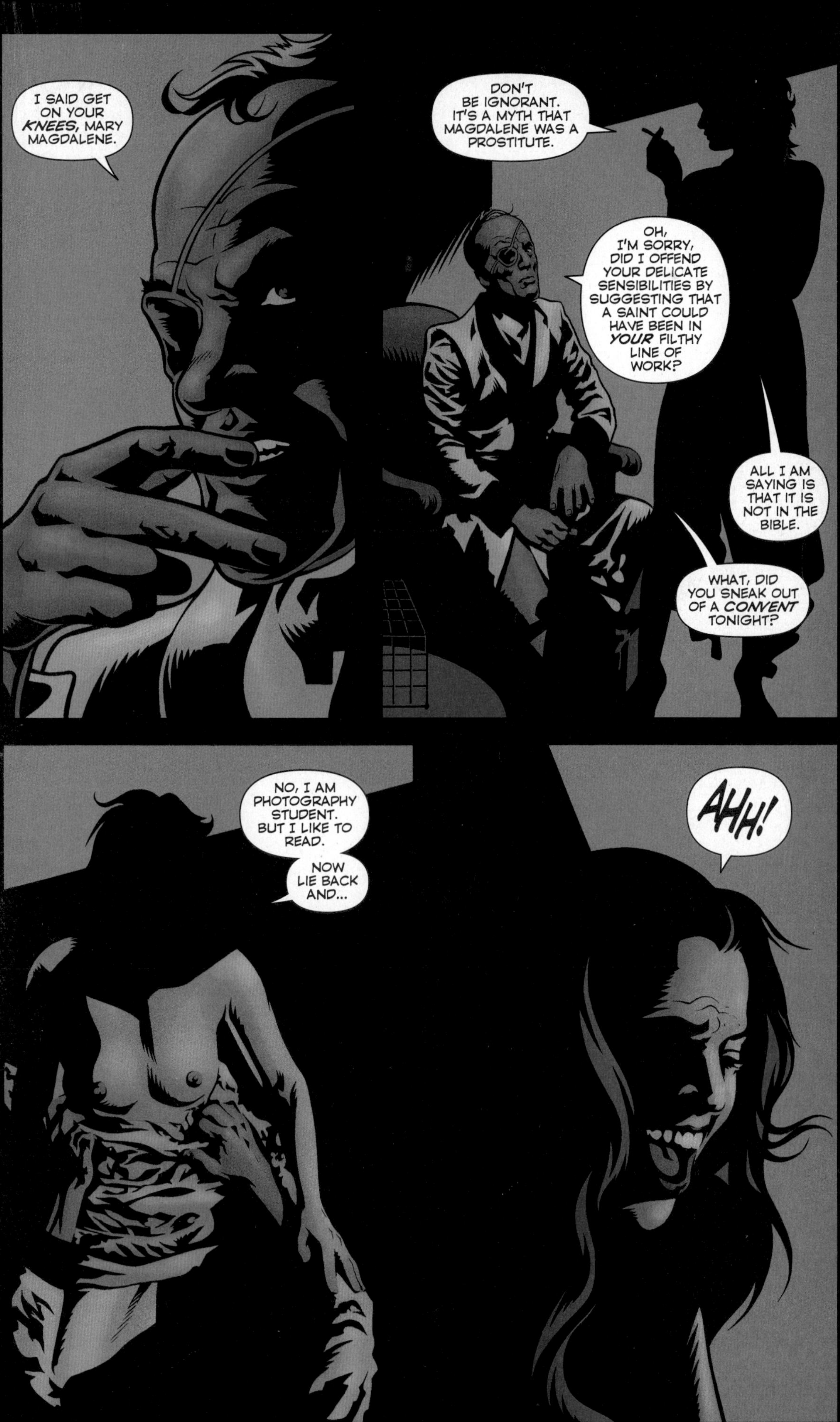
I SAID GET ON YOUR KNEES, MARY MAGDALENE.
DON'T BE IGNORANT. IT'S A MYTH THAT MAGDALENE WAS A PROSTITUTE.
OH, I'M SORRY, DID I OFFEND YOUR DELICATE SENSIBILITIES BY SUGGESTING THAT A SAINT COULD HAVE BEEN IN YOUR FILTHY LINE OF WORK?
ALL I AM SAYING IS THAT IT IS NOT IN THE BIBLE.
WHAT, DID YOU SNEAK OUT OF A CONVENT TONIGHT?
NO, I AM PHOTOGRAPHY STUDENT. BUT I LIKE TO READ.
NOW LIE BACK AND...
AHH!

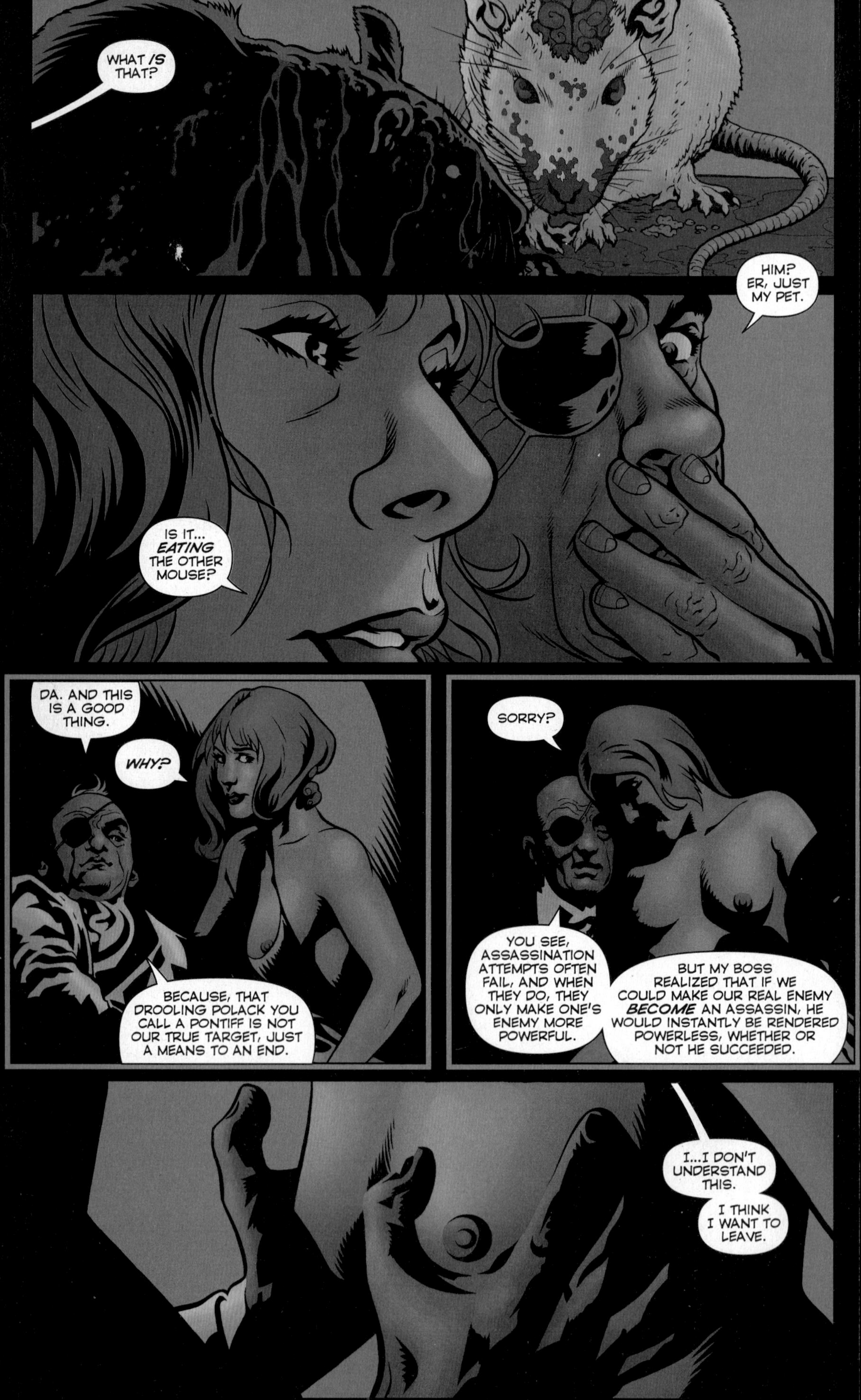
WHAT *IS* THAT?
HIM? ER, JUST MY PET.
IS IT... *EATING* THE OTHER MOUSE?
DA. AND THIS IS A GOOD THING.
WHY?
BECAUSE, THAT DROOLING POLACK YOU CALL A PONTIFF IS NOT OUR TRUE TARGET, JUST A MEANS TO AN END.
SORRY?
YOU SEE, ASSASSINATION ATTEMPTS OFTEN FAIL, AND WHEN THEY DO, THEY ONLY MAKE ONE'S ENEMY MORE POWERFUL.
BUT MY BOSS REALIZED THAT IF WE COULD MAKE OUR REAL ENEMY *BECOME* AN ASSASSIN, HE WOULD INSTANTLY BE RENDERED POWERLESS, WHETHER OR NOT HE SUCCEEDED.
I...I DON'T UNDERSTAND THIS.
I THINK I WANT TO LEAVE.

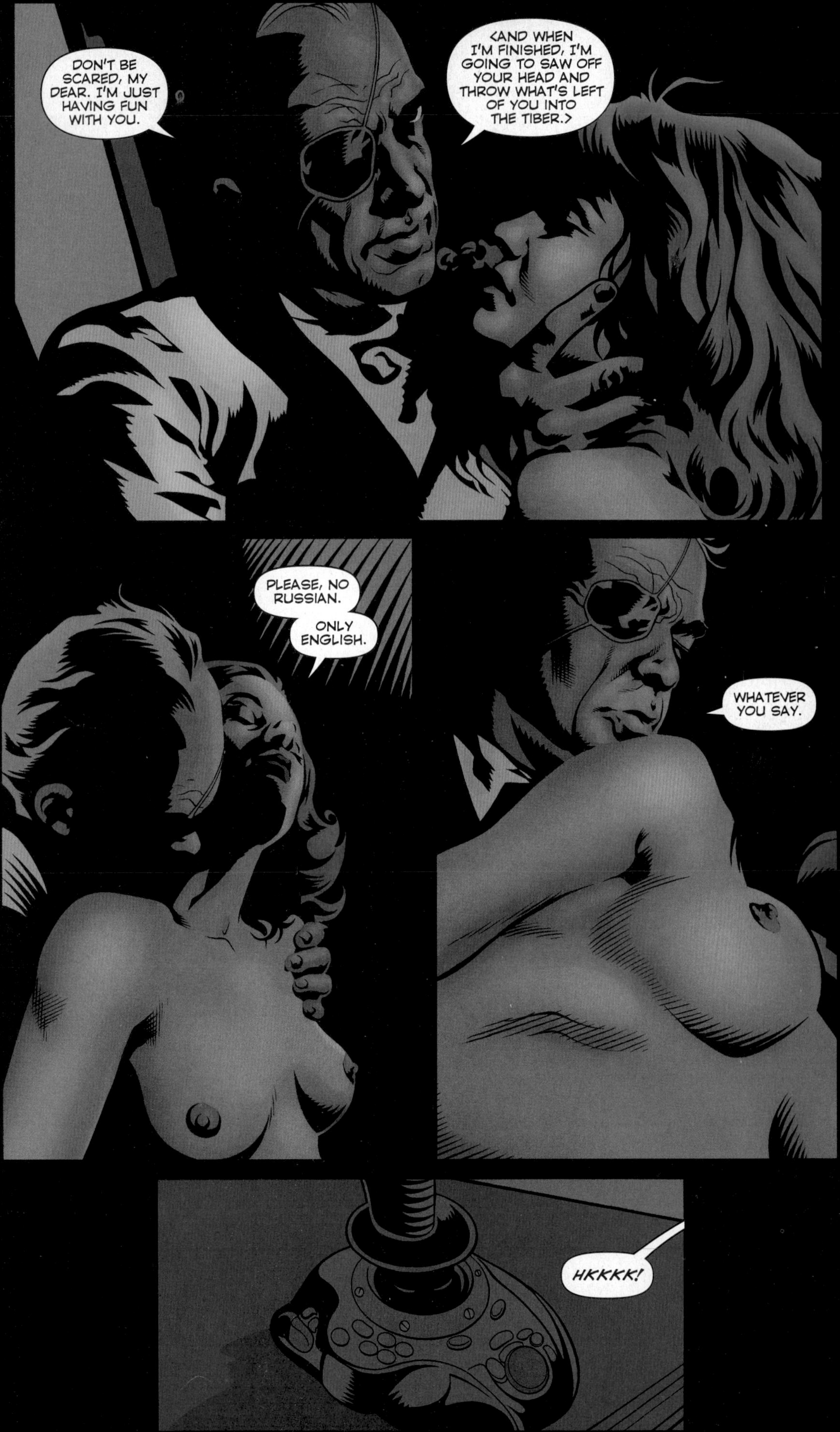
DON'T BE SCARED, MY DEAR. I'M JUST HAVING FUN WITH YOU.
<AND WHEN I'M FINISHED, I'M GOING TO SAW OFF YOUR HEAD AND THROW WHAT'S LEFT OF YOU INTO THE TIBER.>
PLEASE, NO RUSSIAN.
ONLY ENGLISH.
WHATEVER YOU SAY.
HKKKK!

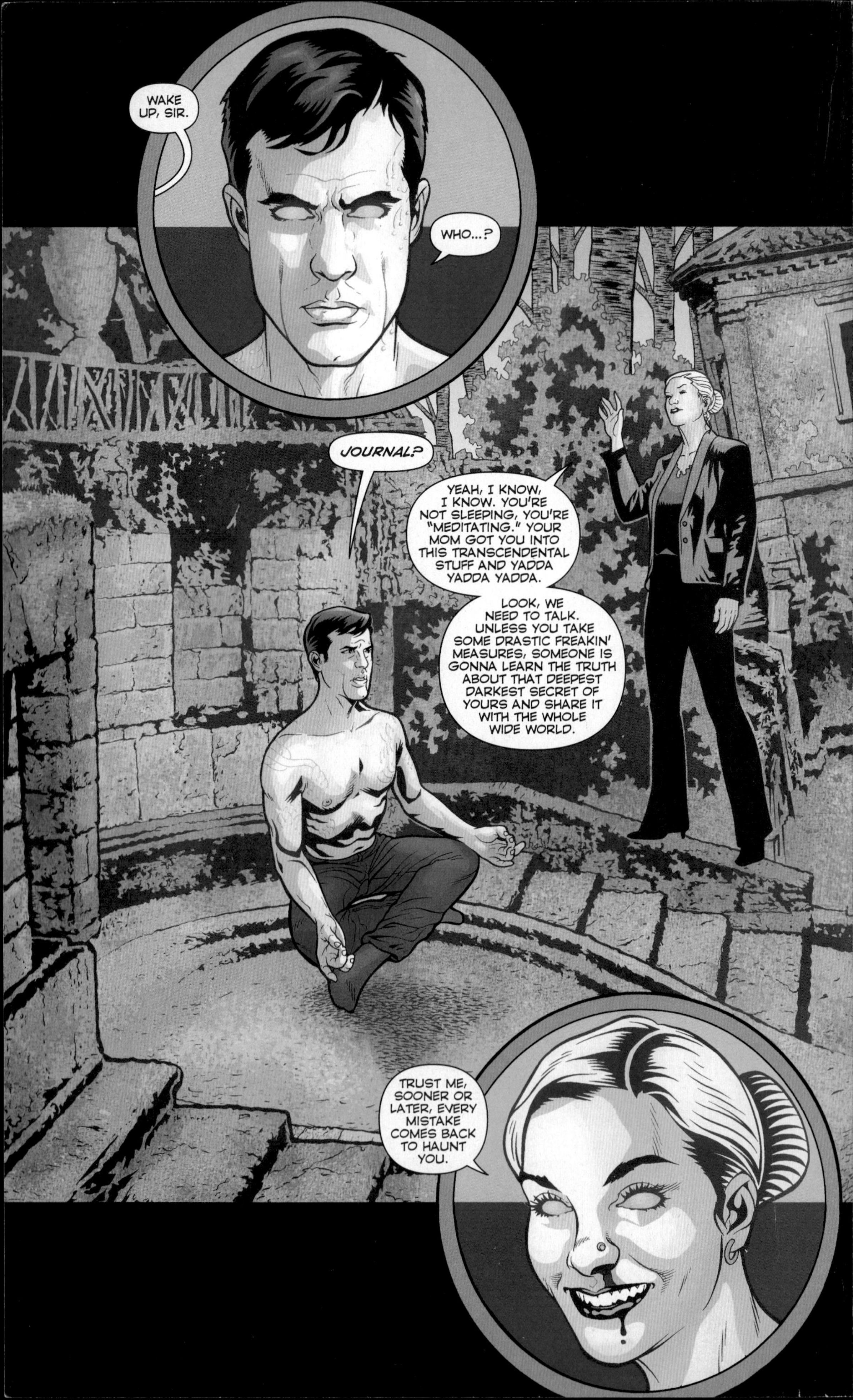
WAKE UP, SIR.
WHO...?
JOURNAL?
YEAH, I KNOW, I KNOW. YOU'RE NOT SLEEPING, YOU'RE "MEDITATING." YOUR MOM GOT YOU INTO THIS TRANSCENDENTAL STUFF AND YADDA YADDA YADDA.
LOOK, WE NEED TO TALK. UNLESS YOU TAKE SOME DRASTIC FREAKIN' MEASURES, SOMEONE IS GONNA LEARN THE TRUTH ABOUT THAT DEEPEST DARKEST SECRET OF YOURS AND SHARE IT WITH THE WHOLE WIDE WORLD.
TRUST ME, SOONER OR LATER, EVERY MISTAKE COMES BACK TO HAUNT YOU.

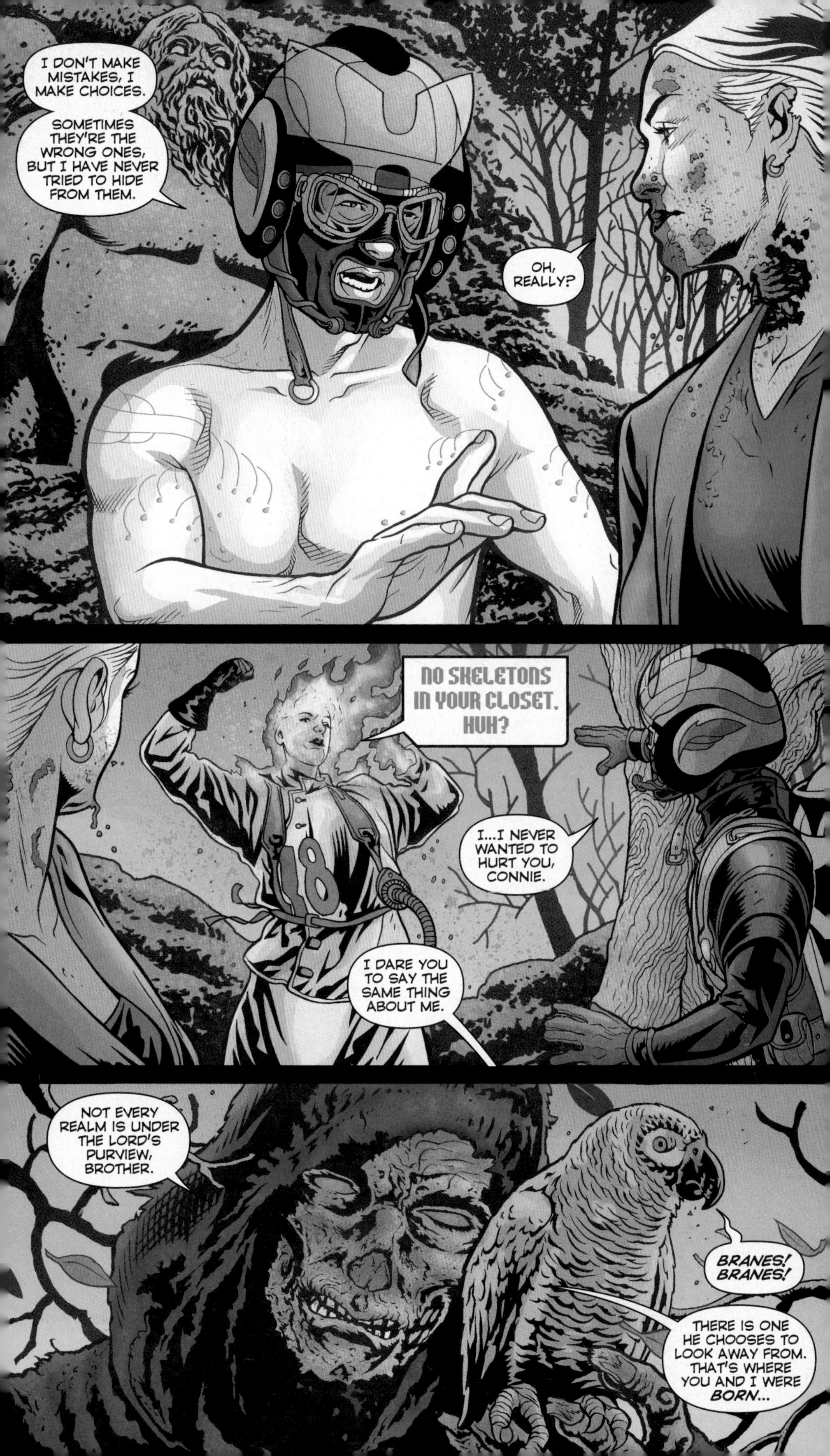

I DON'T MAKE MISTAKES, I MAKE CHOICES.
SOMETIMES THEY'RE THE WRONG ONES, BUT I HAVE NEVER TRIED TO HIDE FROM THEM.
OH, REALLY?
NO SKELETONS IN YOUR CLOSET, HUH?
I...I NEVER WANTED TO HURT YOU, CONNIE.
I DARE YOU TO SAY THE SAME THING ABOUT ME.
NOT EVERY REALM IS UNDER THE LORD'S PURVIEW, BROTHER.
BRANES! BRANES!
THERE IS ONE HE CHOOSES TO LOOK AWAY FROM. THAT'S WHERE YOU AND I WERE BORN...

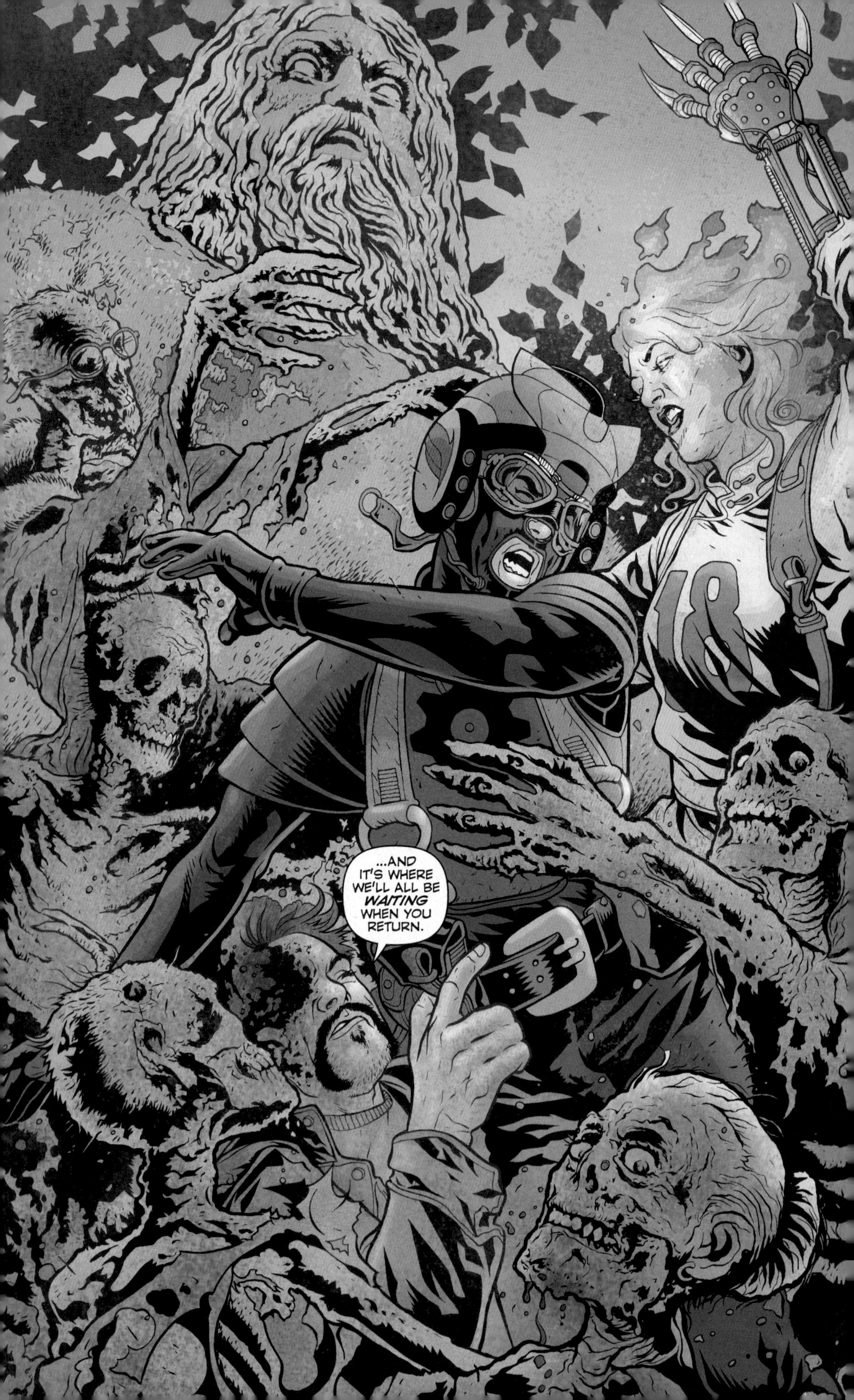
...AND IT'S WHERE WE'LL ALL BE *WAITING* WHEN YOU RETURN.

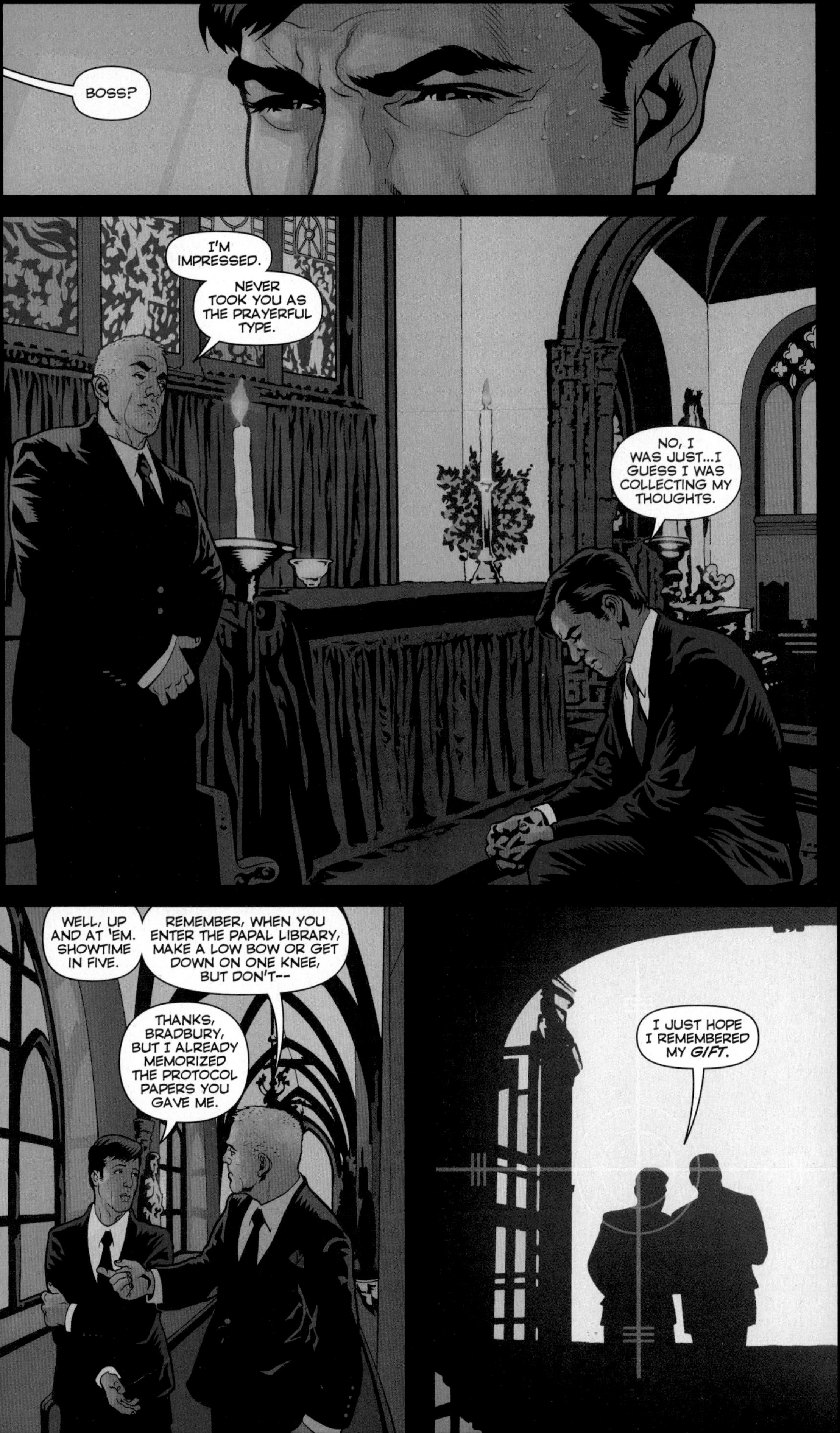
BOSS?
I'M IMPRESSED.
NEVER TOOK YOU AS THE PRAYERFUL TYPE.
NO, I WAS JUST...I GUESS I WAS COLLECTING MY THOUGHTS.
WELL, UP AND AT 'EM. SHOWTIME IN FIVE.
REMEMBER, WHEN YOU ENTER THE PAPAL LIBRARY, MAKE A LOW BOW OR GET DOWN ON ONE KNEE, BUT DON'T--
THANKS, BRADBURY, BUT I ALREADY MEMORIZED THE PROTOCOL PAPERS YOU GAVE ME.
I JUST HOPE I REMEMBERED MY *GIFT*.

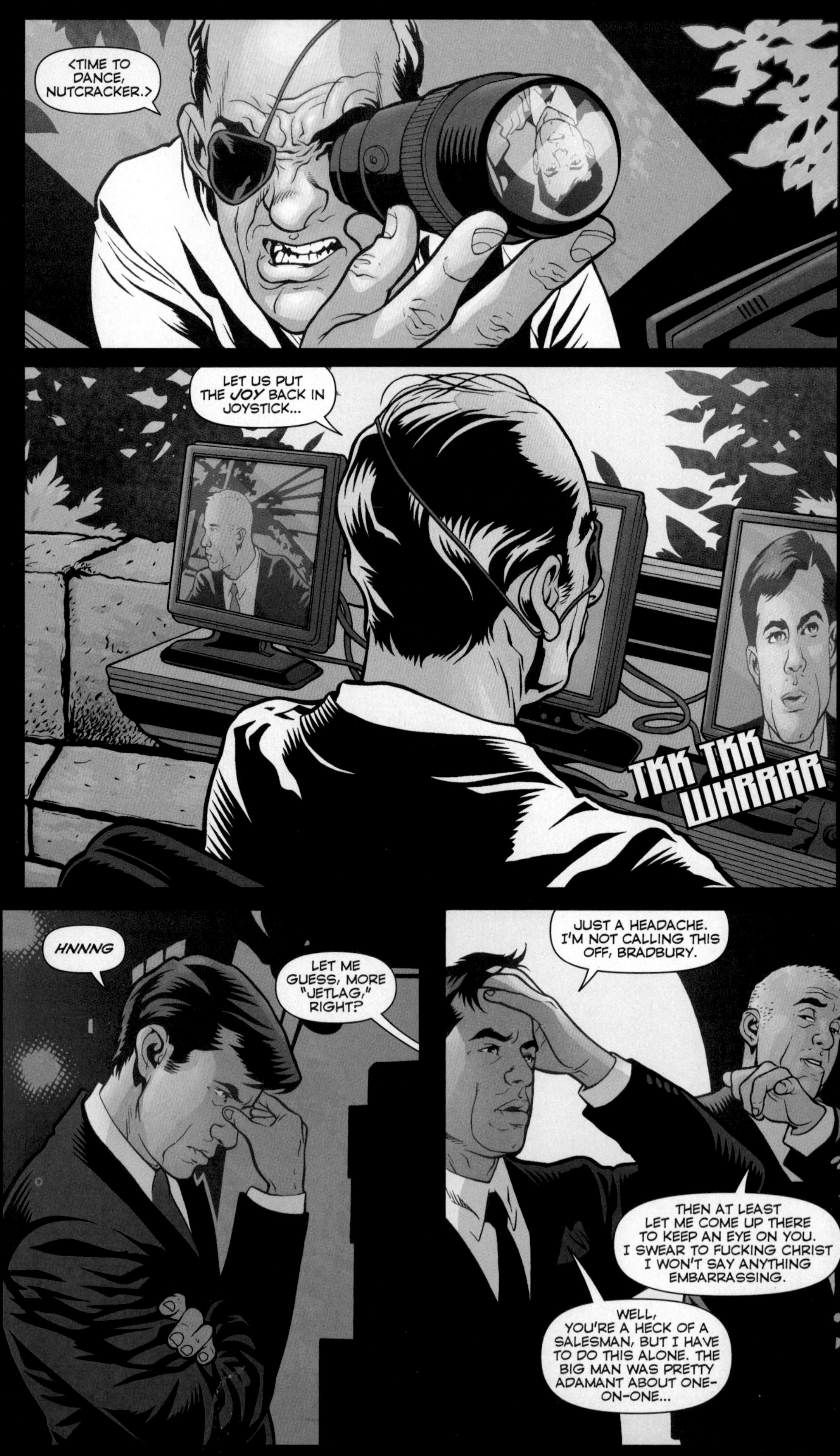
<TIME TO DANCE, NUTCRACKER.>
LET US PUT THE JOY BACK IN JOYSTICK...
TKK TKK WHRRRR
HNNNG
LET ME GUESS, MORE "JETLAG," RIGHT?
JUST A HEADACHE. I'M NOT CALLING THIS OFF, BRADBURY.
THEN AT LEAST LET ME COME UP THERE TO KEEP AN EYE ON YOU. I SWEAR TO FUCKING CHRIST I WON'T SAY ANYTHING EMBARRASSING.
WELL, YOU'RE A HECK OF A SALESMAN, BUT I HAVE TO DO THIS ALONE. THE BIG MAN WAS PRETTY ADAMANT ABOUT ONE-ON-ONE...

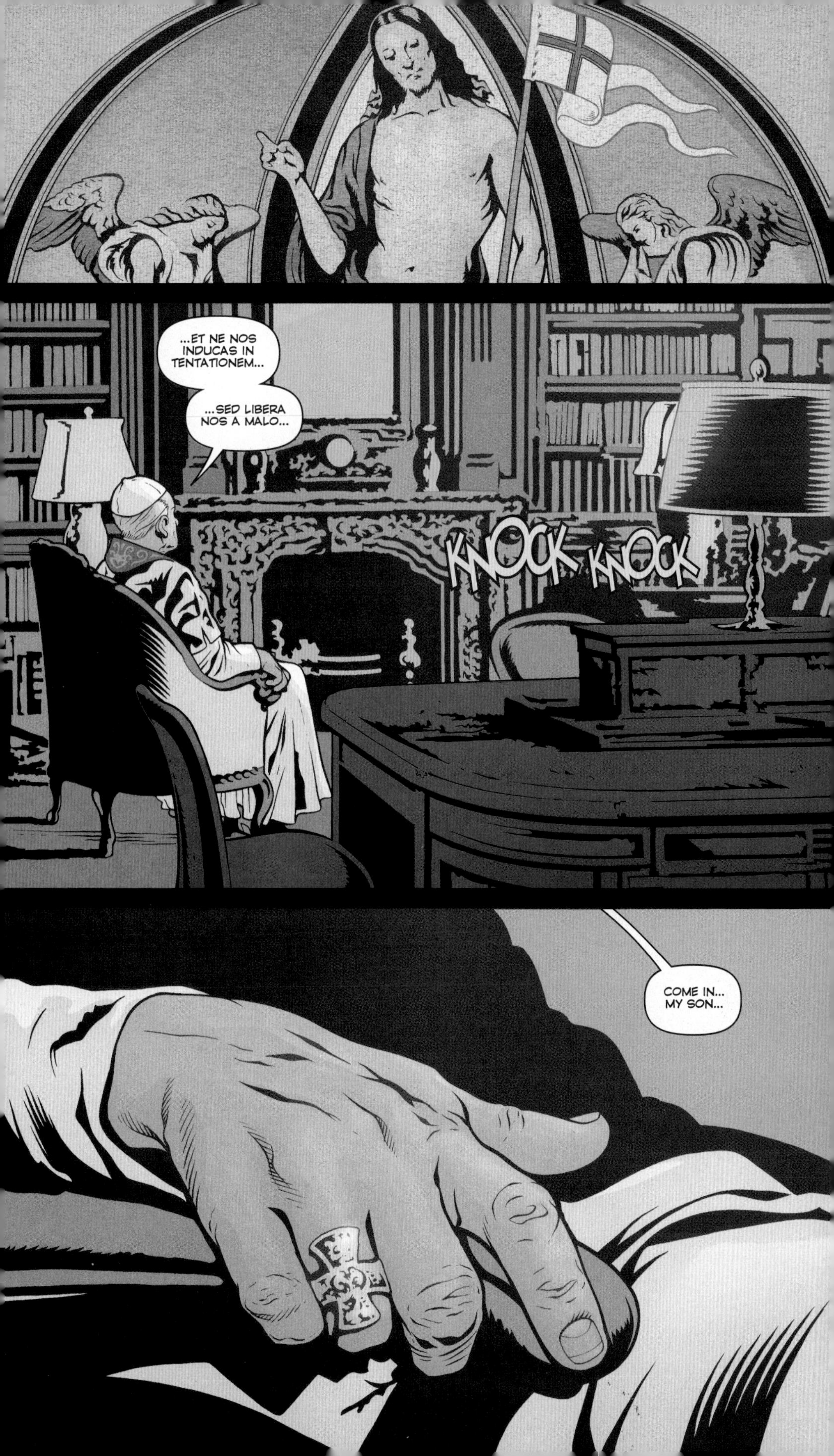
...ET NE NOS INDUCAS IN TENTATIONEM...
...SED LIBERA NOS A MALO...
KNOCK KNOCK
COME IN... MY SON...

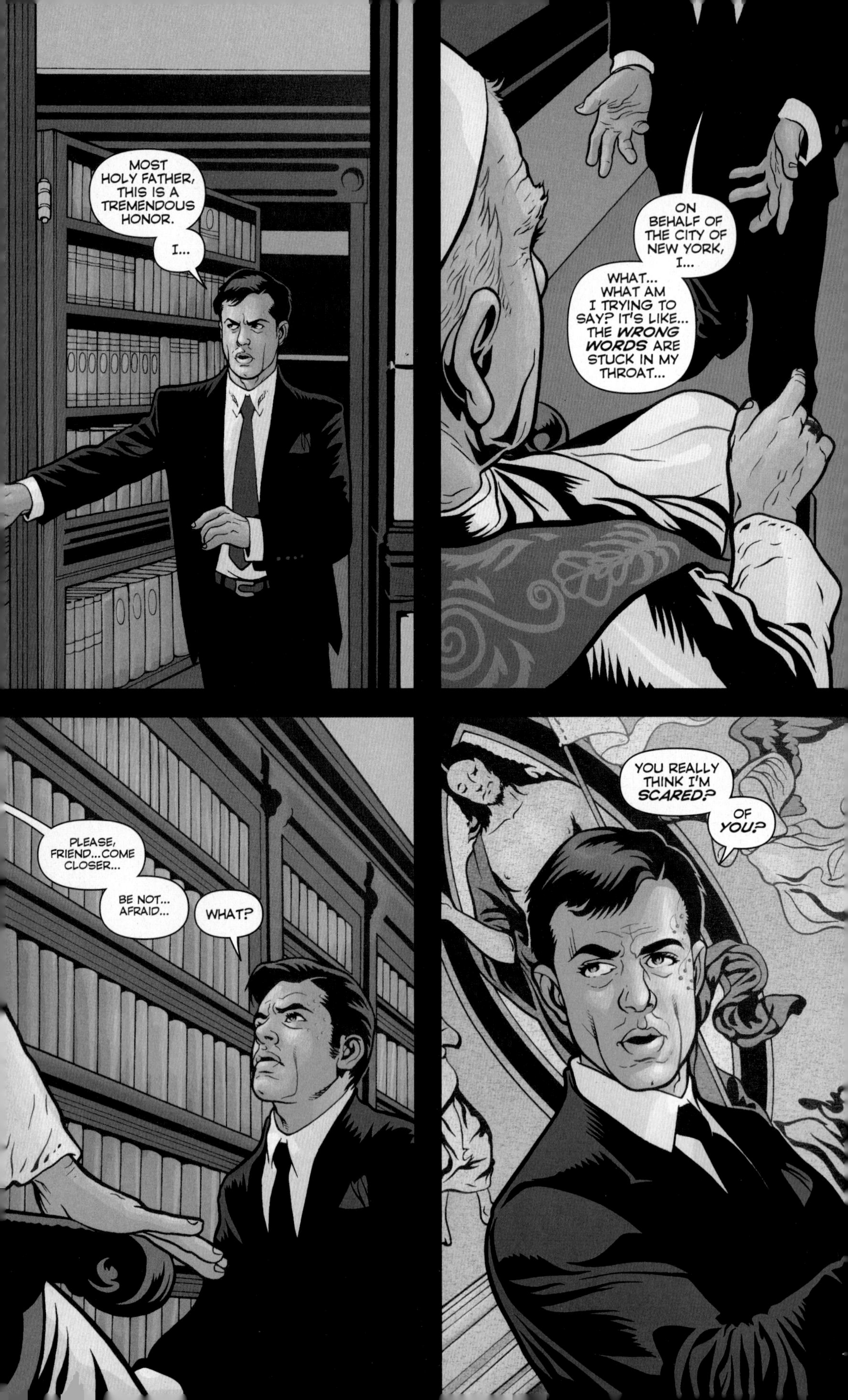
MOST HOLY FATHER, THIS IS A TREMENDOUS HONOR.
I...
ON BEHALF OF THE CITY OF NEW YORK, I...
WHAT... WHAT AM I TRYING TO SAY? IT'S LIKE... THE WRONG WORDS ARE STUCK IN MY THROAT...
PLEASE, FRIEND...COME CLOSER...
BE NOT... AFRAID...
WHAT?
YOU REALLY THINK I'M SCARED?
OF YOU?

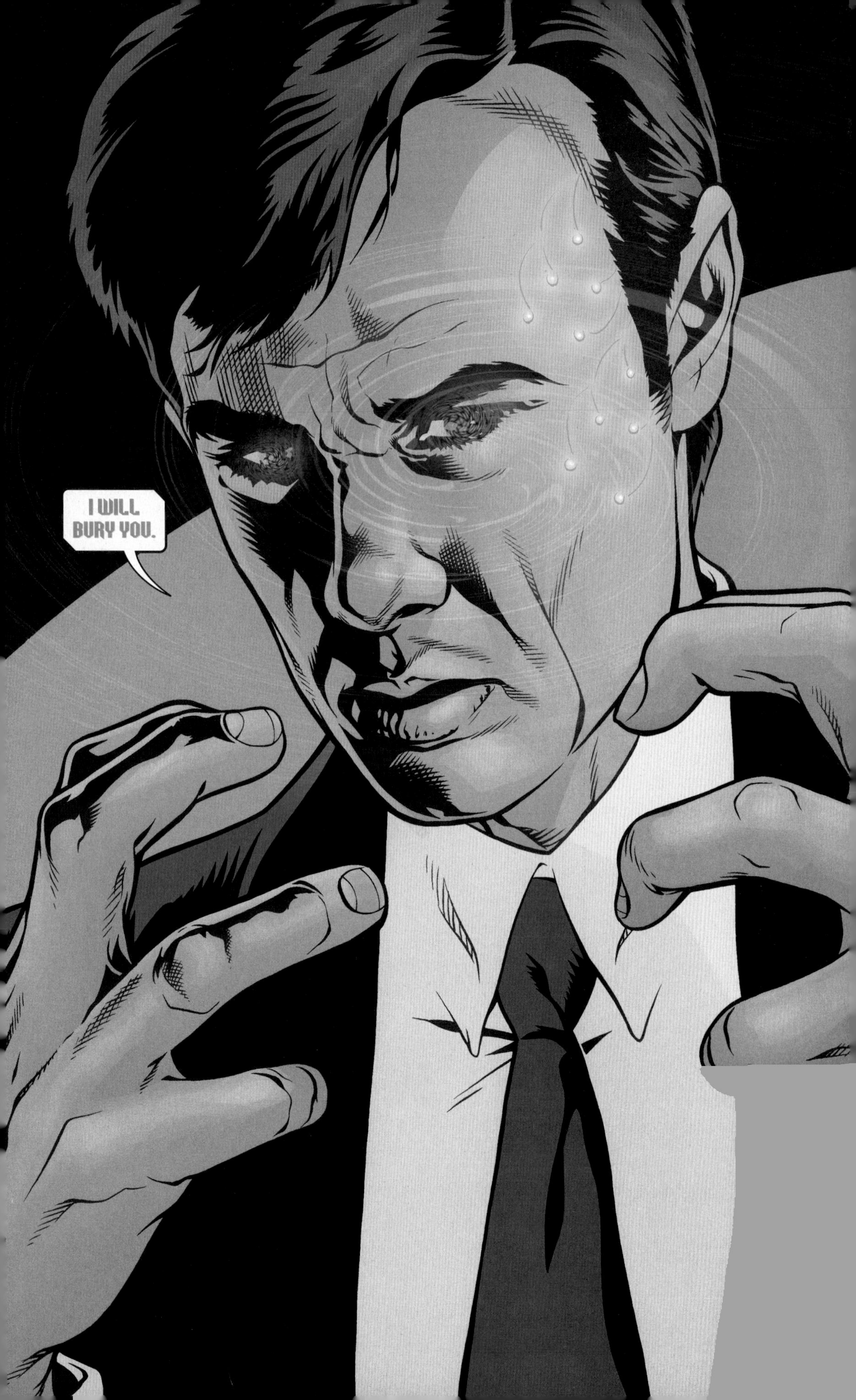
I WILL BURY YOU.

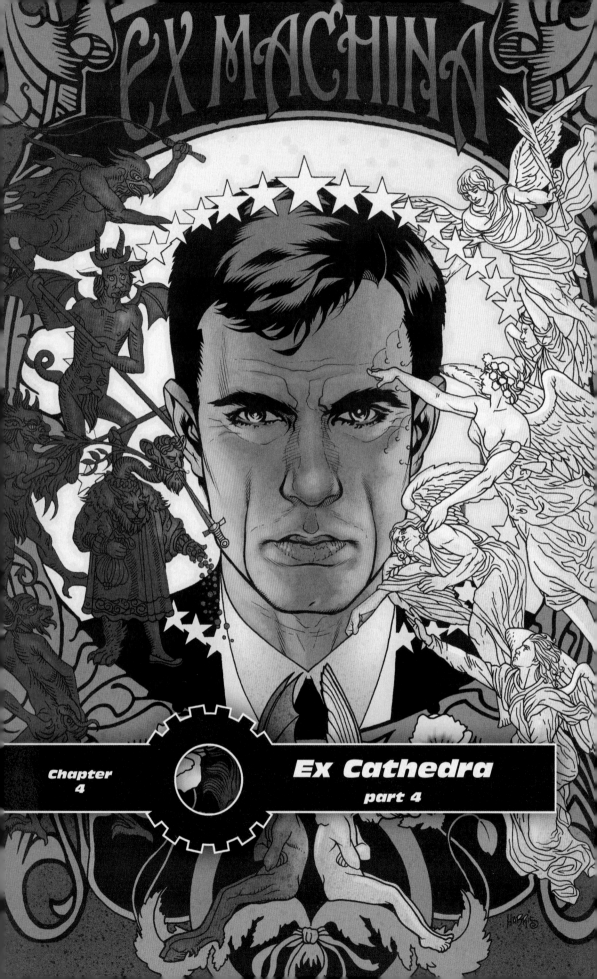

EX MACHINA

Chapter 4

Ex Cathedra
part 4

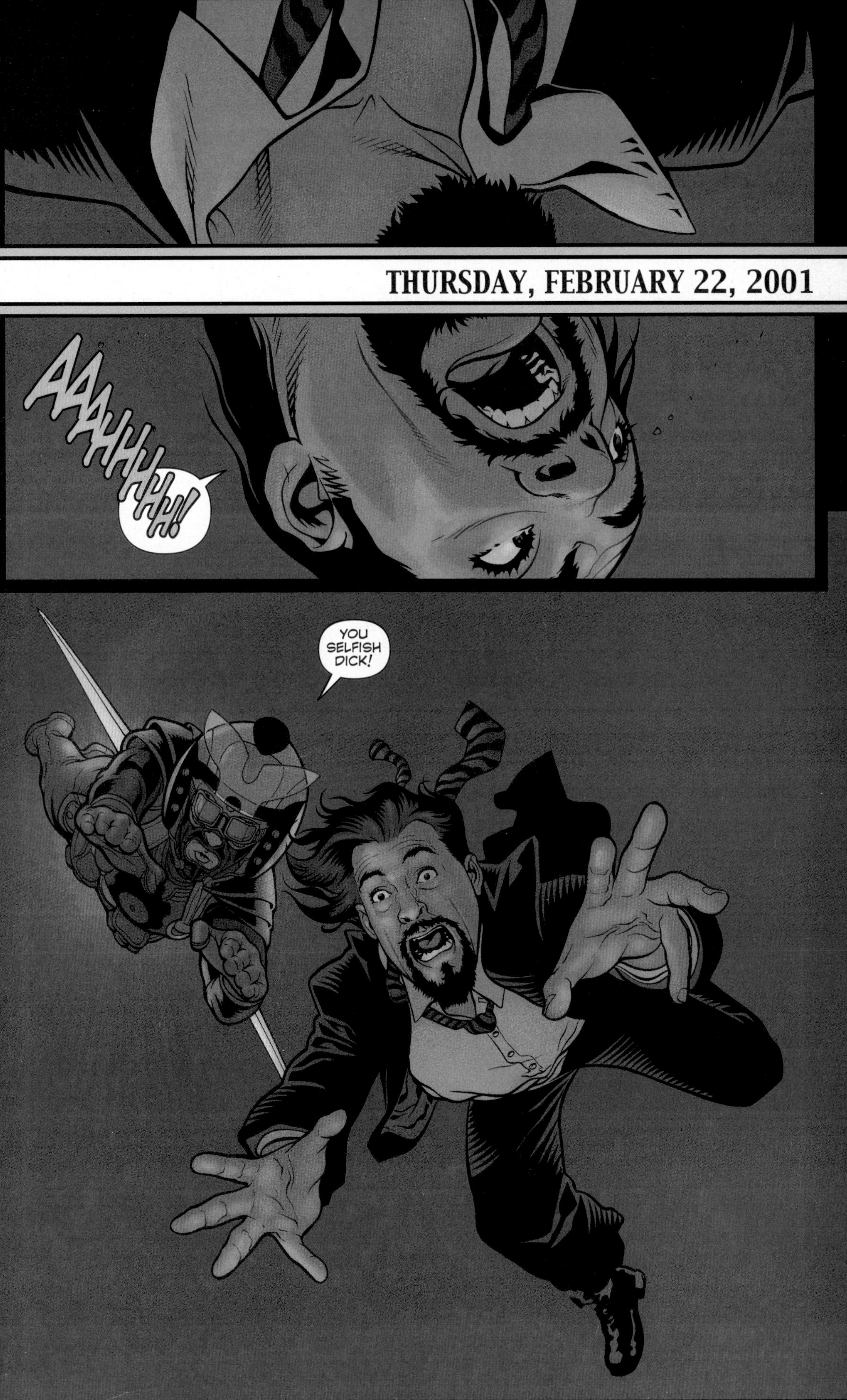
THURSDAY, FEBRUARY 22, 2001
AAAHHHHH!
YOU SELFISH DICK!

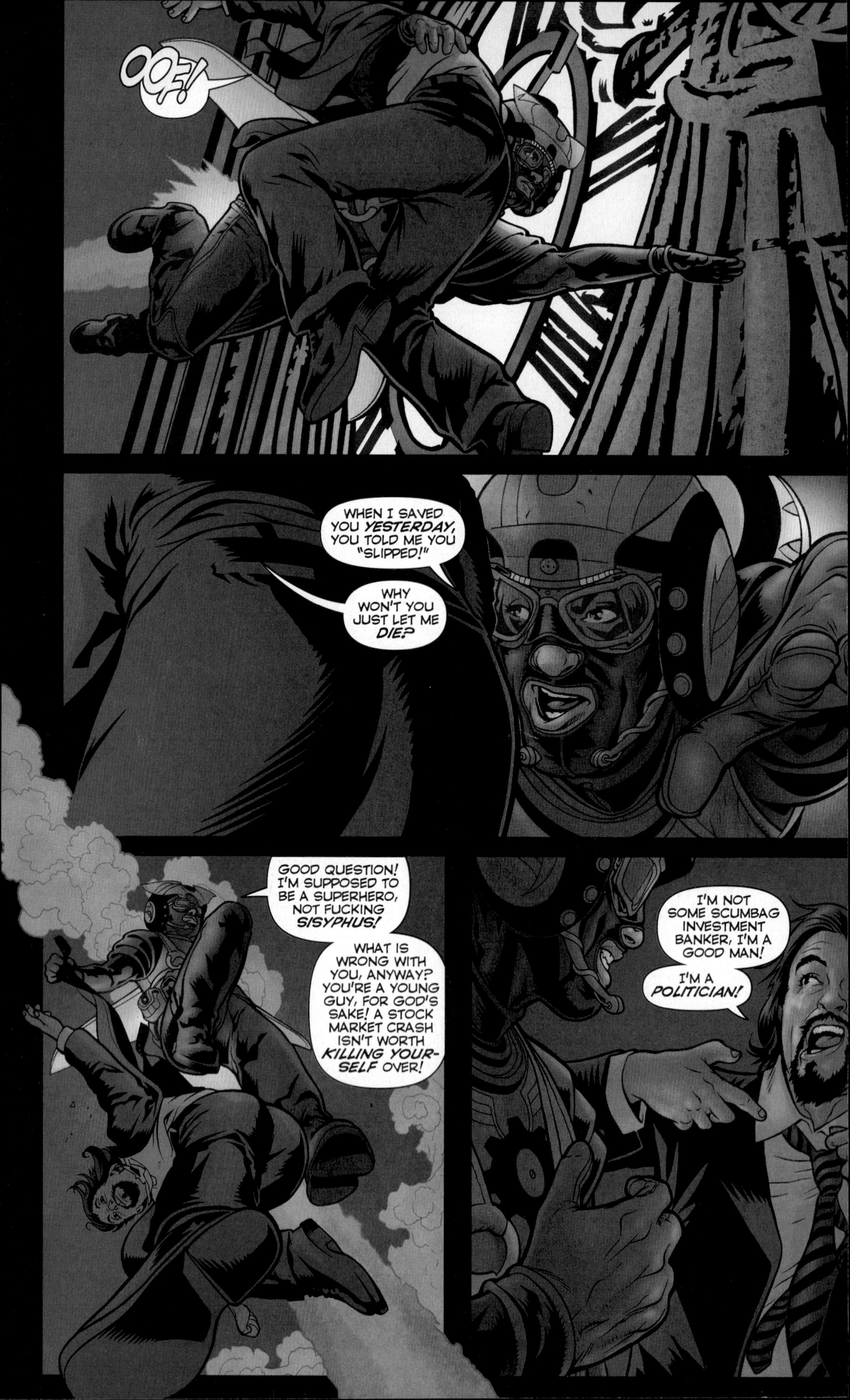
OOF!
WHEN I SAVED YOU YESTERDAY, YOU TOLD ME YOU "SLIPPED!"
WHY WON'T YOU JUST LET ME DIE?
GOOD QUESTION! I'M SUPPOSED TO BE A SUPERHERO, NOT FUCKING SISYPHUS!
WHAT IS WRONG WITH YOU, ANYWAY? YOU'RE A YOUNG GUY, FOR GOD'S SAKE! A STOCK MARKET CRASH ISN'T WORTH KILLING YOURSELF OVER!
I'M NOT SOME SCUMBAG INVESTMENT BANKER, I'M A GOOD MAN!
I'M A POLITICIAN!

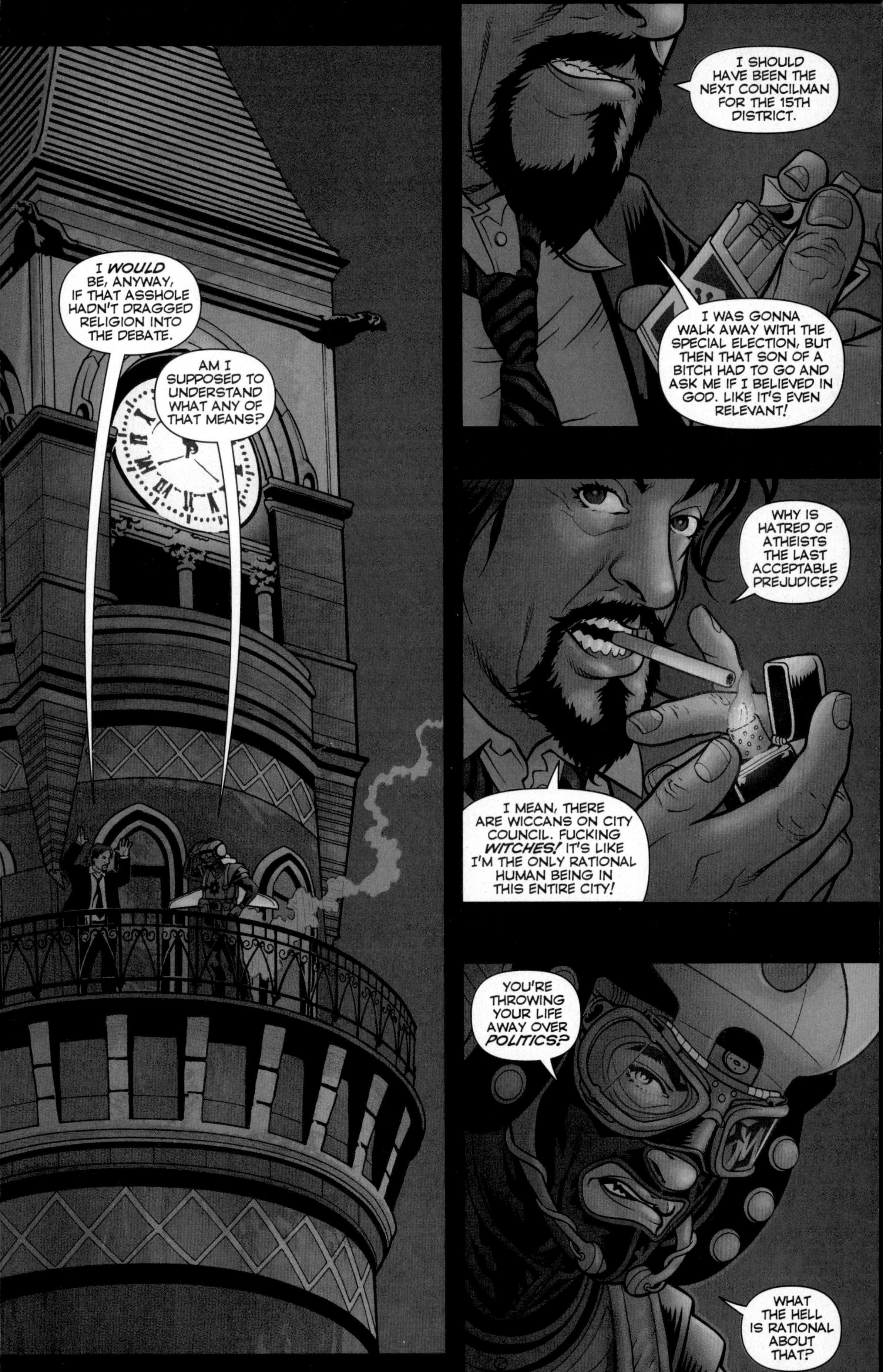
I WOULD BE, ANYWAY, IF THAT ASSHOLE HADN'T DRAGGED RELIGION INTO THE DEBATE.
AM I SUPPOSED TO UNDERSTAND WHAT ANY OF THAT MEANS?
I SHOULD HAVE BEEN THE NEXT COUNCILMAN FOR THE 15TH DISTRICT.
I WAS GONNA WALK AWAY WITH THE SPECIAL ELECTION, BUT THEN THAT SON OF A BITCH HAD TO GO AND ASK ME IF I BELIEVED IN GOD. LIKE IT'S EVEN RELEVANT!
WHY IS HATRED OF ATHEISTS THE LAST ACCEPTABLE PREJUDICE?
I MEAN, THERE ARE WICCANS ON CITY COUNCIL. FUCKING WITCHES! IT'S LIKE I'M THE ONLY RATIONAL HUMAN BEING IN THIS ENTIRE CITY!
YOU'RE THROWING YOUR LIFE AWAY OVER POLITICS?
WHAT THE HELL IS RATIONAL ABOUT THAT?

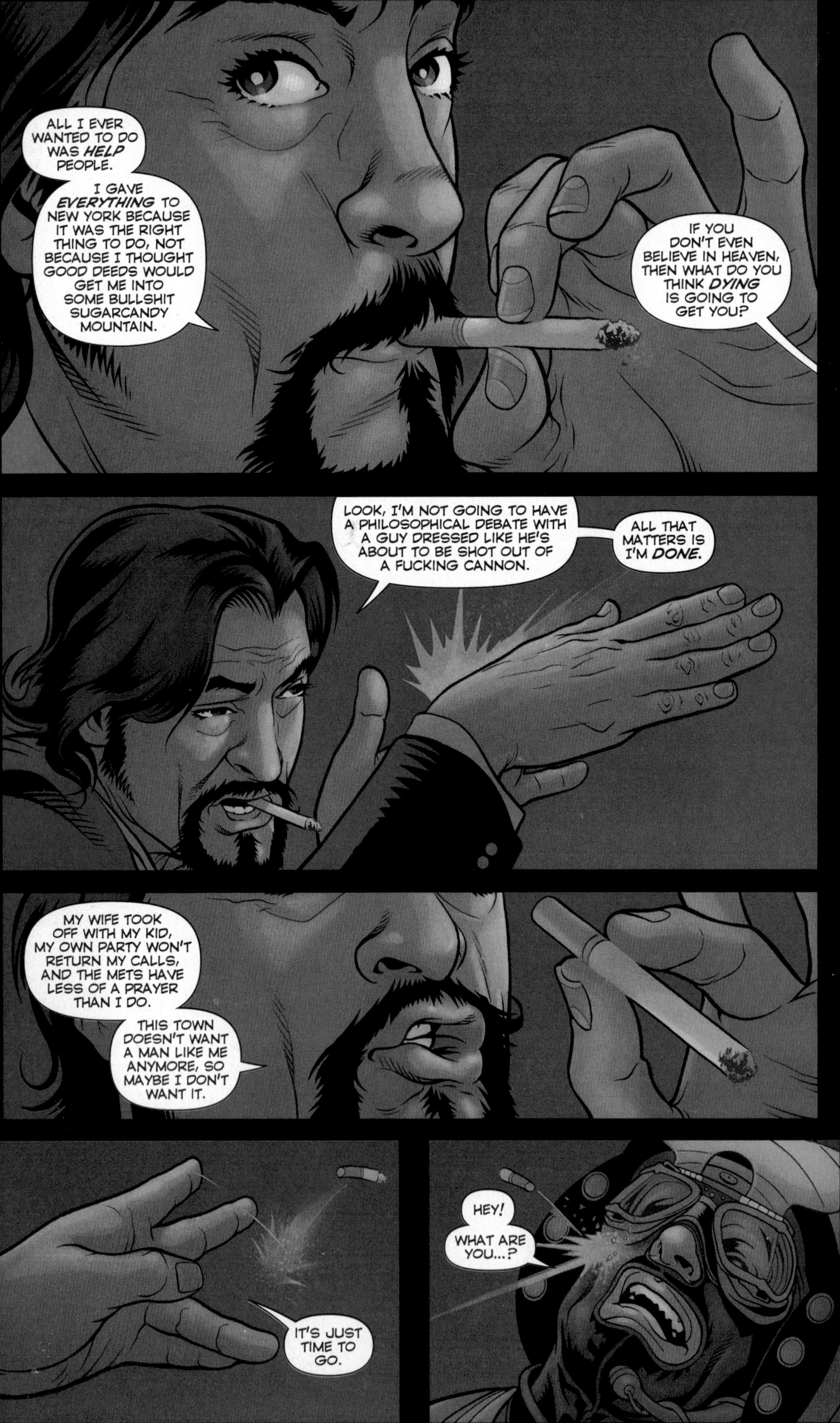
ALL I EVER WANTED TO DO WAS *HELP* PEOPLE.
I GAVE *EVERYTHING* TO NEW YORK BECAUSE IT WAS THE RIGHT THING TO DO, NOT BECAUSE I THOUGHT GOOD DEEDS WOULD GET ME INTO SOME BULLSHIT SUGARCANDY MOUNTAIN.
IF YOU DON'T EVEN BELIEVE IN HEAVEN, THEN WHAT DO YOU THINK *DYING* IS GOING TO GET YOU?
LOOK, I'M NOT GOING TO HAVE A PHILOSOPHICAL DEBATE WITH A GUY DRESSED LIKE HE'S ABOUT TO BE SHOT OUT OF A FUCKING CANNON.
ALL THAT MATTERS IS I'M ***DONE.***
MY WIFE TOOK OFF WITH MY KID, MY OWN PARTY WON'T RETURN MY CALLS, AND THE METS HAVE LESS OF A PRAYER THAN I DO.
THIS TOWN DOESN'T WANT A MAN LIKE ME ANYMORE, SO MAYBE I DON'T WANT IT.
IT'S JUST TIME TO GO.
HEY!
WHAT ARE YOU...?

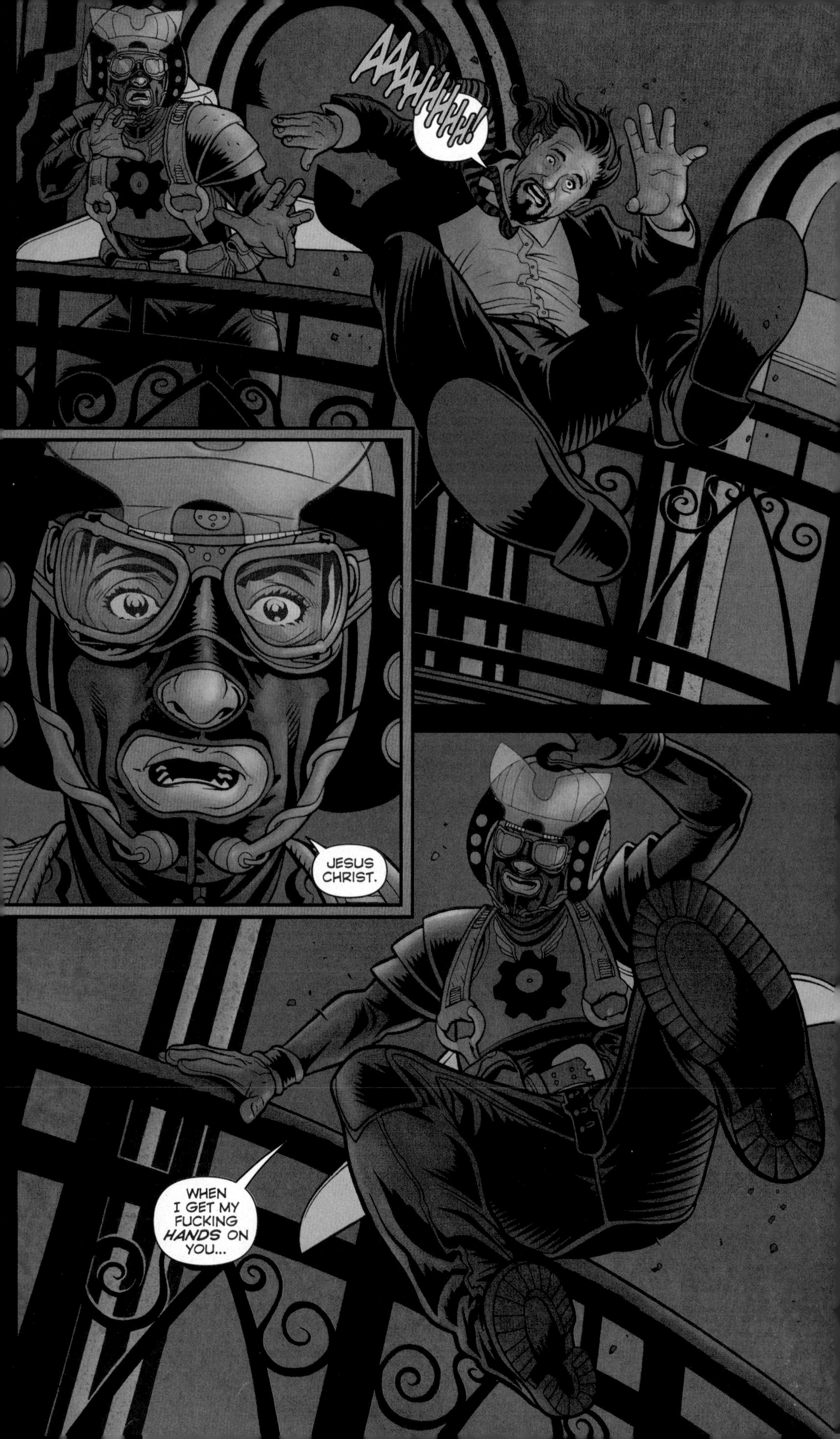
AAAHHHH!!
JESUS CHRIST.
WHEN I GET MY FUCKING *HANDS* ON YOU...

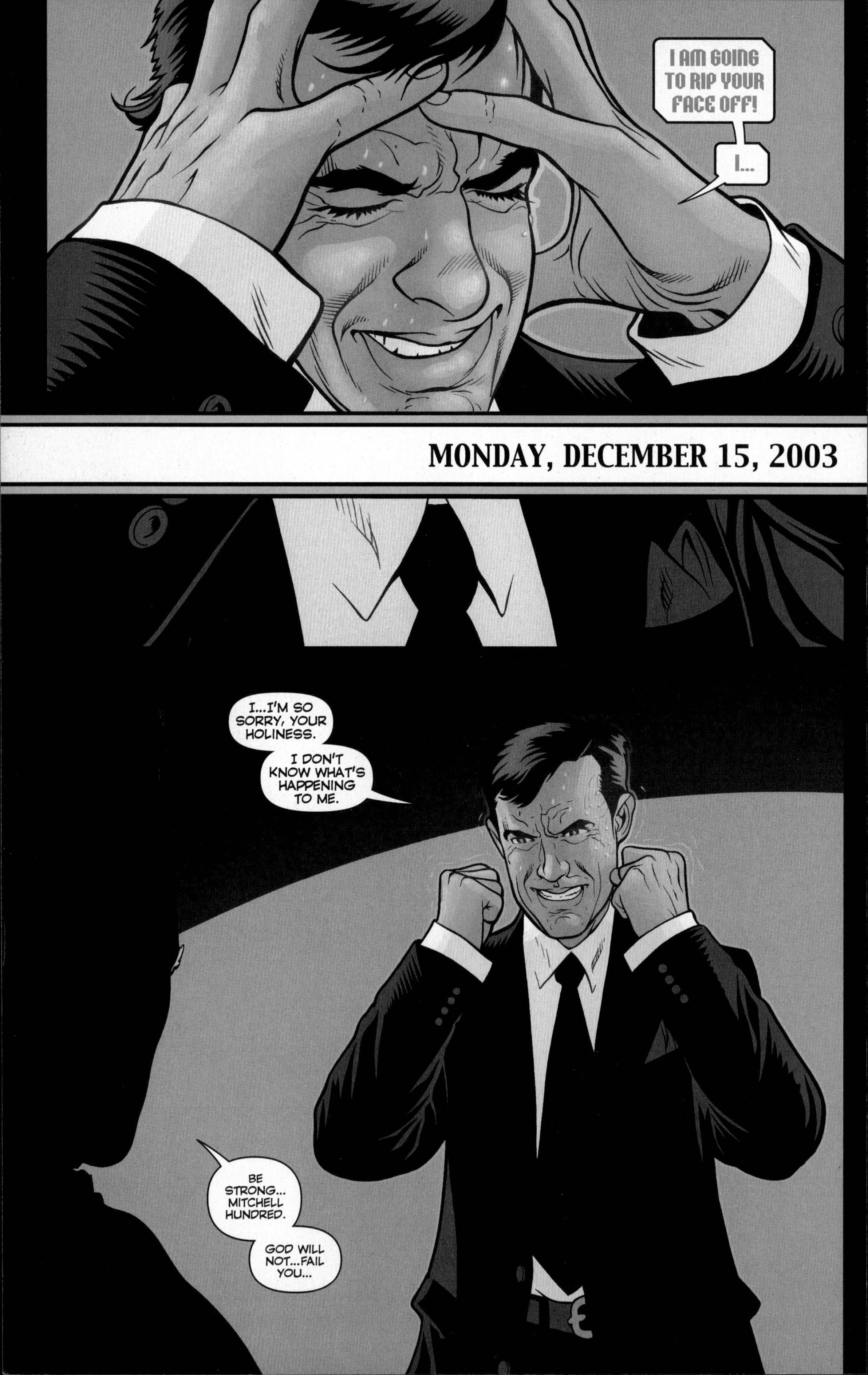
I AM GOING TO RIP YOUR FACE OFF!
I...
MONDAY, DECEMBER 15, 2003
I...I'M SO SORRY, YOUR HOLINESS.
I DON'T KNOW WHAT'S HAPPENING TO ME.
BE STRONG... MITCHELL HUNDRED.
GOD WILL NOT...FAIL YOU...

MY HANDS.

IT'S LIKE...

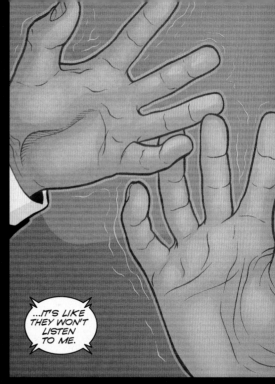

...IT'S LIKE THEY WON'T LISTEN TO ME.

<THAT A BOY, MR. MAYOR.>

<JUST DO WHAT FEELS RIGHT.>

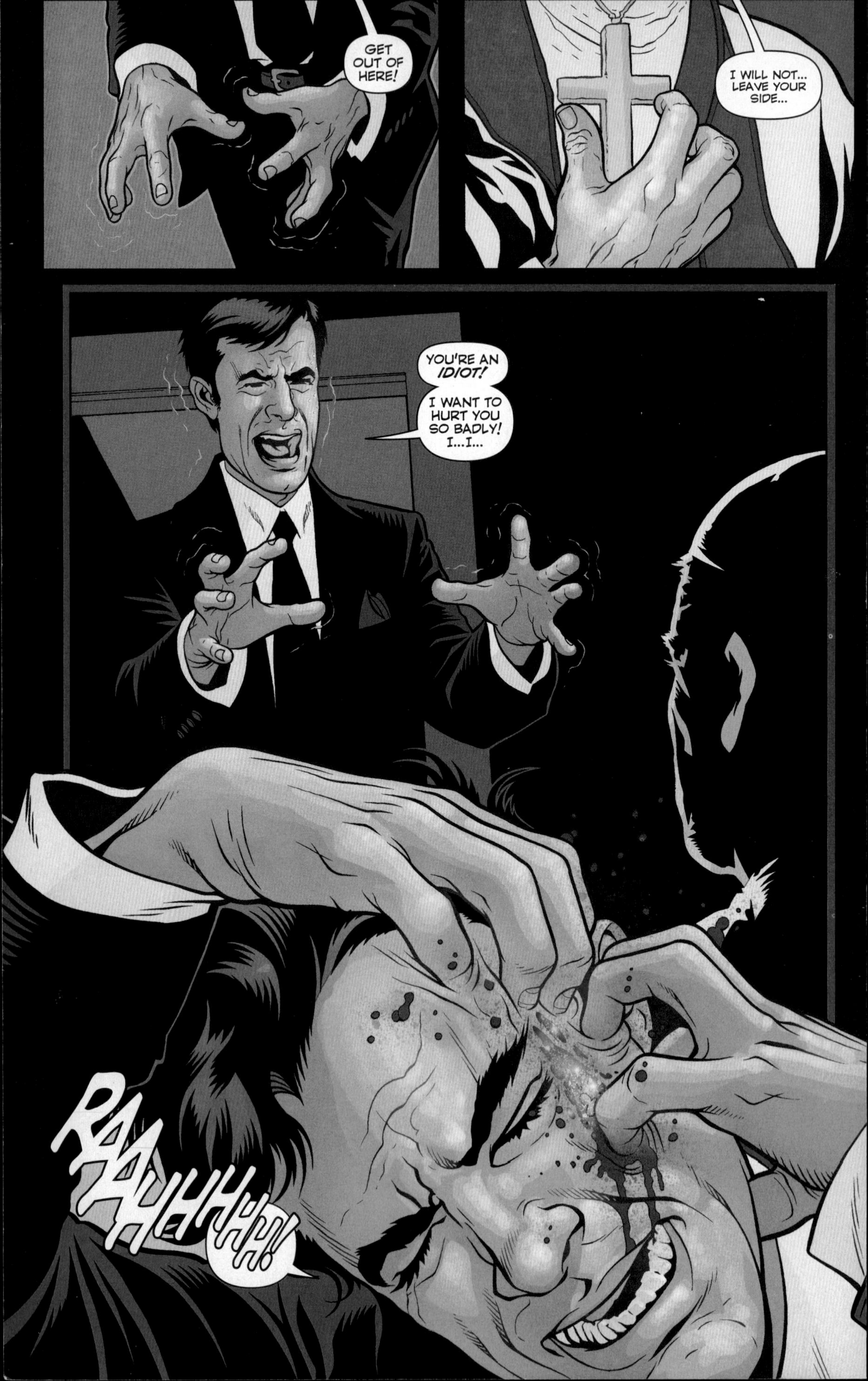
GET OUT OF HERE!
I WILL NOT... LEAVE YOUR SIDE...
YOU'RE AN *IDIOT!*
I WANT TO HURT YOU SO BADLY! I...I...
RAAHHHHH!

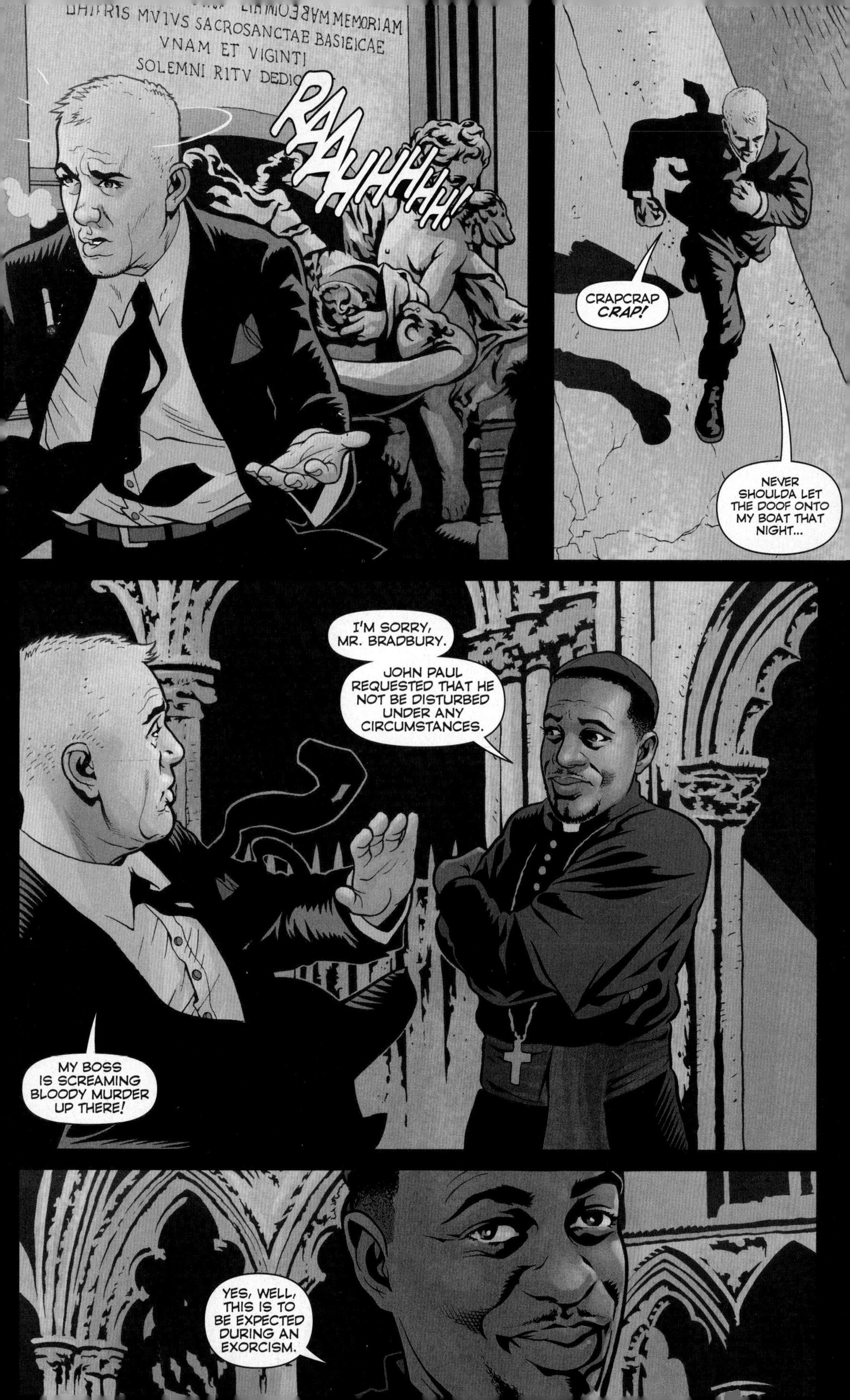
SACROSANCTAE BASIEICAE
VNAM ET VIGINTI
RAAAHHHHHH!
CRAPCRAP *CRAP!*
NEVER SHOULDA LET THE DOOF ONTO MY BOAT THAT NIGHT...
I'M SORRY, MR. BRADBURY.
JOHN PAUL REQUESTED THAT HE NOT BE DISTURBED UNDER ANY CIRCUMSTANCES.
MY BOSS IS SCREAMING BLOODY MURDER UP THERE!
YES, WELL, THIS IS TO BE EXPECTED DURING AN EXORCISM.

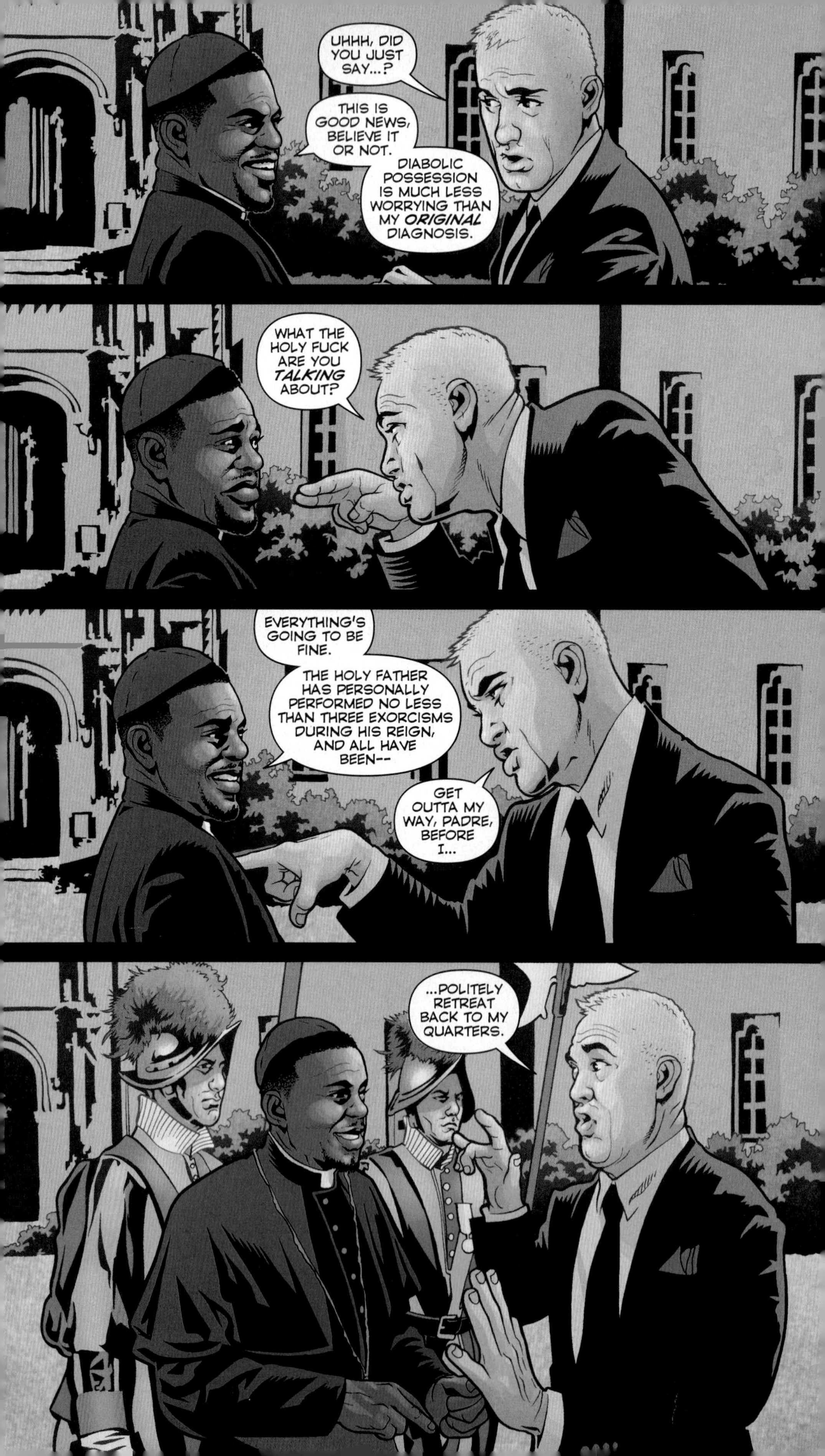
UHHH, DID YOU JUST SAY...?
THIS IS GOOD NEWS, BELIEVE IT OR NOT.
DIABOLIC POSSESSION IS MUCH LESS WORRYING THAN MY *ORIGINAL* DIAGNOSIS.
WHAT THE HOLY FUCK ARE YOU *TALKING* ABOUT?
EVERYTHING'S GOING TO BE FINE.
THE HOLY FATHER HAS PERSONALLY PERFORMED NO LESS THAN THREE EXORCISMS DURING HIS REIGN, AND ALL HAVE BEEN--
GET OUTTA MY WAY, PADRE, BEFORE I...
...POLITELY RETREAT BACK TO MY QUARTERS.

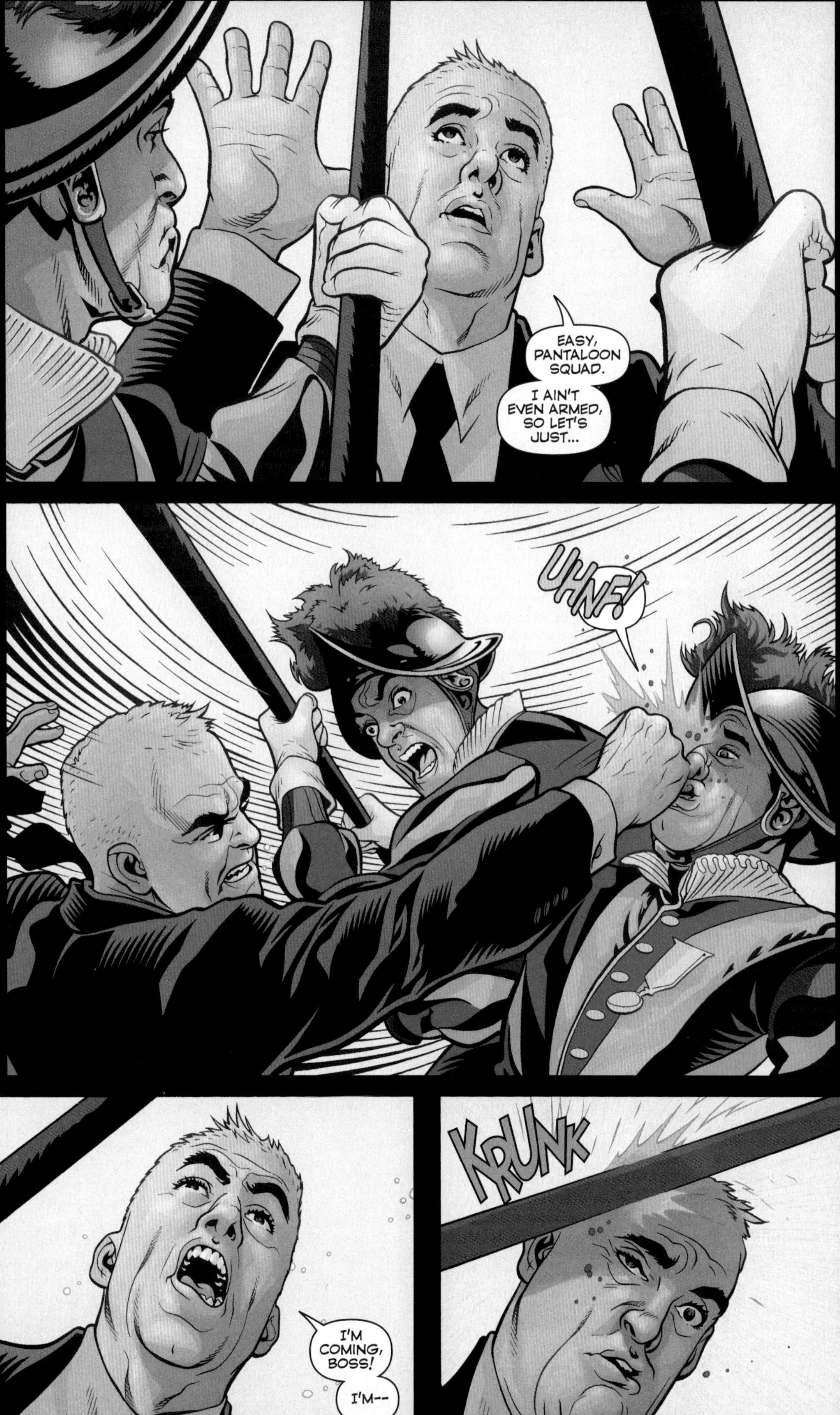

EASY, PANTALOON SQUAD.
I AIN'T EVEN ARMED, SO LET'S JUST...
UHNF!
I'M COMING, BOSS!
I'M--
KRUNK

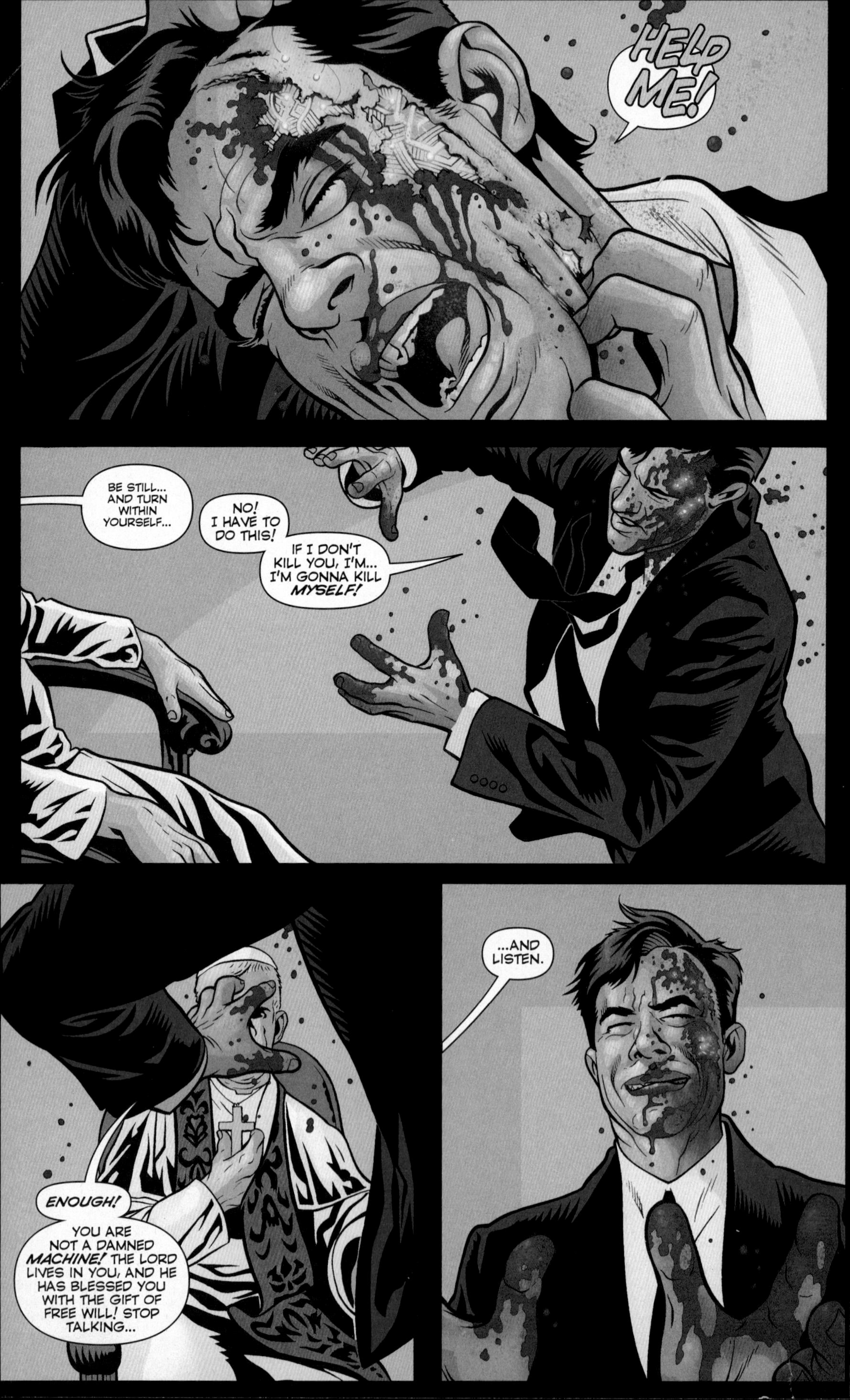
HELP ME!
BE STILL... AND TURN WITHIN YOURSELF...
NO! I HAVE TO DO THIS!
IF I DON'T KILL YOU, I'M... I'M GONNA KILL *MYSELF!*
ENOUGH!
YOU ARE NOT A DAMNED *MACHINE!* THE LORD LIVES IN YOU, AND HE HAS BLESSED YOU WITH THE GIFT OF FREE WILL! STOP TALKING...
...AND LISTEN.

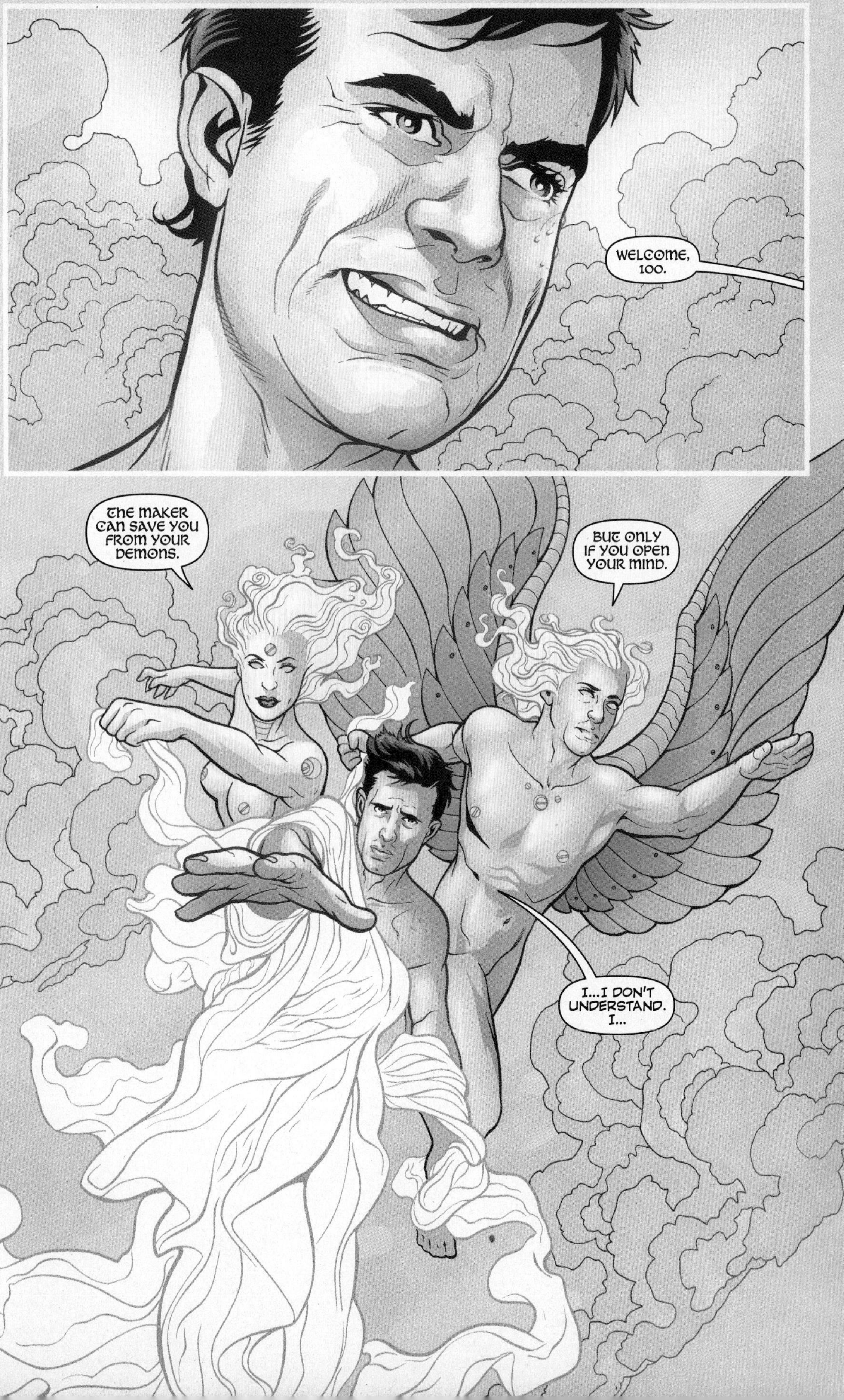
WELCOME, 100.
THE MAKER CAN SAVE YOU FROM YOUR DEMONS.
BUT ONLY IF YOU OPEN YOUR MIND.
I...I DON'T UNDERSTAND. I...

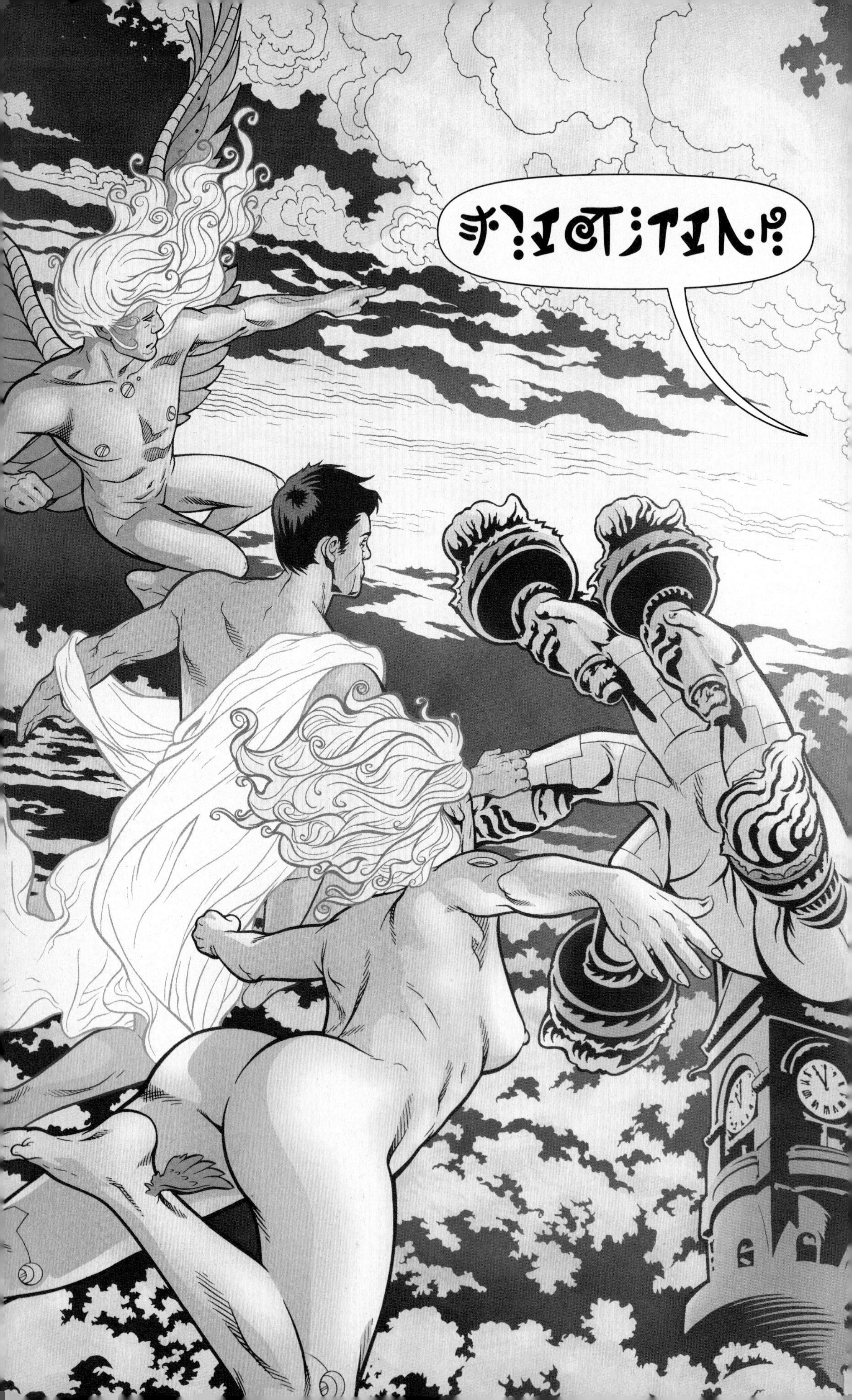

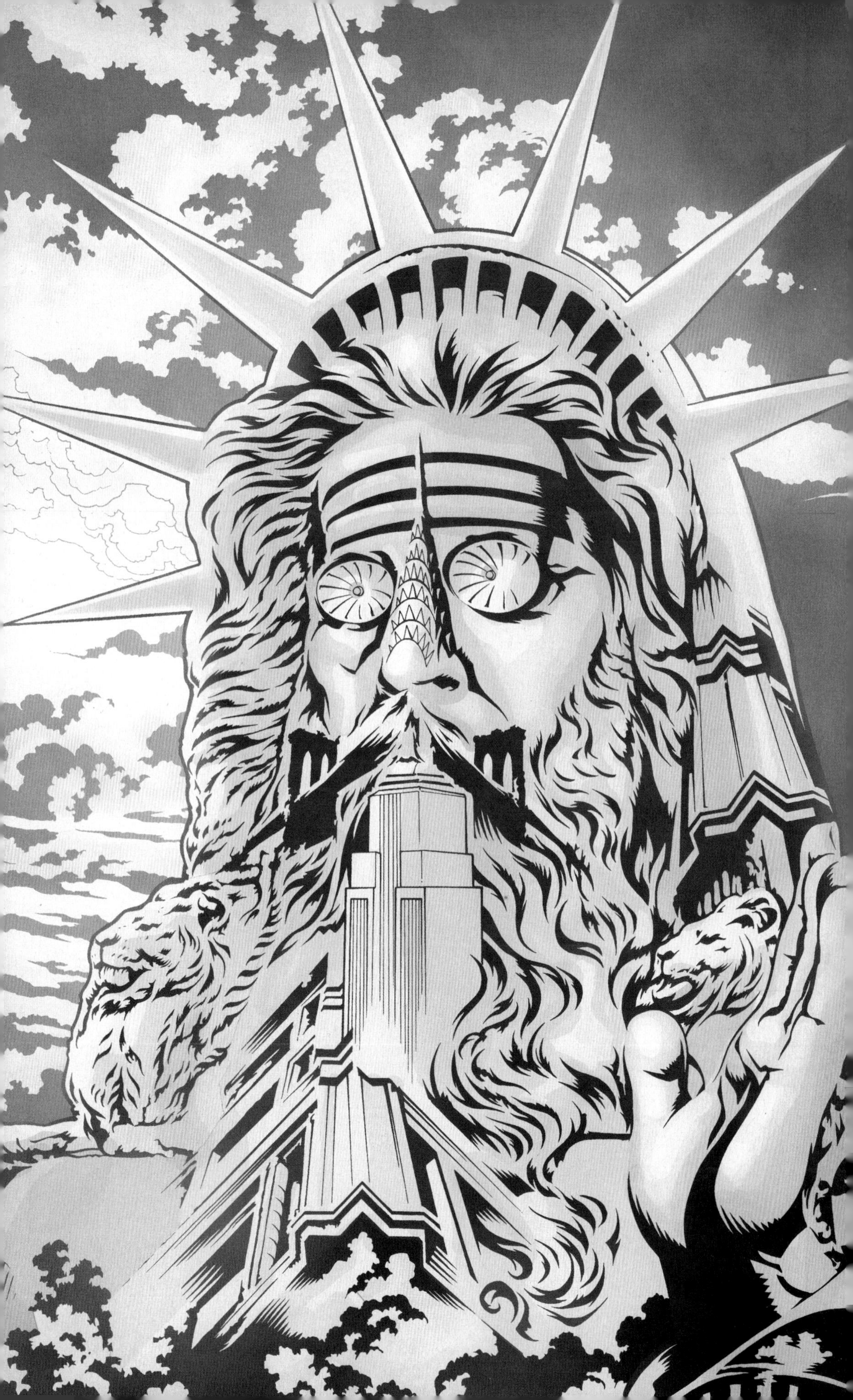

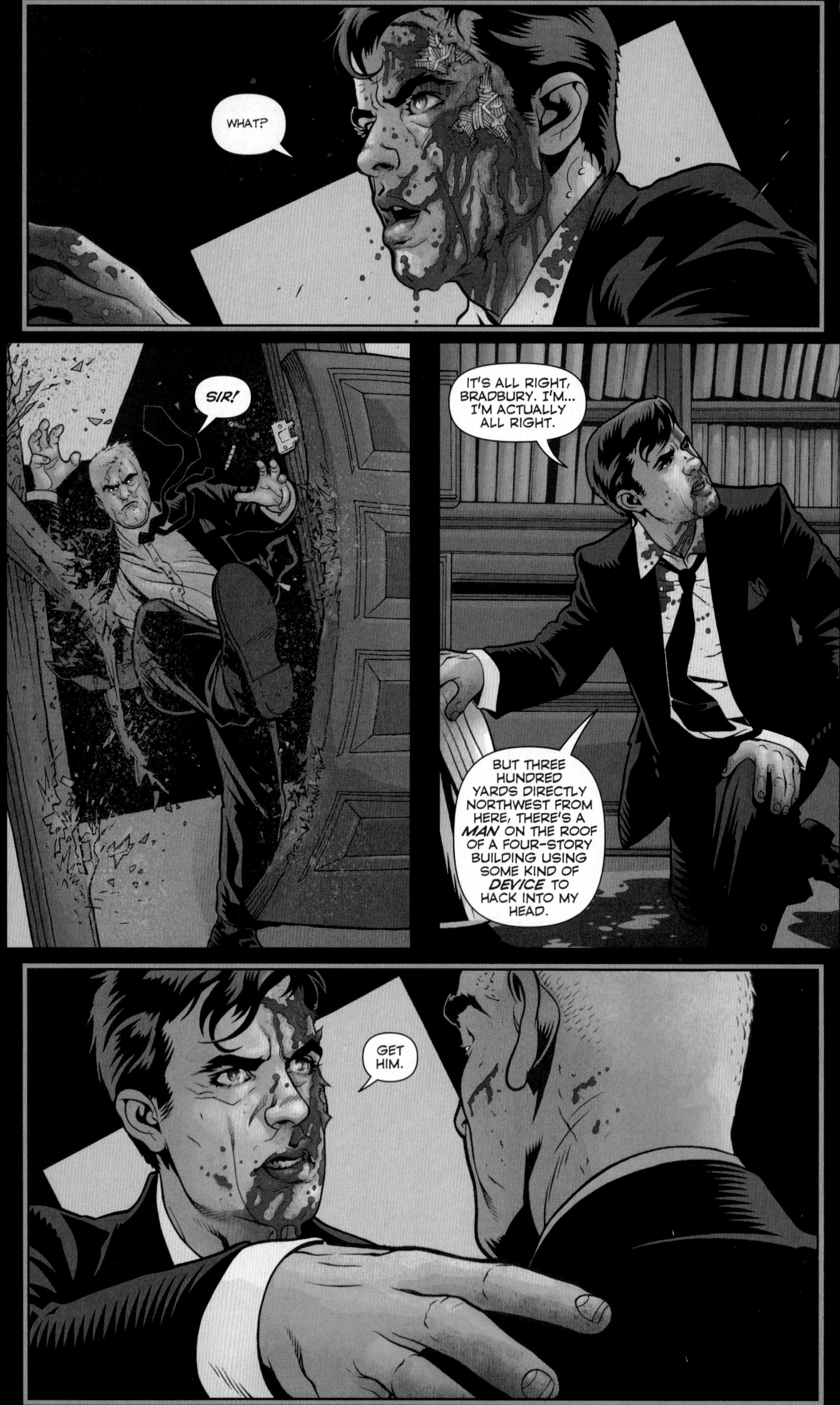

WHAT?
SIR!
IT'S ALL RIGHT, BRADBURY. I'M... I'M ACTUALLY ALL RIGHT.
BUT THREE HUNDRED YARDS DIRECTLY NORTHWEST FROM HERE, THERE'S A *MAN* ON THE ROOF OF A FOUR-STORY BUILDING USING SOME KIND OF *DEVICE* TO HACK INTO MY HEAD.
GET HIM.

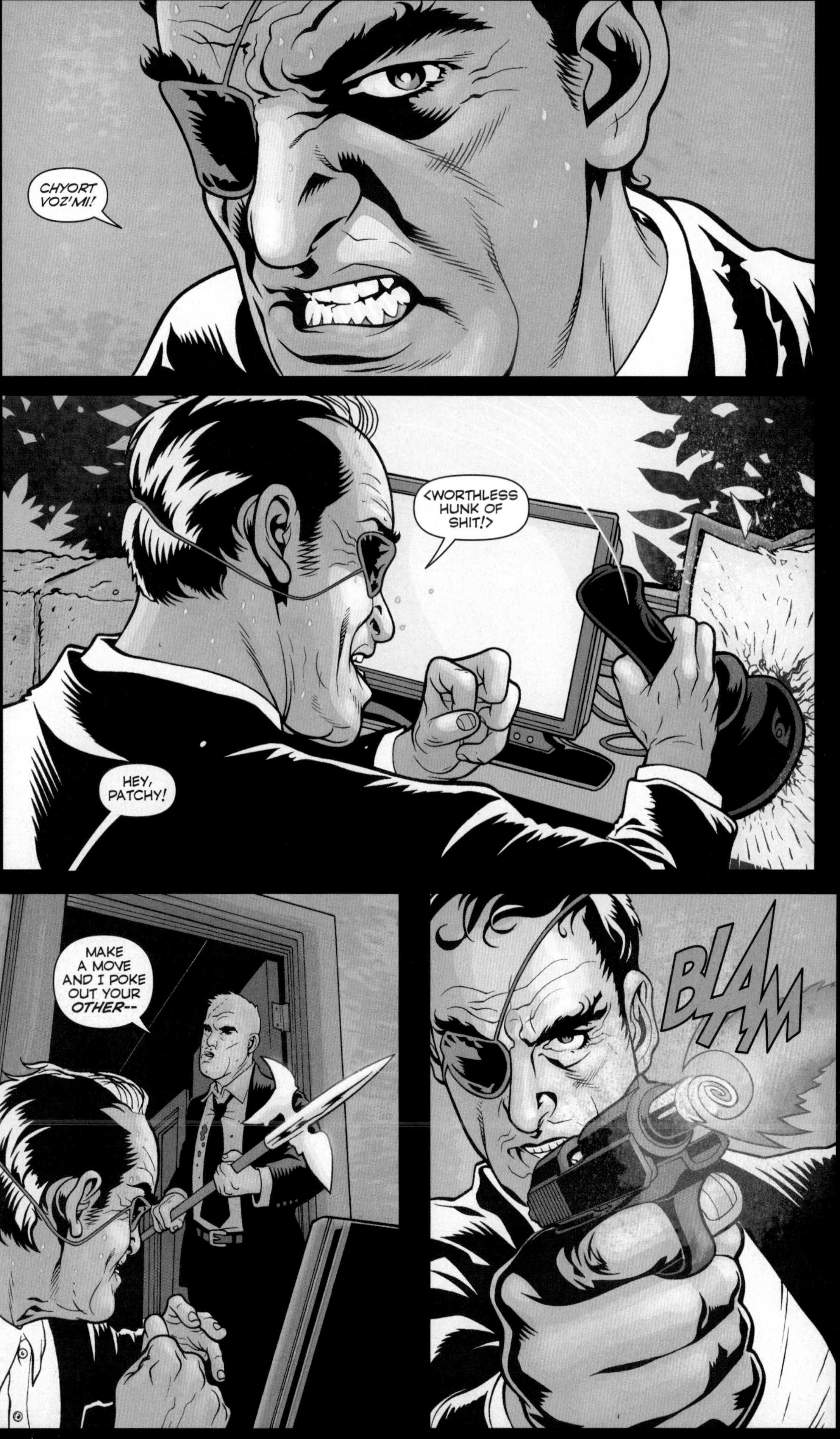
CHYORT VOZ'MI!
<WORTHLESS HUNK OF SHIT!>
HEY, PATCHY!
MAKE A MOVE AND I POKE OUT YOUR *OTHER*--
BLAM

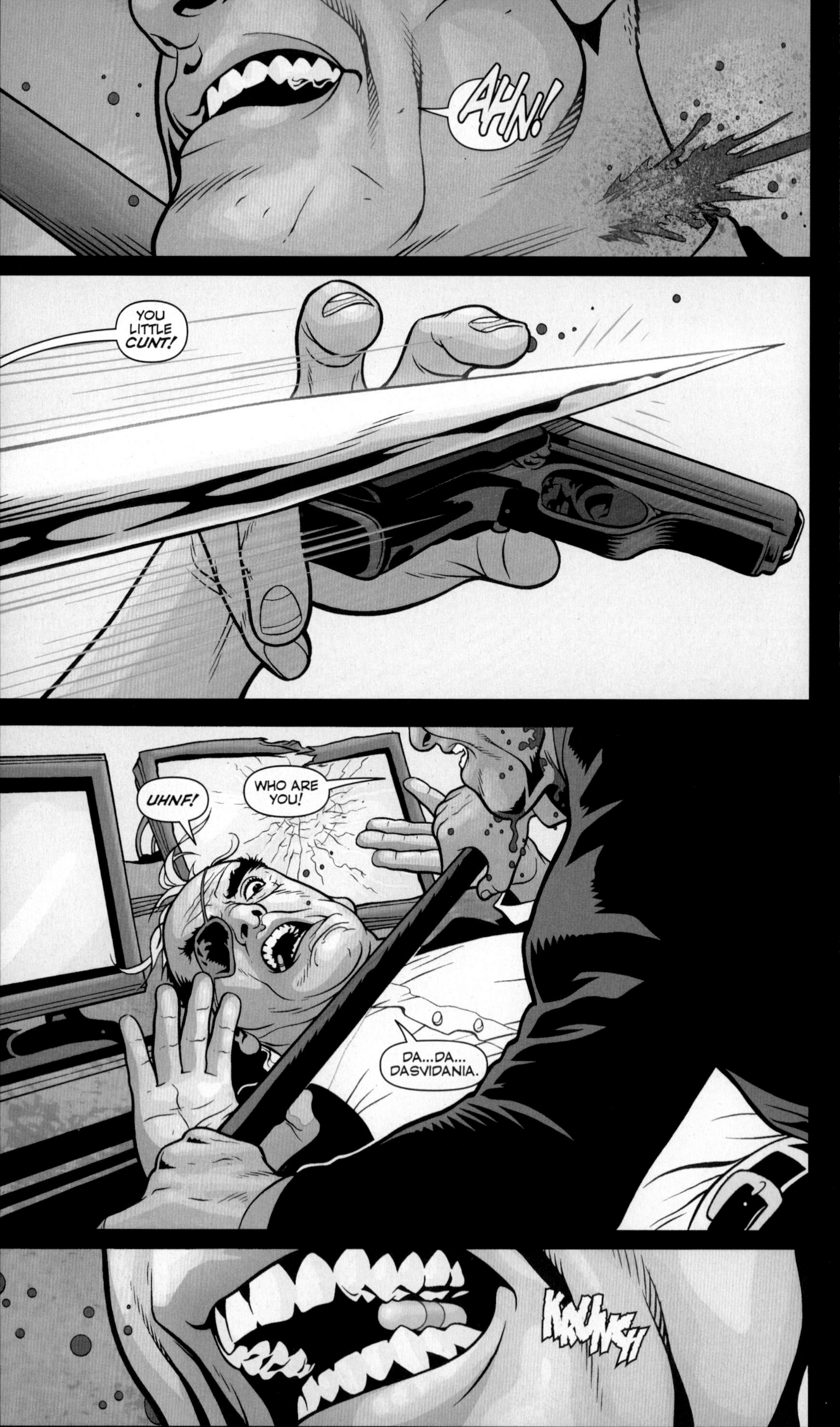
AHN!
YOU LITTLE CUNT!
UHNF!
WHO ARE YOU!
DA...DA... DASVIDANIA.
KRUNCH

A RUSSKIE?

DID...DID *KREMLIN* SEND YOU?

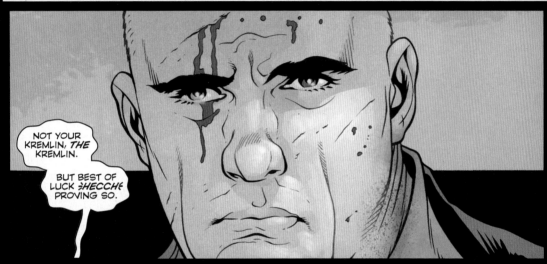

NOT YOUR KREMLIN, *THE* KREMLIN.

BUT BEST OF LUCK *HECCH* PROVING SO.

PLEASE TELL...YOUR EMPLOYER...

...THAT COMRADE *PUTIN* SAYS......*

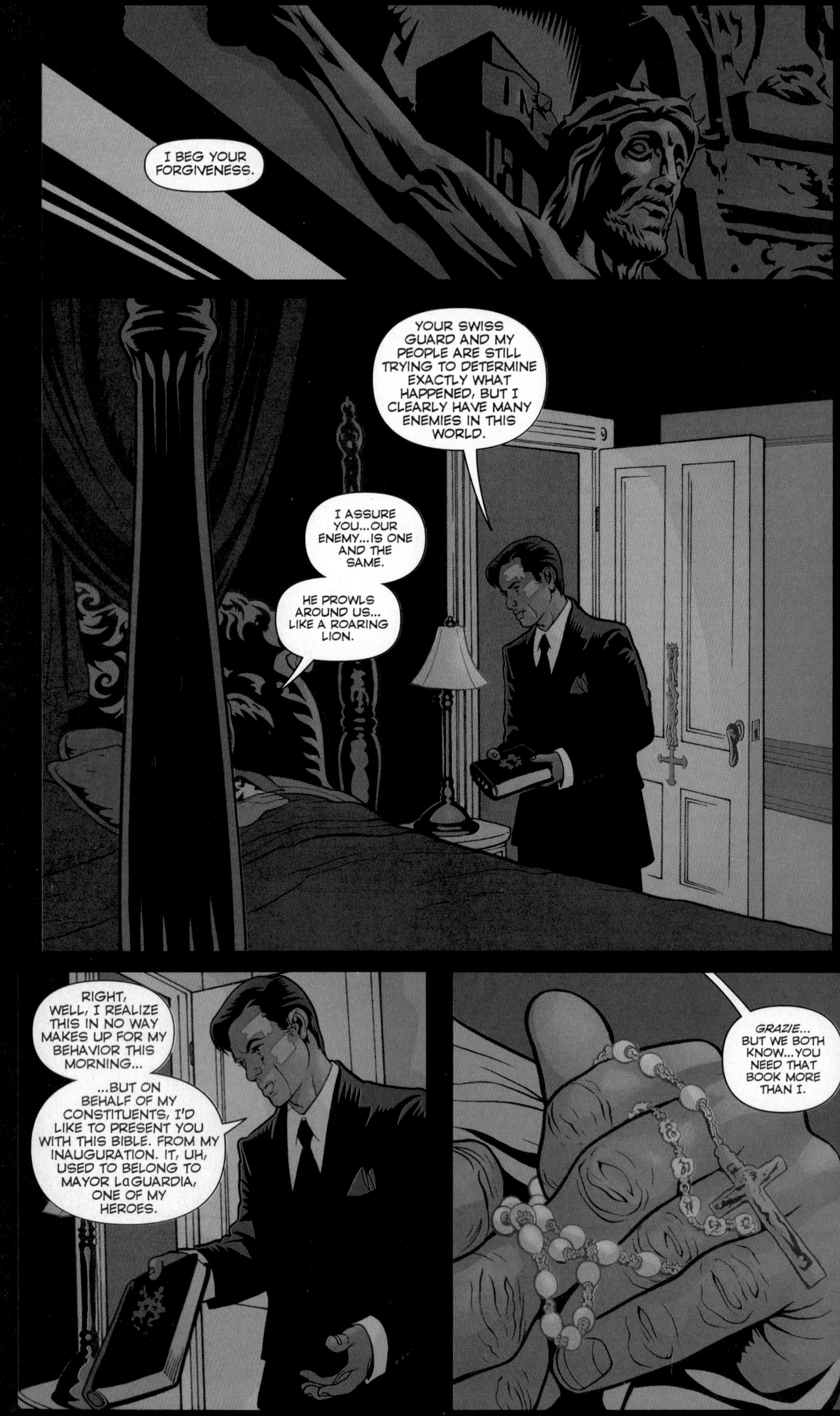
I BEG YOUR FORGIVENESS.
YOUR SWISS GUARD AND MY PEOPLE ARE STILL TRYING TO DETERMINE EXACTLY WHAT HAPPENED, BUT I CLEARLY HAVE MANY ENEMIES IN THIS WORLD.
I ASSURE YOU...OUR ENEMY...IS ONE AND THE SAME.
HE PROWLS AROUND US... LIKE A ROARING LION.
RIGHT, WELL, I REALIZE THIS IN NO WAY MAKES UP FOR MY BEHAVIOR THIS MORNING...
...BUT ON BEHALF OF MY CONSTITUENTS, I'D LIKE TO PRESENT YOU WITH THIS BIBLE. FROM MY INAUGURATION. IT, UH, USED TO BELONG TO MAYOR LaGUARDIA, ONE OF MY HEROES.
GRAZIE... BUT WE BOTH KNOW...YOU NEED THAT BOOK MORE THAN I.

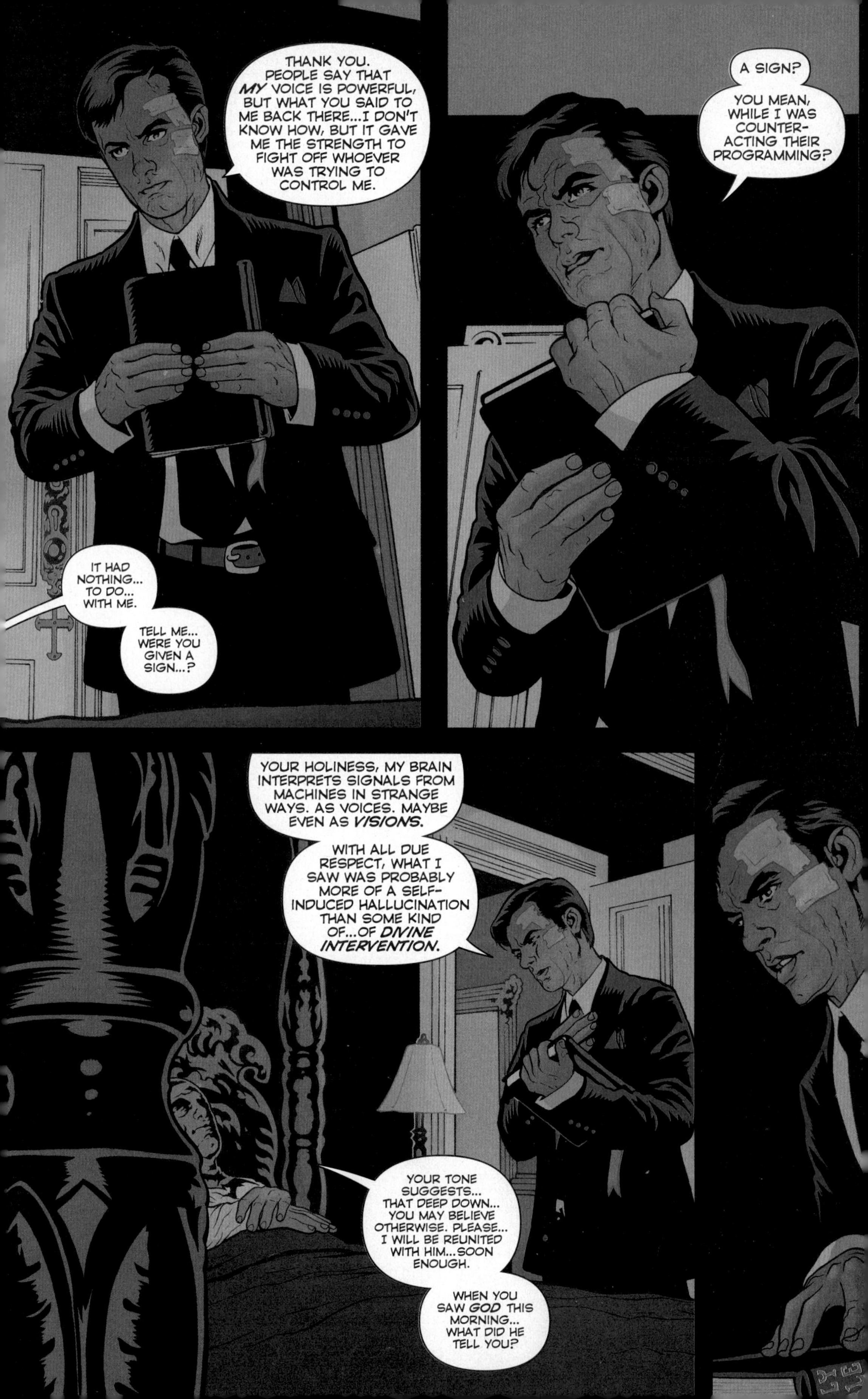
THANK YOU. PEOPLE SAY THAT *MY* VOICE IS POWERFUL, BUT WHAT YOU SAID TO ME BACK THERE...I DON'T KNOW HOW, BUT IT GAVE ME THE STRENGTH TO FIGHT OFF WHOEVER WAS TRYING TO CONTROL ME.
IT HAD NOTHING... TO DO... WITH ME.
TELL ME... WERE YOU GIVEN A SIGN...?
A SIGN?
YOU MEAN, WHILE I WAS COUNTER-ACTING THEIR PROGRAMMING?
YOUR HOLINESS, MY BRAIN INTERPRETS SIGNALS FROM MACHINES IN STRANGE WAYS. AS VOICES. MAYBE EVEN AS *VISIONS*.
WITH ALL DUE RESPECT, WHAT I SAW WAS PROBABLY MORE OF A SELF-INDUCED HALLUCINATION THAN SOME KIND OF...OF *DIVINE INTERVENTION*.
YOUR TONE SUGGESTS... THAT DEEP DOWN... YOU MAY BELIEVE OTHERWISE. PLEASE... I WILL BE REUNITED WITH HIM...SOON ENOUGH.
WHEN YOU SAW *GOD* THIS MORNING... WHAT DID HE TELL YOU?

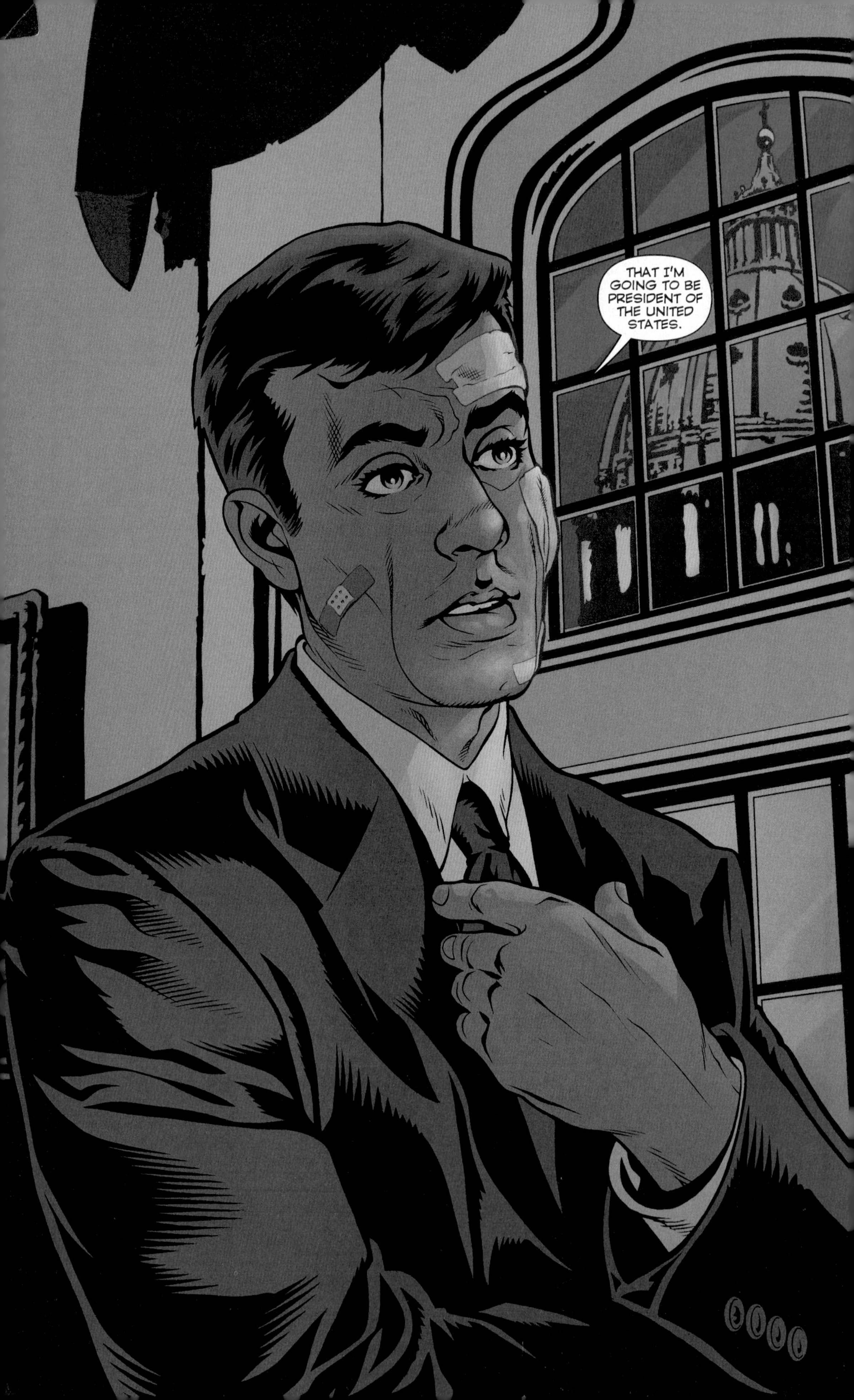
THAT I'M GOING TO BE PRESIDENT OF THE UNITED STATES.

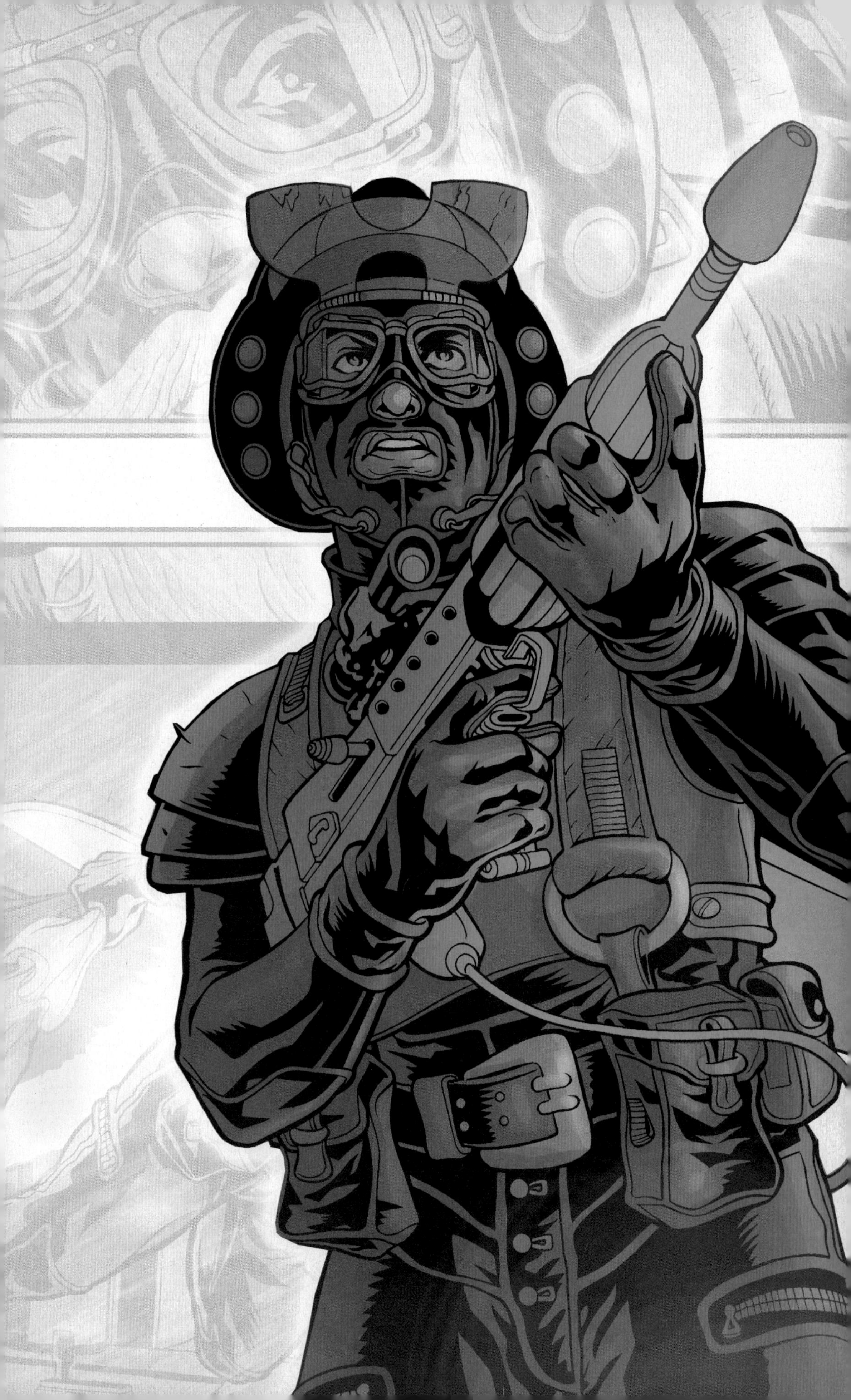

Chapter 5

World's Finest

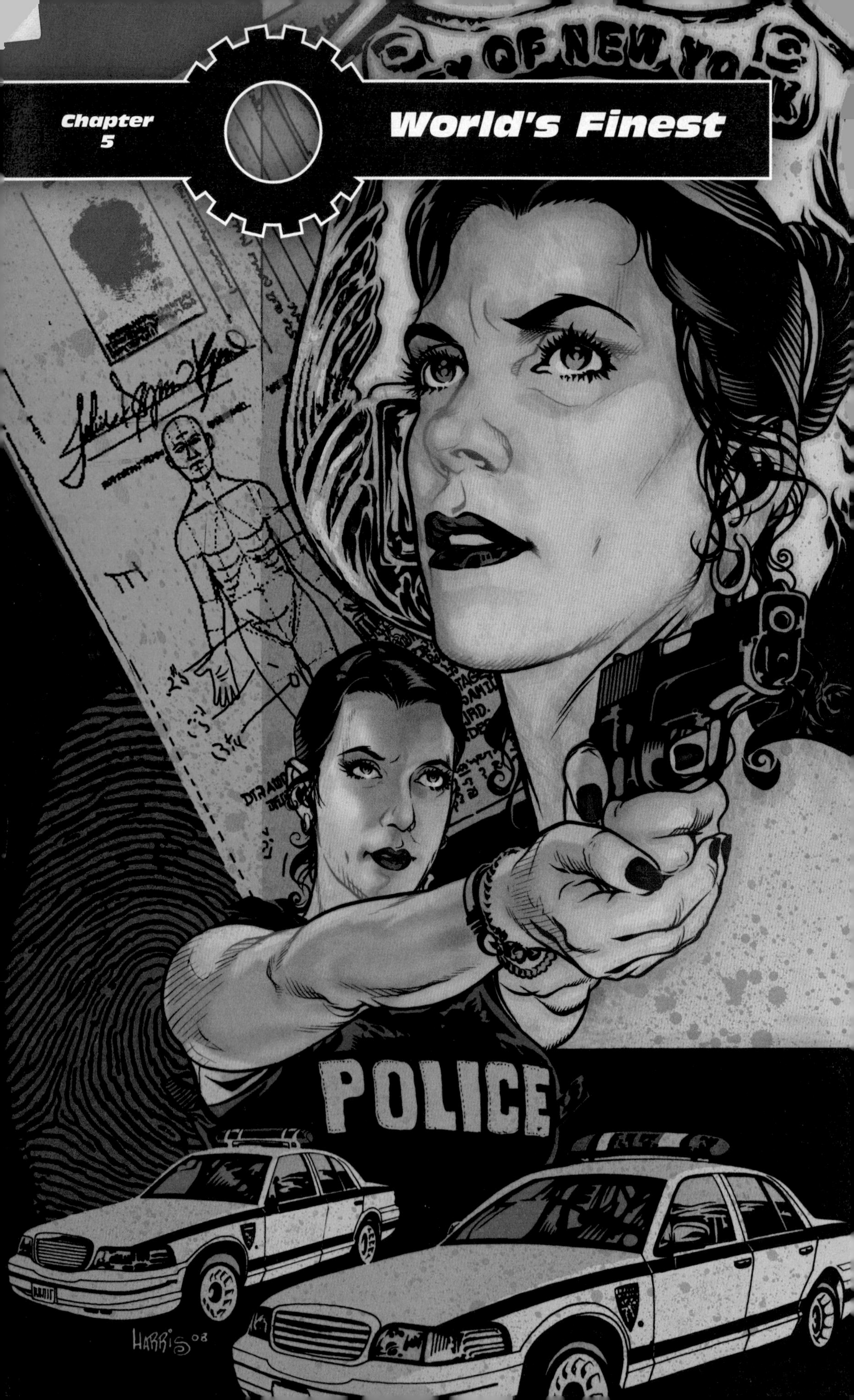
OF NEW YORK
POLICE
HARRIS 08

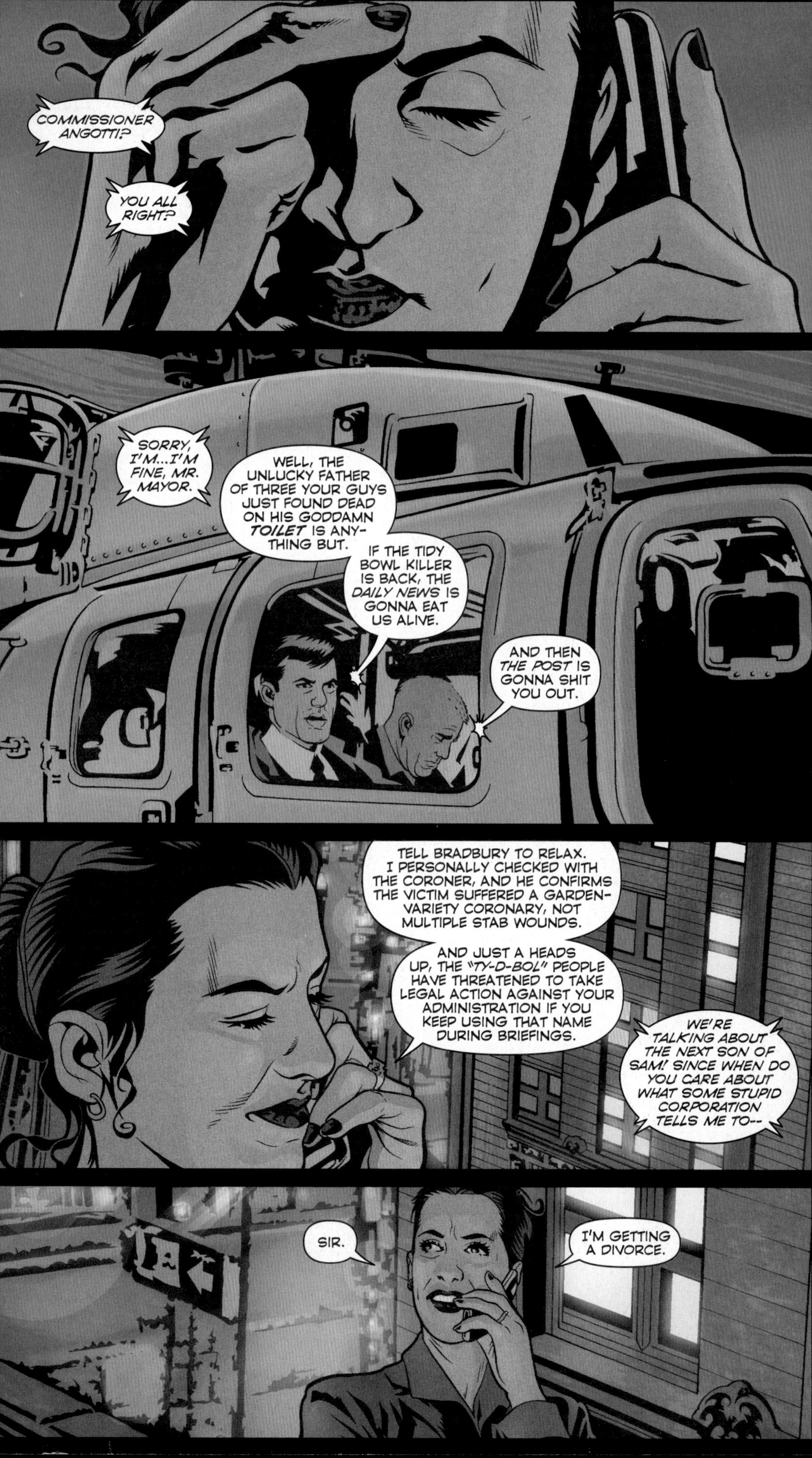
COMMISSIONER ANGOTTI?
YOU ALL RIGHT?
SORRY, I'M...I'M FINE, MR. MAYOR.
WELL, THE UNLUCKY FATHER OF THREE YOUR GUYS JUST FOUND DEAD ON HIS GODDAMN *TOILET* IS ANYTHING BUT.
IF THE TIDY BOWL KILLER IS BACK, THE *DAILY NEWS* IS GONNA EAT US ALIVE.
AND THEN *THE POST* IS GONNA SHIT YOU OUT.
TELL BRADBURY TO RELAX. I PERSONALLY CHECKED WITH THE CORONER, AND HE CONFIRMS THE VICTIM SUFFERED A GARDEN-VARIETY CORONARY, NOT MULTIPLE STAB WOUNDS.
AND JUST A HEADS UP, THE "*TY-D-BOL*" PEOPLE HAVE THREATENED TO TAKE LEGAL ACTION AGAINST YOUR ADMINISTRATION IF YOU KEEP USING THAT NAME DURING BRIEFINGS.
WE'RE TALKING ABOUT THE NEXT SON OF SAM! SINCE WHEN DO YOU CARE ABOUT WHAT SOME STUPID CORPORATION TELLS ME TO--
SIR.
I'M GETTING A DIVORCE.

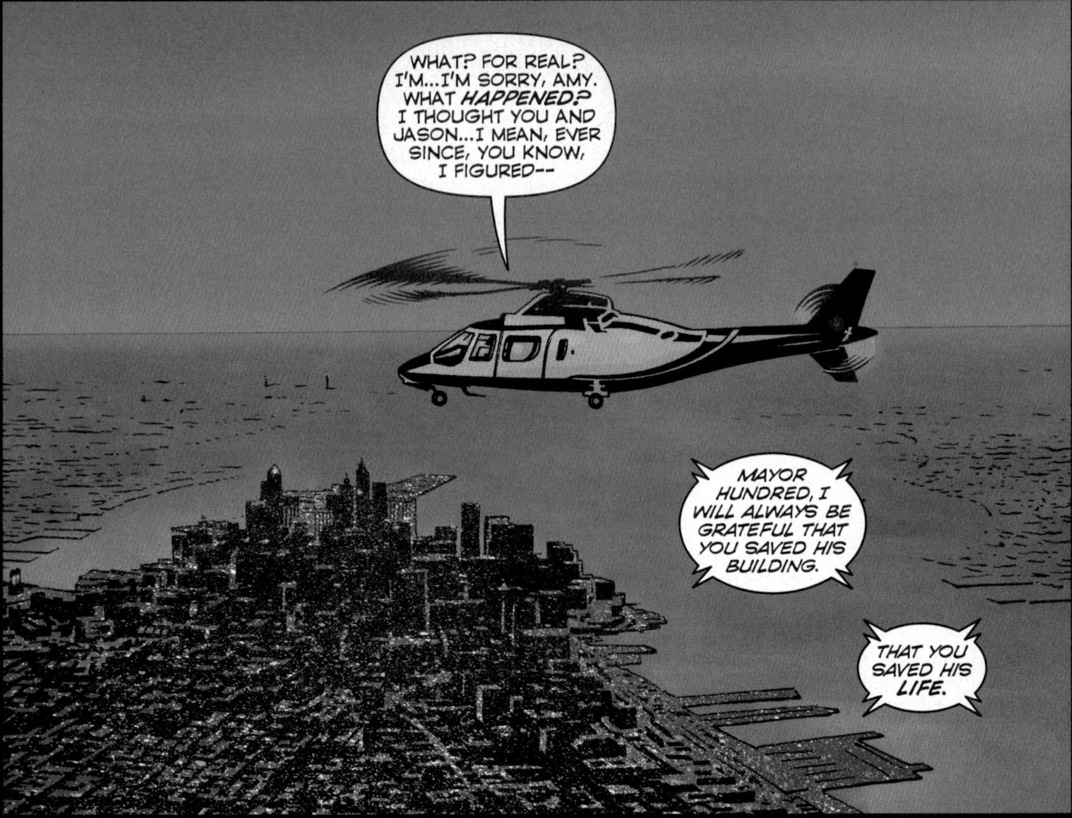
WHAT? FOR REAL? I'M...I'M SORRY, AMY. WHAT *HAPPENED?* I THOUGHT YOU AND JASON...I MEAN, EVER SINCE, YOU KNOW, I FIGURED--
MAYOR HUNDRED, I WILL ALWAYS BE GRATEFUL THAT YOU SAVED HIS BUILDING.
THAT YOU SAVED HIS ***LIFE.***

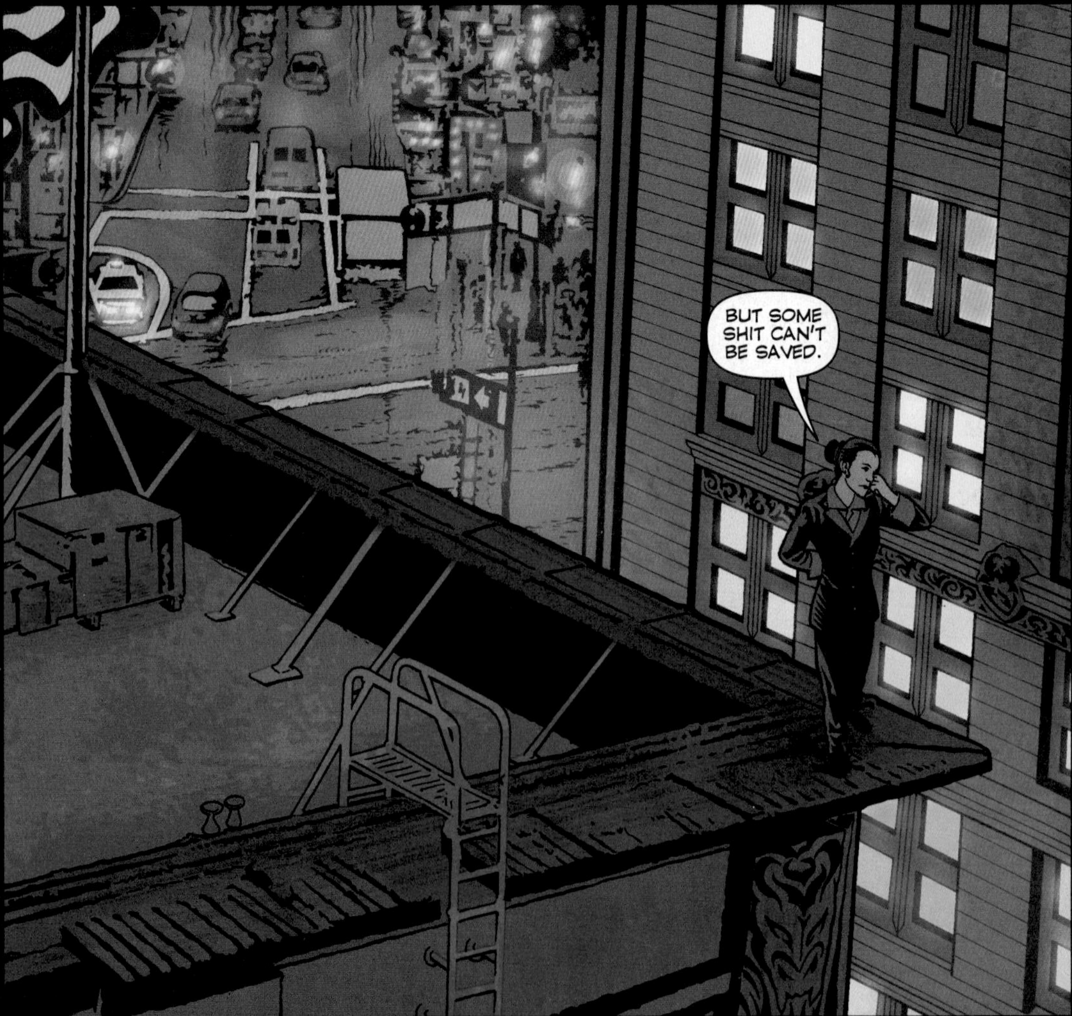
BUT SOME SHIT CAN'T BE SAVED.

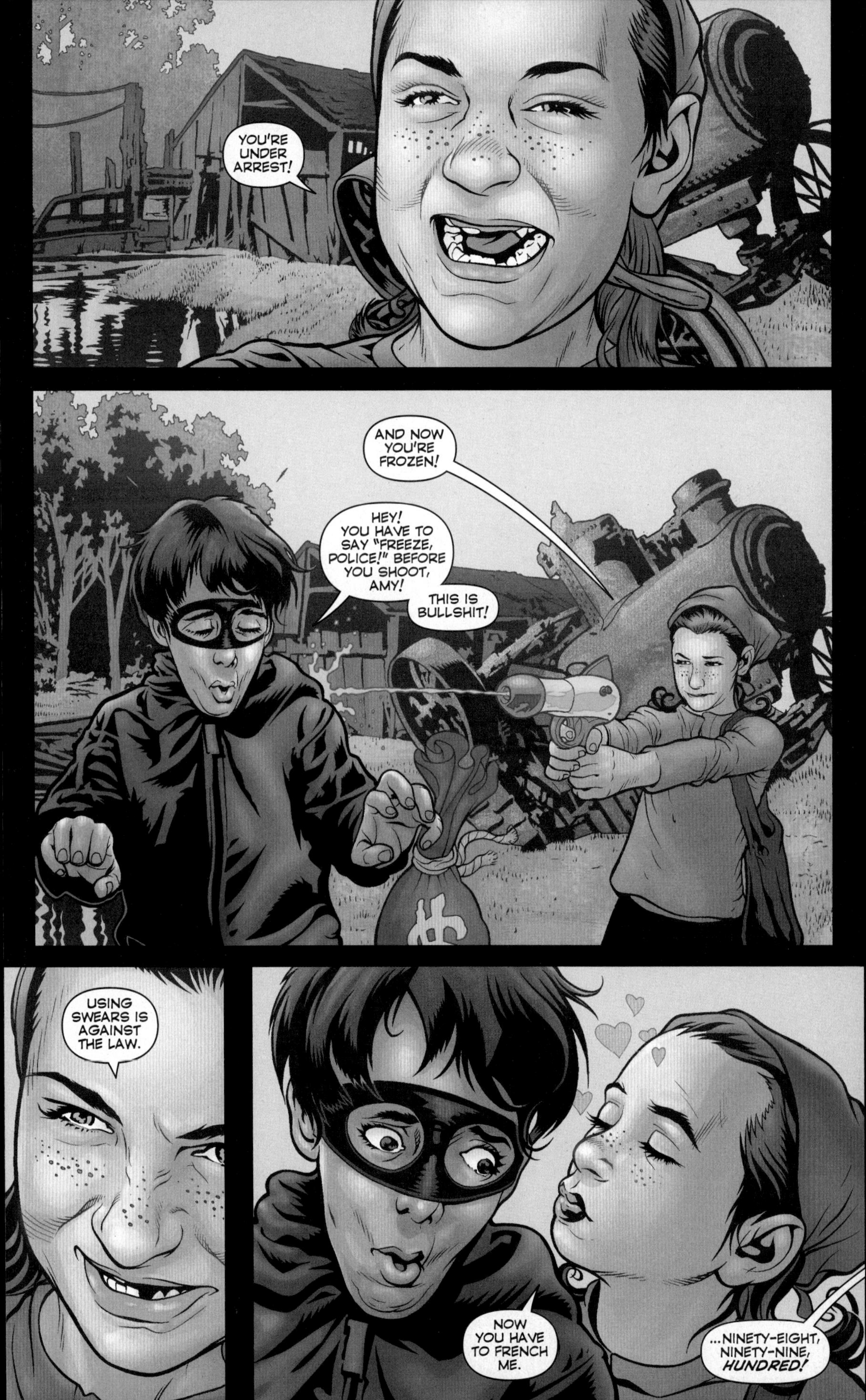

YOU'RE UNDER ARREST!
AND NOW YOU'RE FROZEN!
HEY! YOU HAVE TO SAY "FREEZE, POLICE!" BEFORE YOU SHOOT, AMY!
THIS IS BULLSHIT!
USING SWEARS IS AGAINST THE LAW.
NOW YOU HAVE TO FRENCH ME.
...NINETY-EIGHT, NINETY-NINE, HUNDRED!

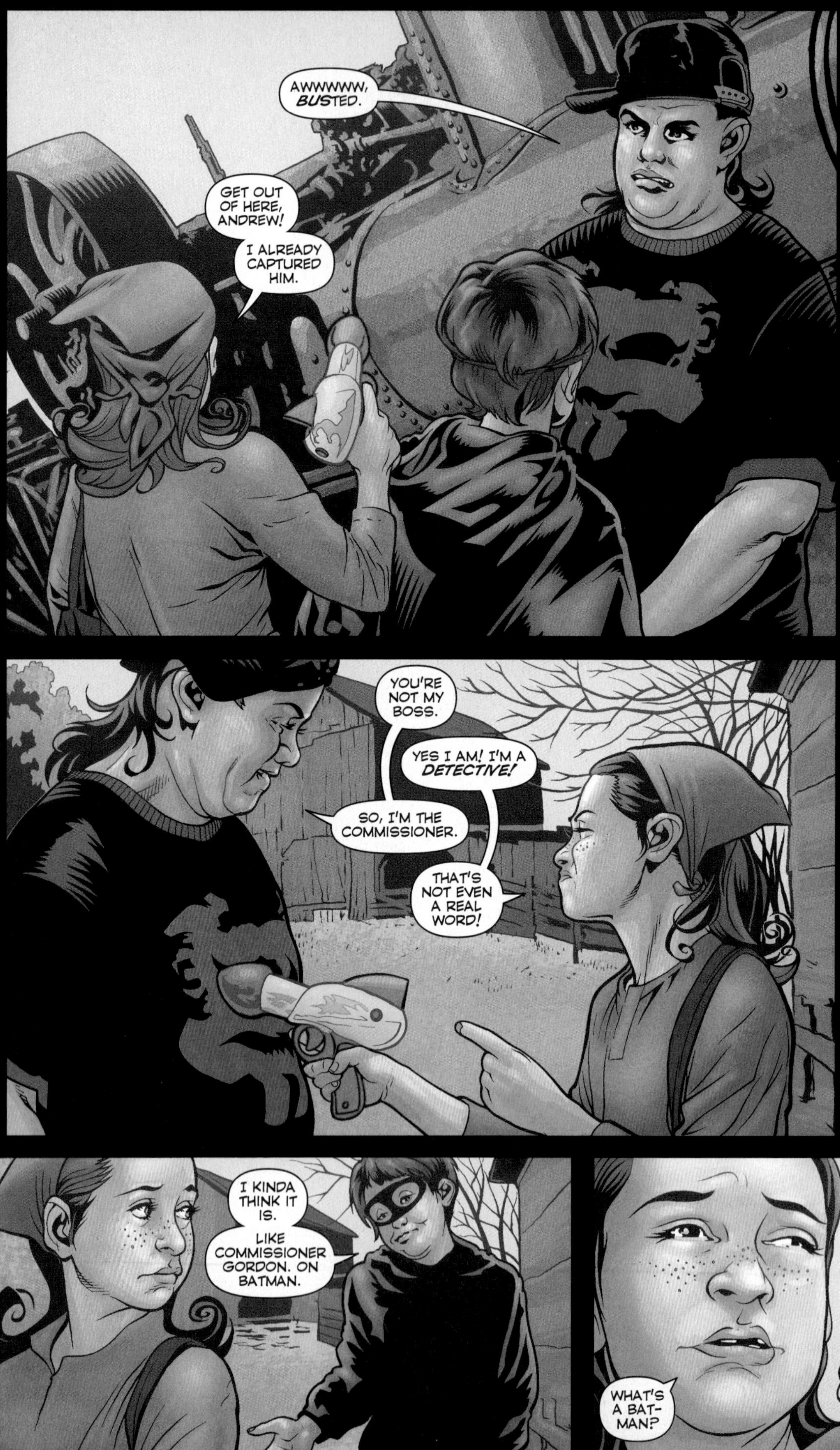
AWWWWW, BUSTED.
GET OUT OF HERE, ANDREW!
I ALREADY CAPTURED HIM.
YOU'RE NOT MY BOSS.
YES I AM! I'M A DETECTIVE!
SO, I'M THE COMMISSIONER.
THAT'S NOT EVEN A REAL WORD!
I KINDA THINK IT IS.
LIKE COMMISSIONER GORDON. ON BATMAN.
WHAT'S A BAT-MAN?

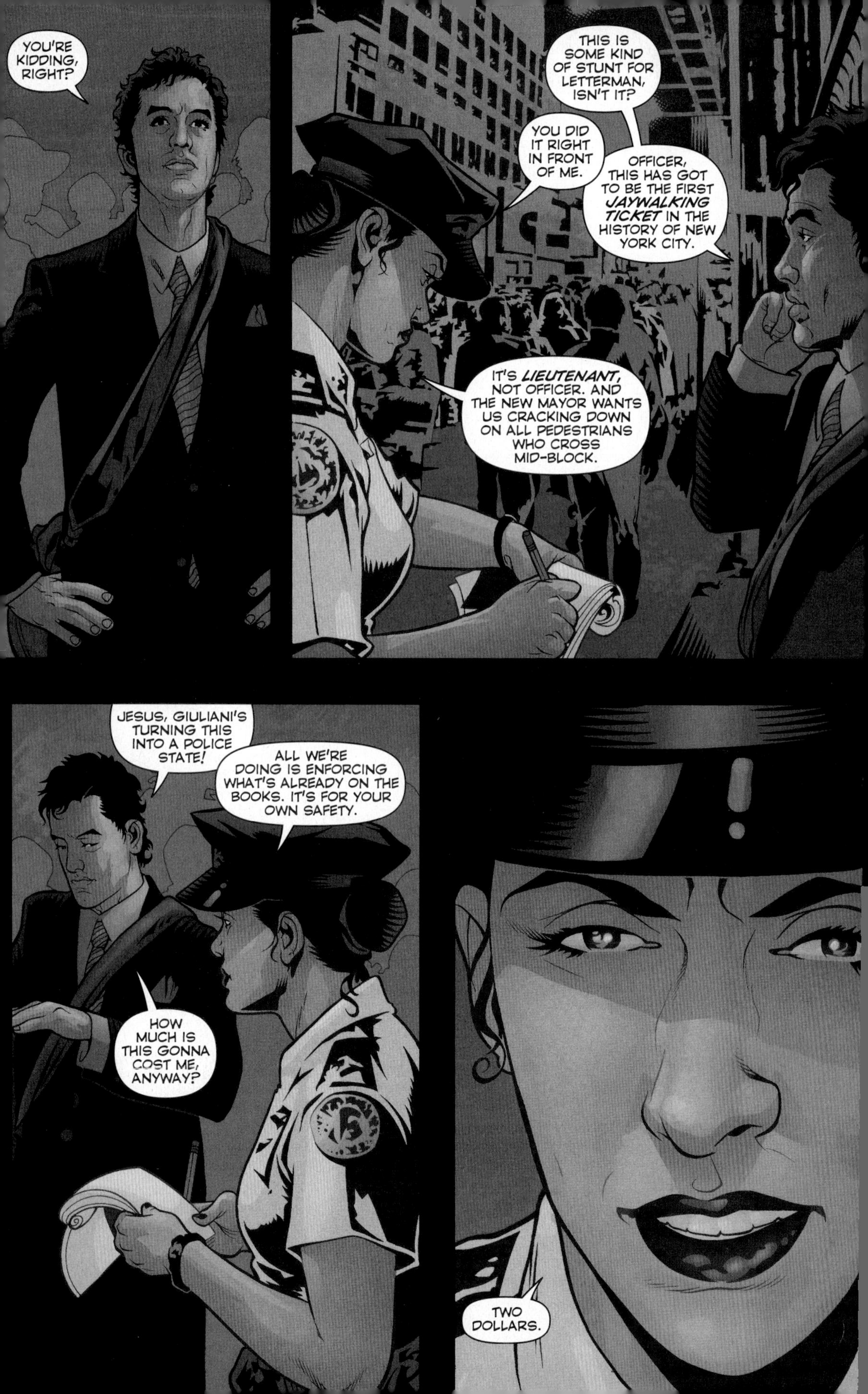
YOU'RE KIDDING, RIGHT?
THIS IS SOME KIND OF STUNT FOR LETTERMAN, ISN'T IT?
YOU DID IT RIGHT IN FRONT OF ME.
OFFICER, THIS HAS GOT TO BE THE FIRST *JAYWALKING TICKET* IN THE HISTORY OF NEW YORK CITY.
IT'S *LIEUTENANT,* NOT OFFICER. AND THE NEW MAYOR WANTS US CRACKING DOWN ON ALL PEDESTRIANS WHO CROSS MID-BLOCK.
JESUS, GIULIANI'S TURNING THIS INTO A POLICE STATE!
ALL WE'RE DOING IS ENFORCING WHAT'S ALREADY ON THE BOOKS. IT'S FOR YOUR OWN SAFETY.
HOW MUCH IS THIS GONNA COST ME, ANYWAY?
TWO DOLLARS.

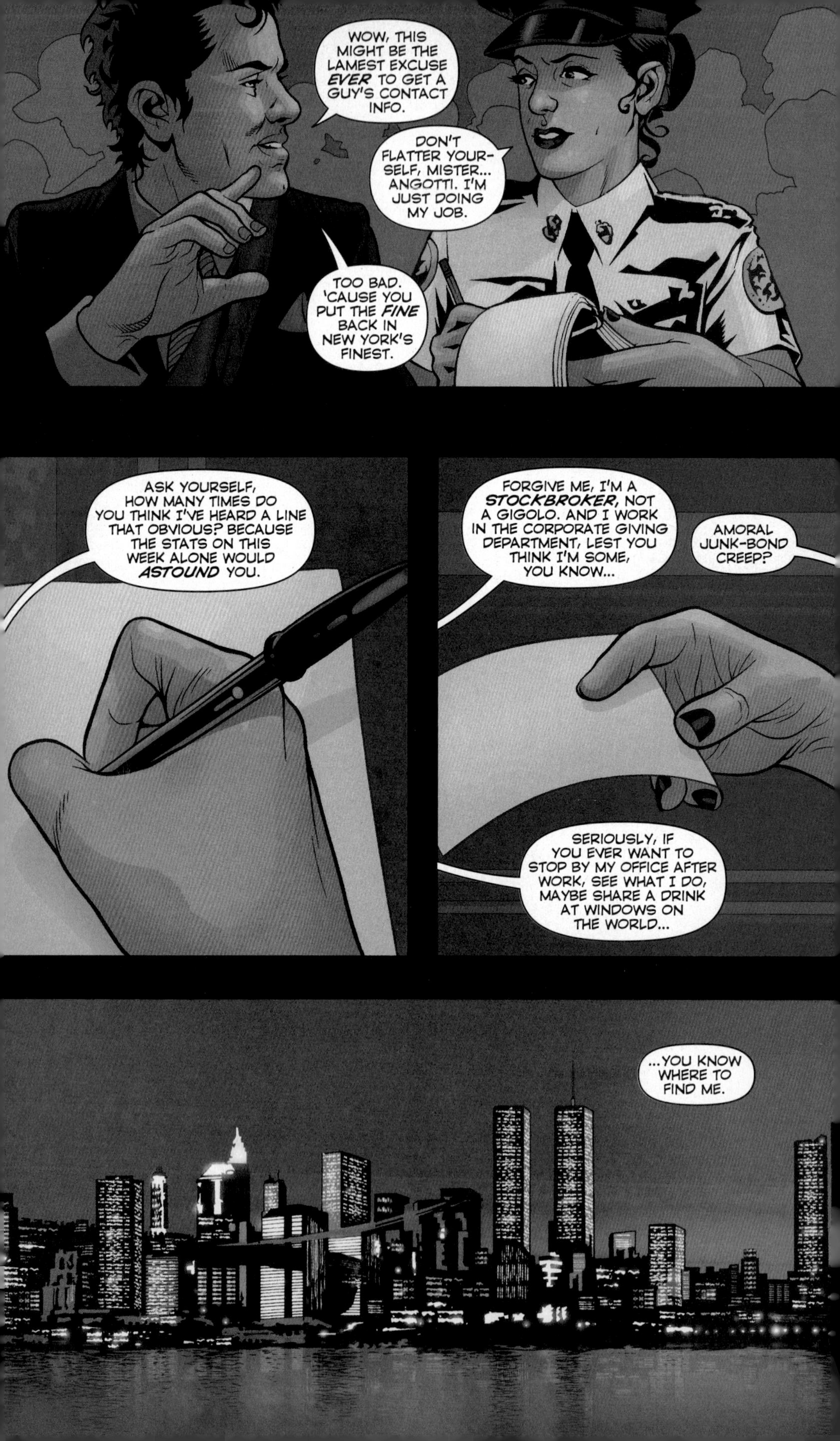
WOW, THIS MIGHT BE THE LAMEST EXCUSE *EVER* TO GET A GUY'S CONTACT INFO.
DON'T FLATTER YOURSELF, MISTER... ANGOTTI. I'M JUST DOING MY JOB.
TOO BAD. 'CAUSE YOU PUT THE *FINE* BACK IN NEW YORK'S FINEST.
ASK YOURSELF, HOW MANY TIMES DO YOU THINK I'VE HEARD A LINE THAT OBVIOUS? BECAUSE THE STATS ON THIS WEEK ALONE WOULD *ASTOUND* YOU.
FORGIVE ME, I'M A *STOCKBROKER,* NOT A GIGOLO. AND I WORK IN THE CORPORATE GIVING DEPARTMENT, LEST YOU THINK I'M SOME, YOU KNOW...
AMORAL JUNK-BOND CREEP?
SERIOUSLY, IF YOU EVER WANT TO STOP BY MY OFFICE AFTER WORK, SEE WHAT I DO, MAYBE SHARE A DRINK AT WINDOWS ON THE WORLD...
...YOU KNOW WHERE TO FIND ME.

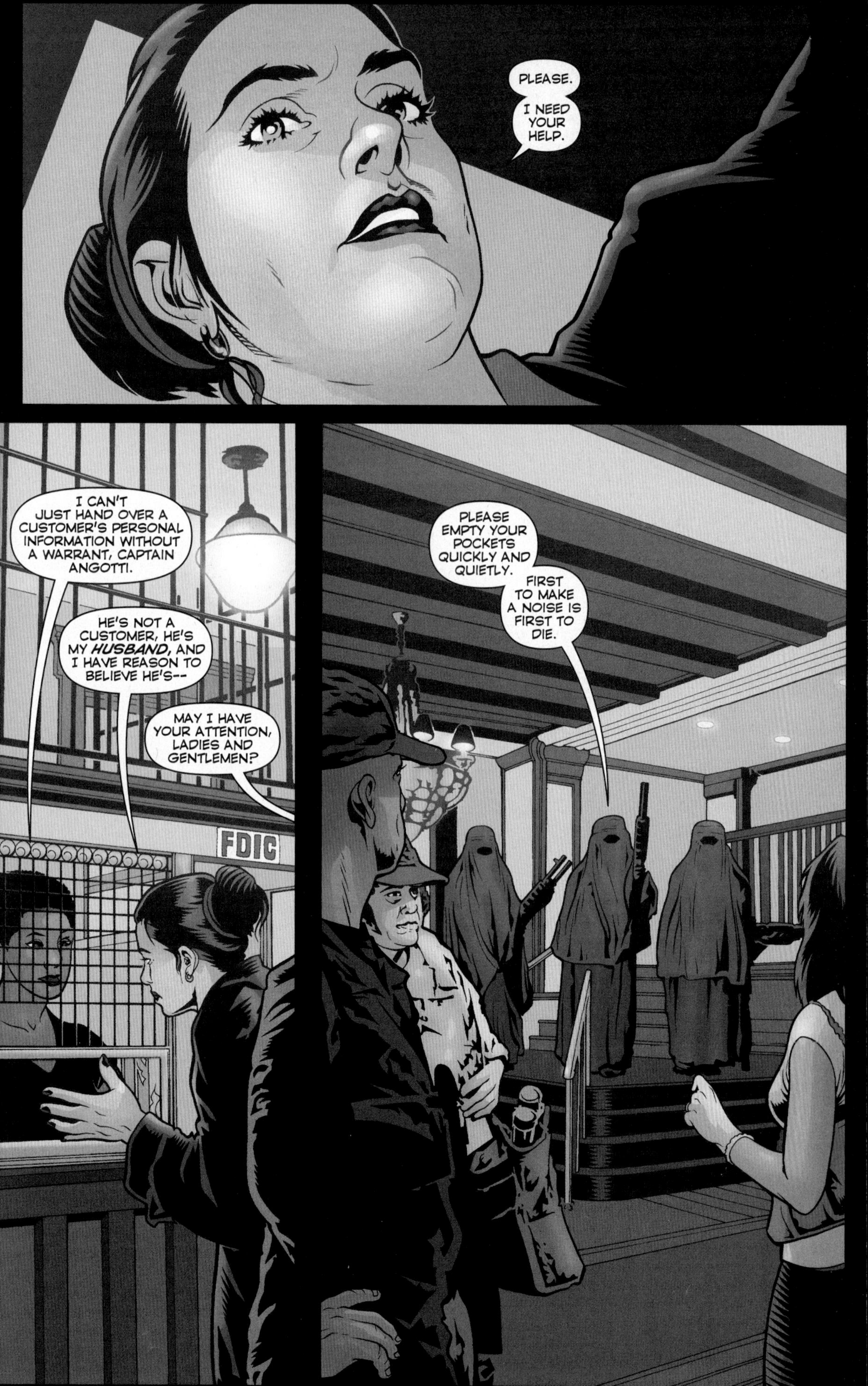
PLEASE.
I NEED YOUR HELP.
I CAN'T JUST HAND OVER A CUSTOMER'S PERSONAL INFORMATION WITHOUT A WARRANT, CAPTAIN ANGOTTI.
HE'S NOT A CUSTOMER, HE'S MY *HUSBAND,* AND I HAVE REASON TO BELIEVE HE'S--
MAY I HAVE YOUR ATTENTION, LADIES AND GENTLEMEN?
FDIC
PLEASE EMPTY YOUR POCKETS QUICKLY AND QUIETLY.
FIRST TO MAKE A NOISE IS FIRST TO DIE.

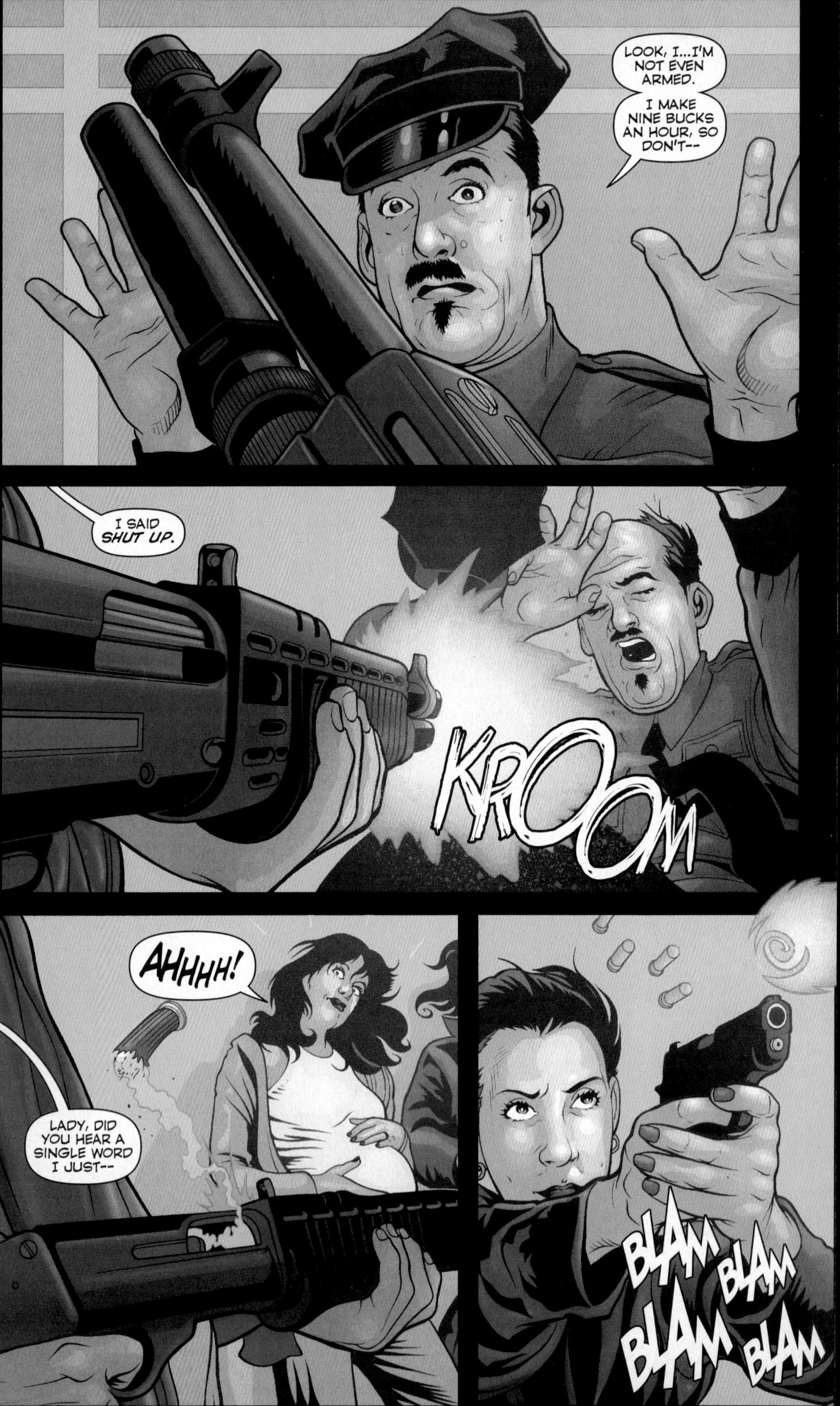
LOOK, I...I'M NOT EVEN ARMED.
I MAKE NINE BUCKS AN HOUR, SO DON'T--
I SAID *SHUT UP.*
KROOOM
AHHHH!
LADY, DID YOU HEAR A SINGLE WORD I JUST--
BLAM BLAM BLAM BLAM

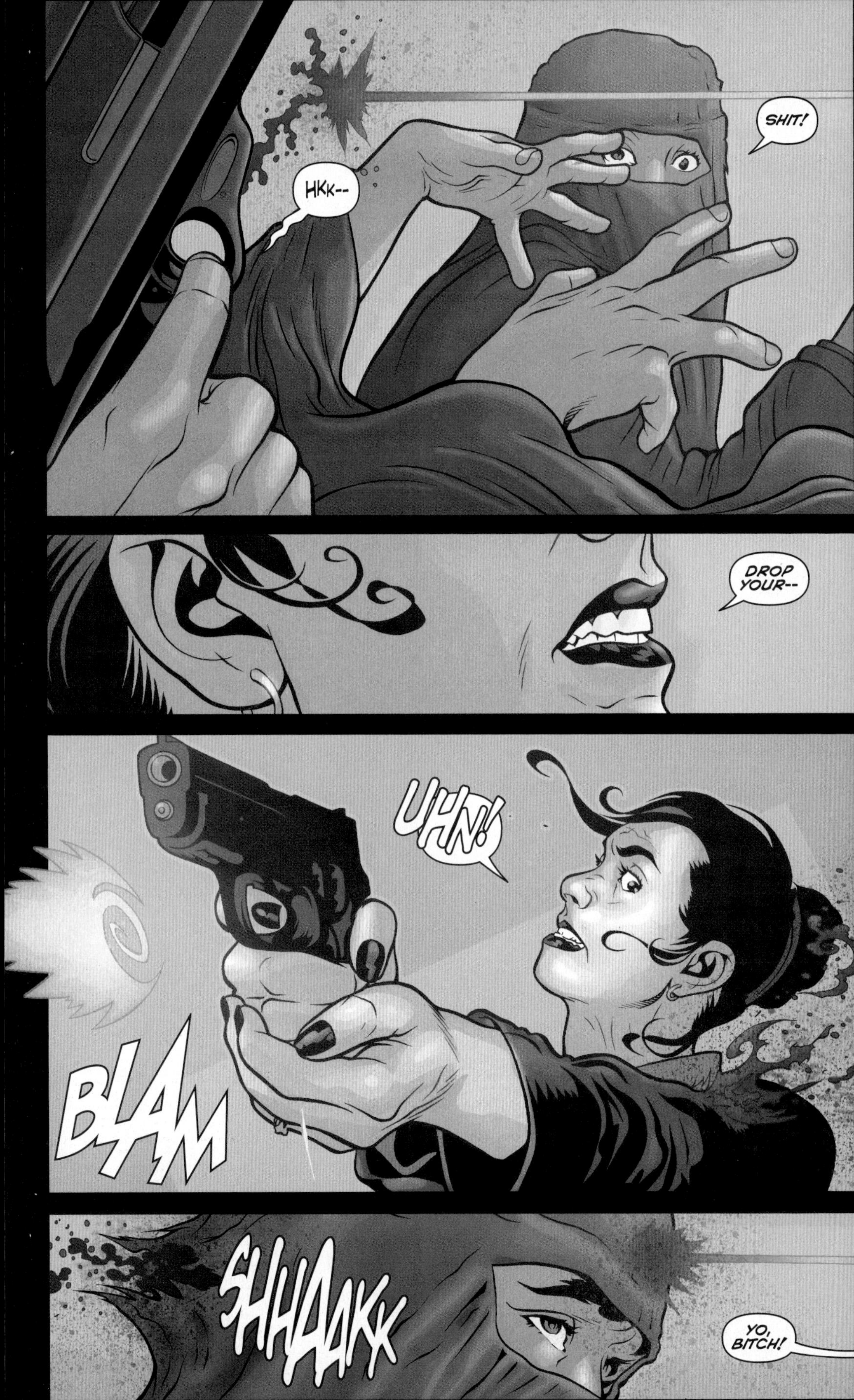
SHIT!
HKK--
DROP YOUR--
UHN!
BLAM
SHHAAKK
YO, BITCH!

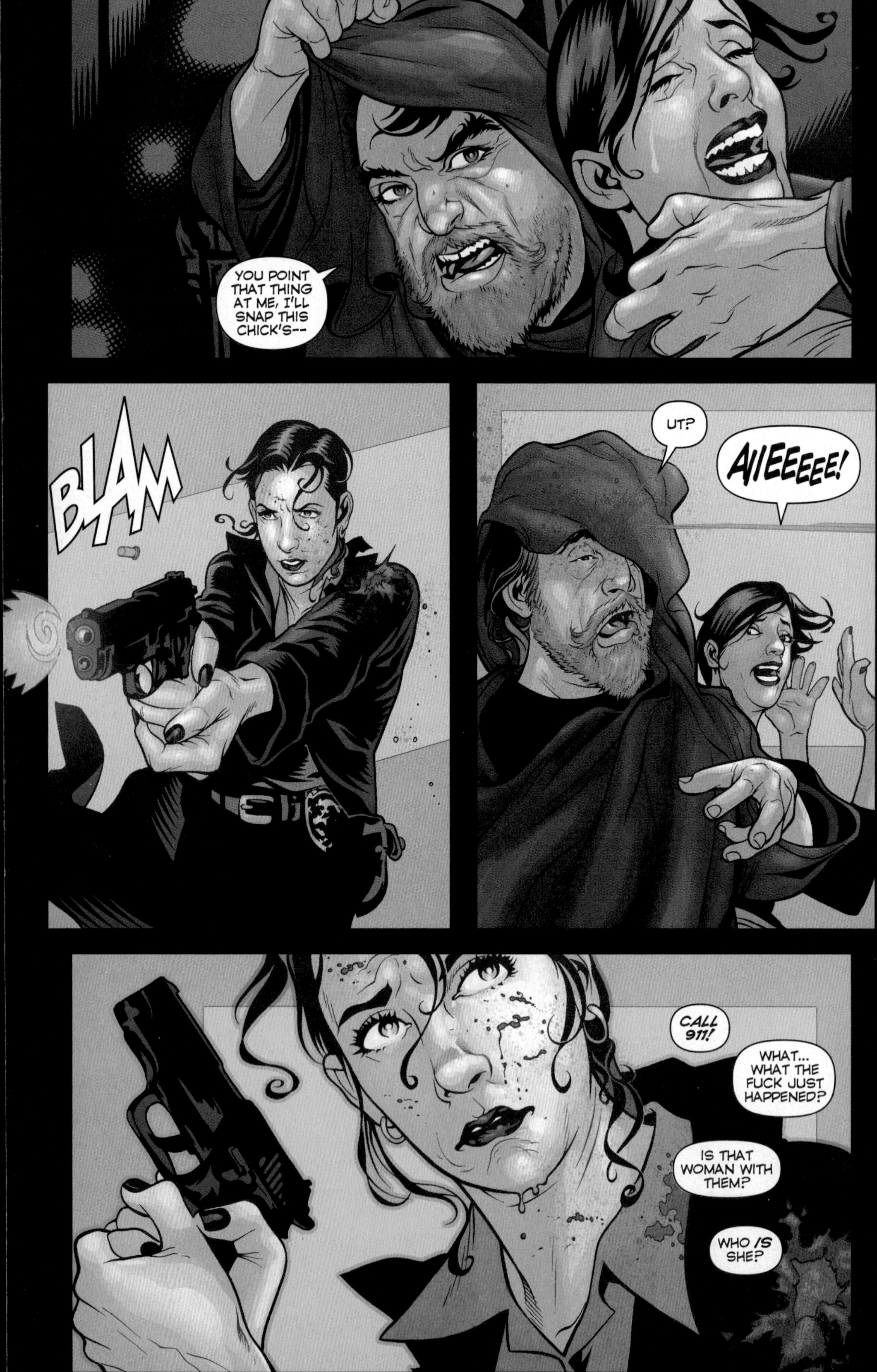
YOU POINT THAT THING AT ME, I'LL SNAP THIS CHICK'S--
BLAM
UT?
AIIEEEEEE!
CALL 911!
WHAT... WHAT THE FUCK JUST HAPPENED?
IS THAT WOMAN WITH THEM?
WHO IS SHE?

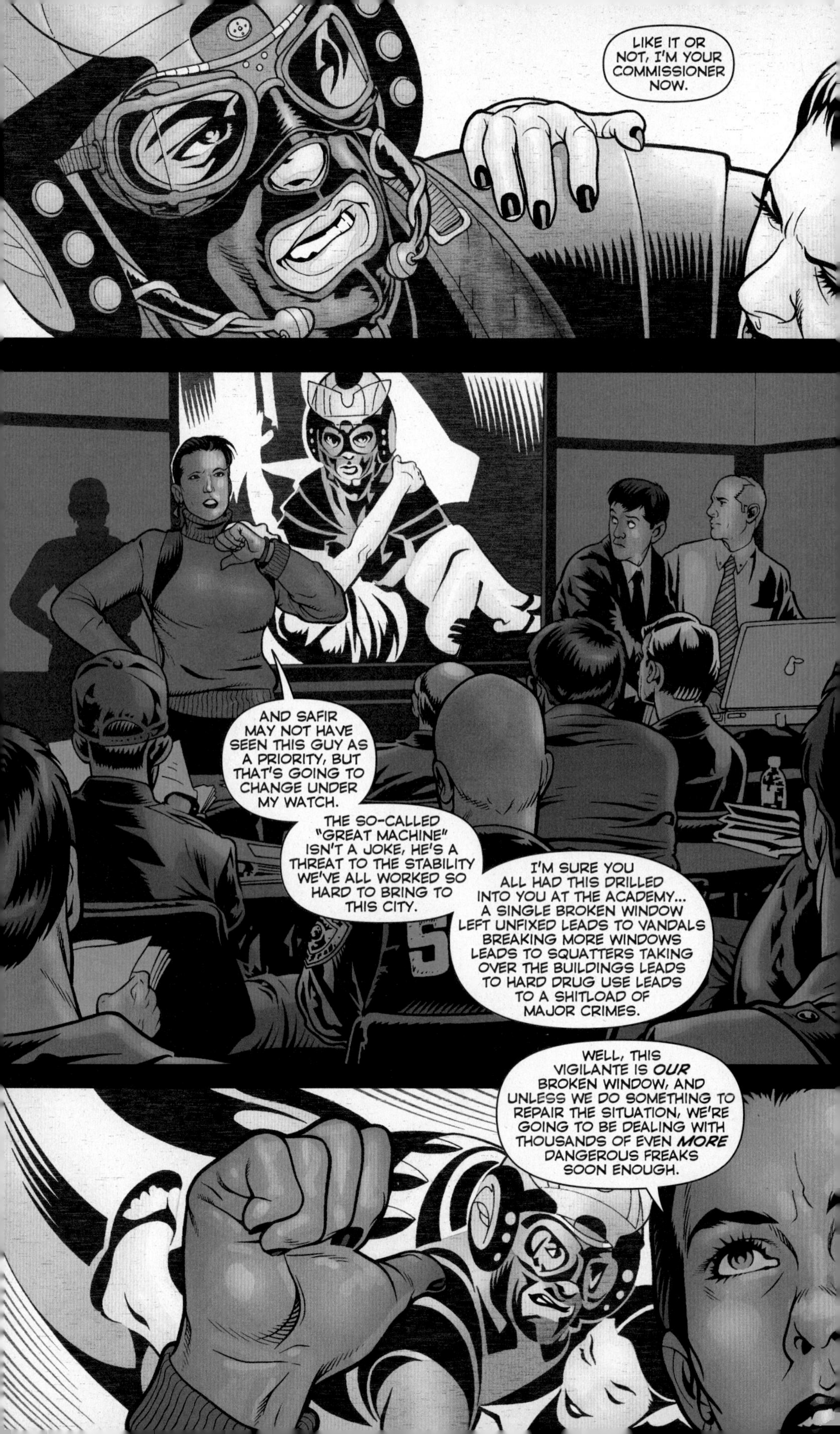

LIKE IT OR NOT, I'M YOUR COMMISSIONER NOW.
AND SAFIR MAY NOT HAVE SEEN THIS GUY AS A PRIORITY, BUT THAT'S GOING TO CHANGE UNDER MY WATCH.
THE SO-CALLED "GREAT MACHINE" ISN'T A JOKE, HE'S A THREAT TO THE STABILITY WE'VE ALL WORKED SO HARD TO BRING TO THIS CITY.
I'M SURE YOU ALL HAD THIS DRILLED INTO YOU AT THE ACADEMY... A SINGLE BROKEN WINDOW LEFT UNFIXED LEADS TO VANDALS BREAKING MORE WINDOWS LEADS TO SQUATTERS TAKING OVER THE BUILDINGS LEADS TO HARD DRUG USE LEADS TO A SHITLOAD OF MAJOR CRIMES.
WELL, THIS VIGILANTE IS *OUR* BROKEN WINDOW, AND UNLESS WE DO SOMETHING TO REPAIR THE SITUATION, WE'RE GOING TO BE DEALING WITH THOUSANDS OF EVEN *MORE* DANGEROUS FREAKS SOON ENOUGH.

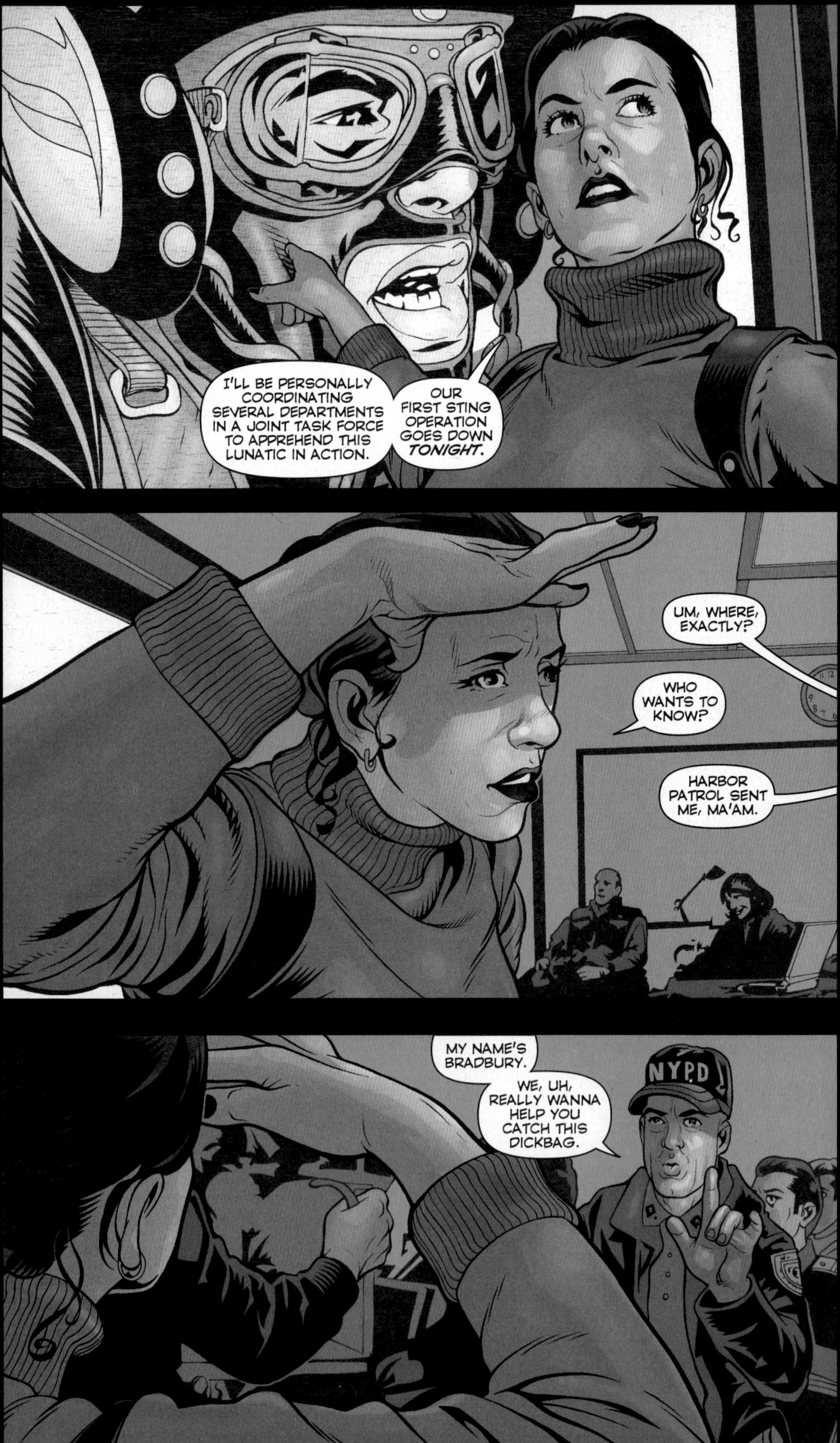
I'LL BE PERSONALLY COORDINATING SEVERAL DEPARTMENTS IN A JOINT TASK FORCE TO APPREHEND THIS LUNATIC IN ACTION.
OUR FIRST STING OPERATION GOES DOWN *TONIGHT*.
UM, WHERE, EXACTLY?
WHO WANTS TO KNOW?
HARBOR PATROL SENT ME, MA'AM.
MY NAME'S BRADBURY.
WE, UH, REALLY WANNA HELP YOU CATCH THIS DICKBAG.
NYPD

ASSHOLE.

AMY?

GOD, COME TO BED ALREADY.

IN A BIT, JASON. SCANNER SAYS PUBLIC ENEMY NUMBER ONE WAS SPOTTED IN OUR NEIGHBORHOOD.

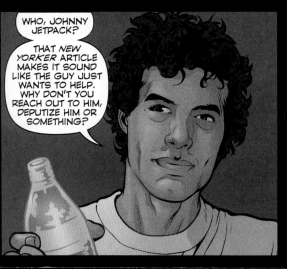

WHO, JOHNNY JETPACK?

THAT *NEW YORKER* ARTICLE MAKES IT SOUND LIKE THE GUY JUST WANTS TO HELP. WHY DON'T YOU REACH OUT TO HIM, DEPUTIZE HIM OR SOMETHING?

WHAT THE FUCK DID YOU SAY?

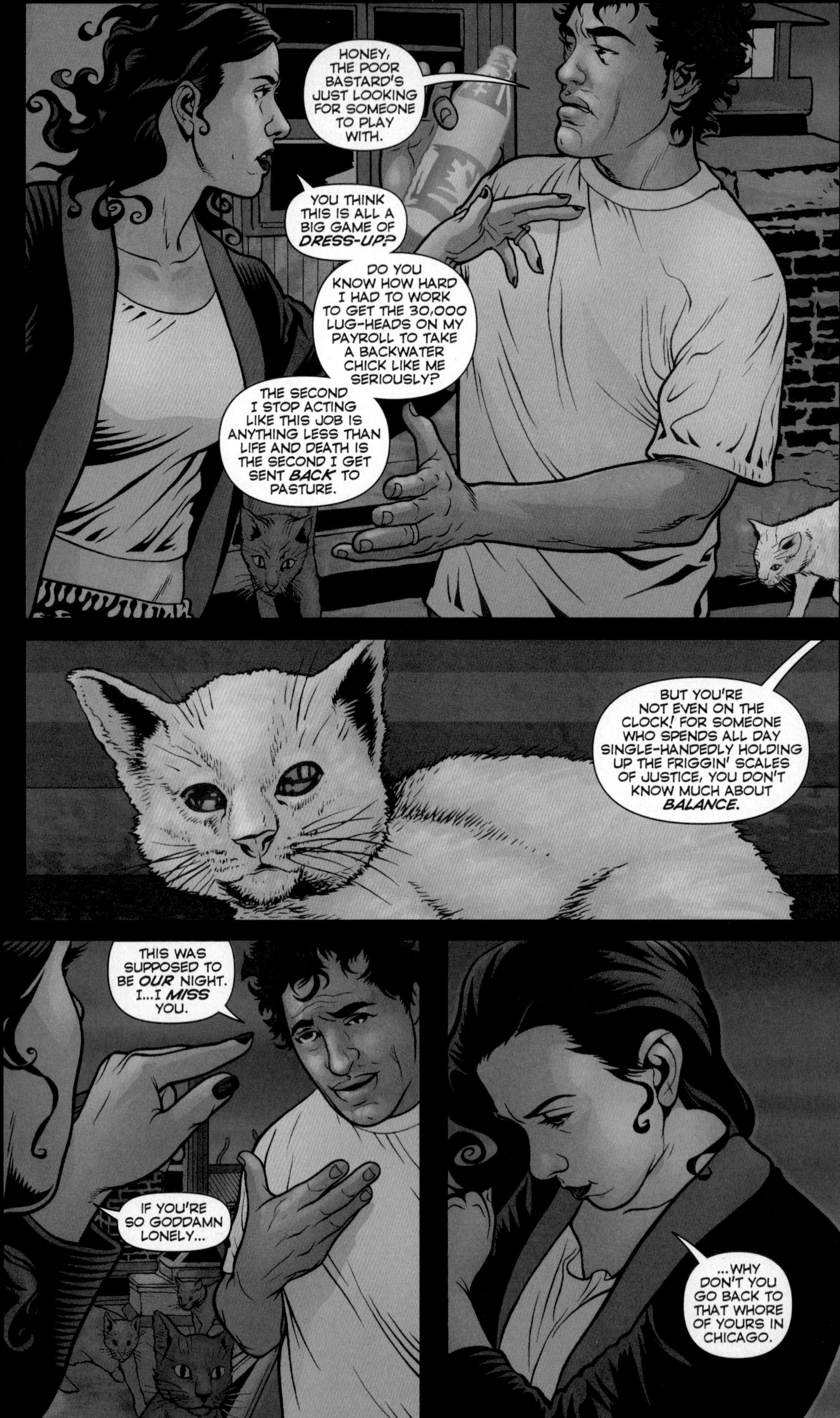
HONEY, THE POOR BASTARD'S JUST LOOKING FOR SOMEONE TO PLAY WITH.
YOU THINK THIS IS ALL A BIG GAME OF DRESS-UP?
DO YOU KNOW HOW HARD I HAD TO WORK TO GET THE 30,000 LUG-HEADS ON MY PAYROLL TO TAKE A BACKWATER CHICK LIKE ME SERIOUSLY?
THE SECOND I STOP ACTING LIKE THIS JOB IS ANYTHING LESS THAN LIFE AND DEATH IS THE SECOND I GET SENT BACK TO PASTURE.
BUT YOU'RE NOT EVEN ON THE CLOCK! FOR SOMEONE WHO SPENDS ALL DAY SINGLE-HANDEDLY HOLDING UP THE FRIGGIN' SCALES OF JUSTICE, YOU DON'T KNOW MUCH ABOUT BALANCE.
THIS WAS SUPPOSED TO BE OUR NIGHT. I...I MISS YOU.
IF YOU'RE SO GODDAMN LONELY...
...WHY DON'T YOU GO BACK TO THAT WHORE OF YOURS IN CHICAGO.

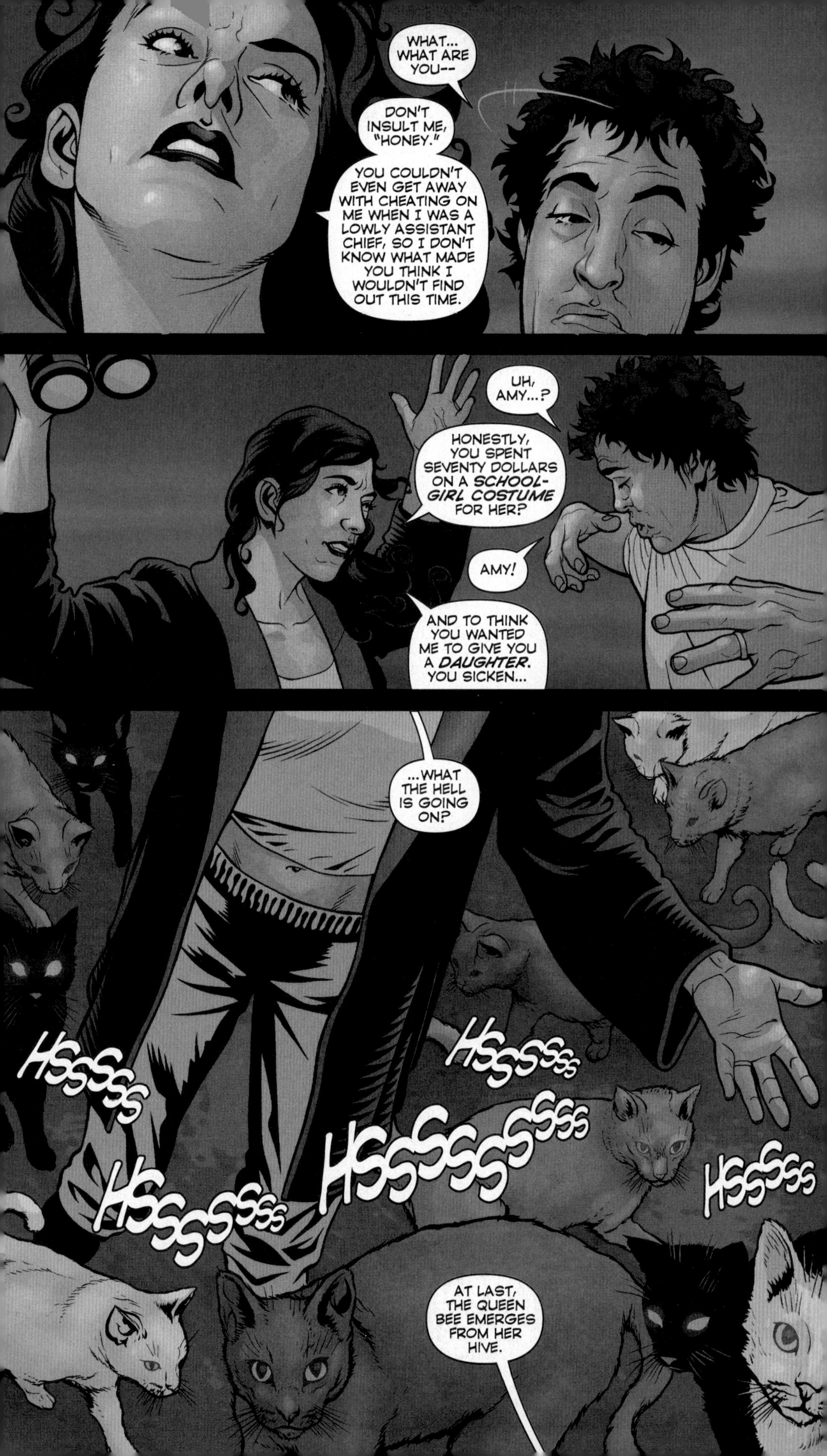
WHAT... WHAT ARE YOU--
DON'T INSULT ME, "HONEY."
YOU COULDN'T EVEN GET AWAY WITH CHEATING ON ME WHEN I WAS A LOWLY ASSISTANT CHIEF, SO I DON'T KNOW WHAT MADE YOU THINK I WOULDN'T FIND OUT THIS TIME.
UH, AMY...?
HONESTLY, YOU SPENT SEVENTY DOLLARS ON A *SCHOOL-GIRL COSTUME* FOR HER?
AMY!
AND TO THINK YOU WANTED ME TO GIVE YOU A *DAUGHTER*. YOU SICKEN...
...WHAT THE HELL IS GOING ON?
HSSSSS
HSSSSSS
HSSSSSSSSSSS
HSSSSSSSS
HSSSSSS
AT LAST, THE QUEEN BEE EMERGES FROM HER HIVE.

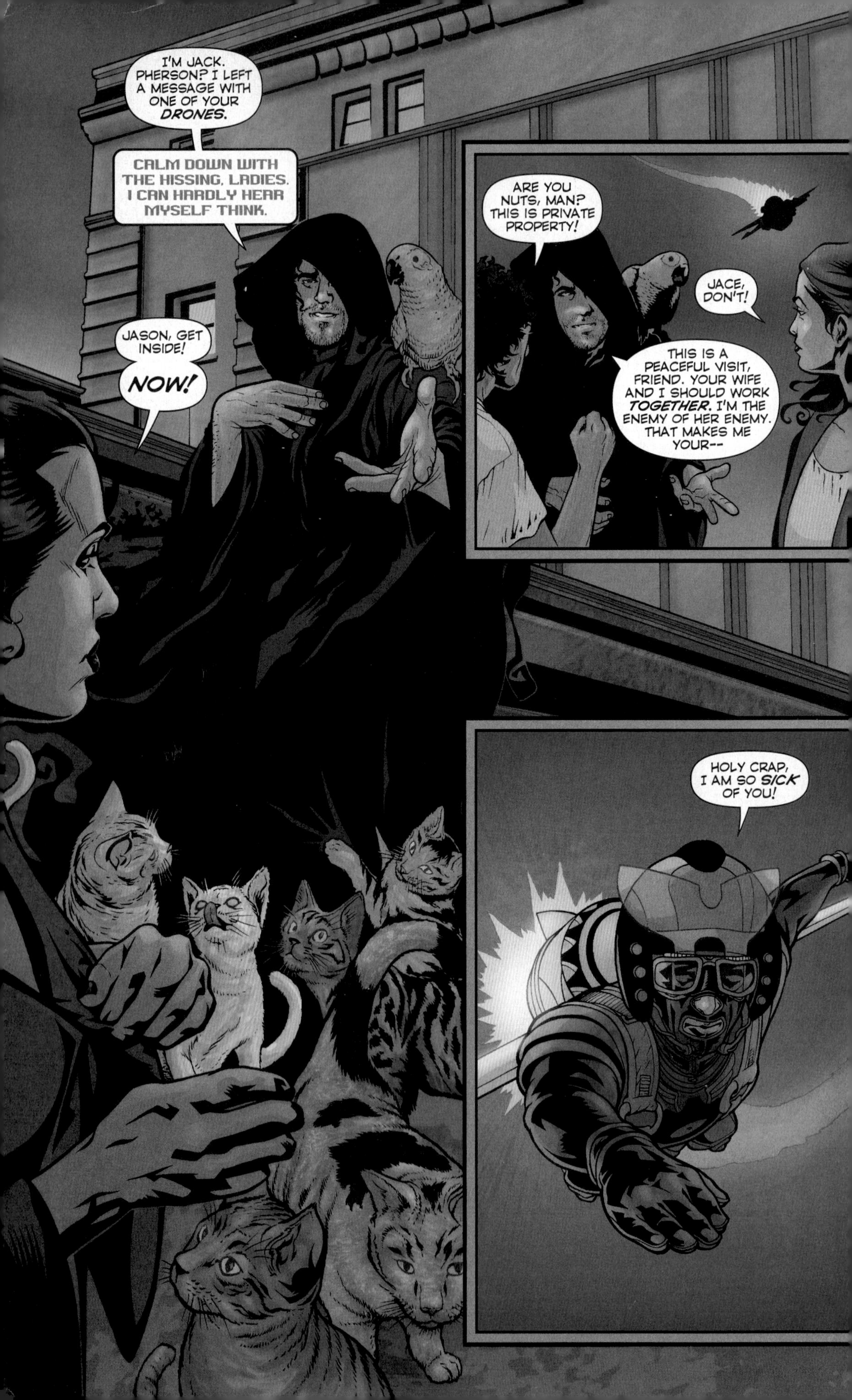
I'M JACK. PHERSON? I LEFT A MESSAGE WITH ONE OF YOUR DRONES.
CALM DOWN WITH THE HISSING, LADIES. I CAN HARDLY HEAR MYSELF THINK.
JASON, GET INSIDE!
NOW!
ARE YOU NUTS, MAN? THIS IS PRIVATE PROPERTY!
JACE, DON'T!
THIS IS A PEACEFUL VISIT, FRIEND. YOUR WIFE AND I SHOULD WORK TOGETHER. I'M THE ENEMY OF HER ENEMY. THAT MAKES ME YOUR--
HOLY CRAP, I AM SO SICK OF YOU!

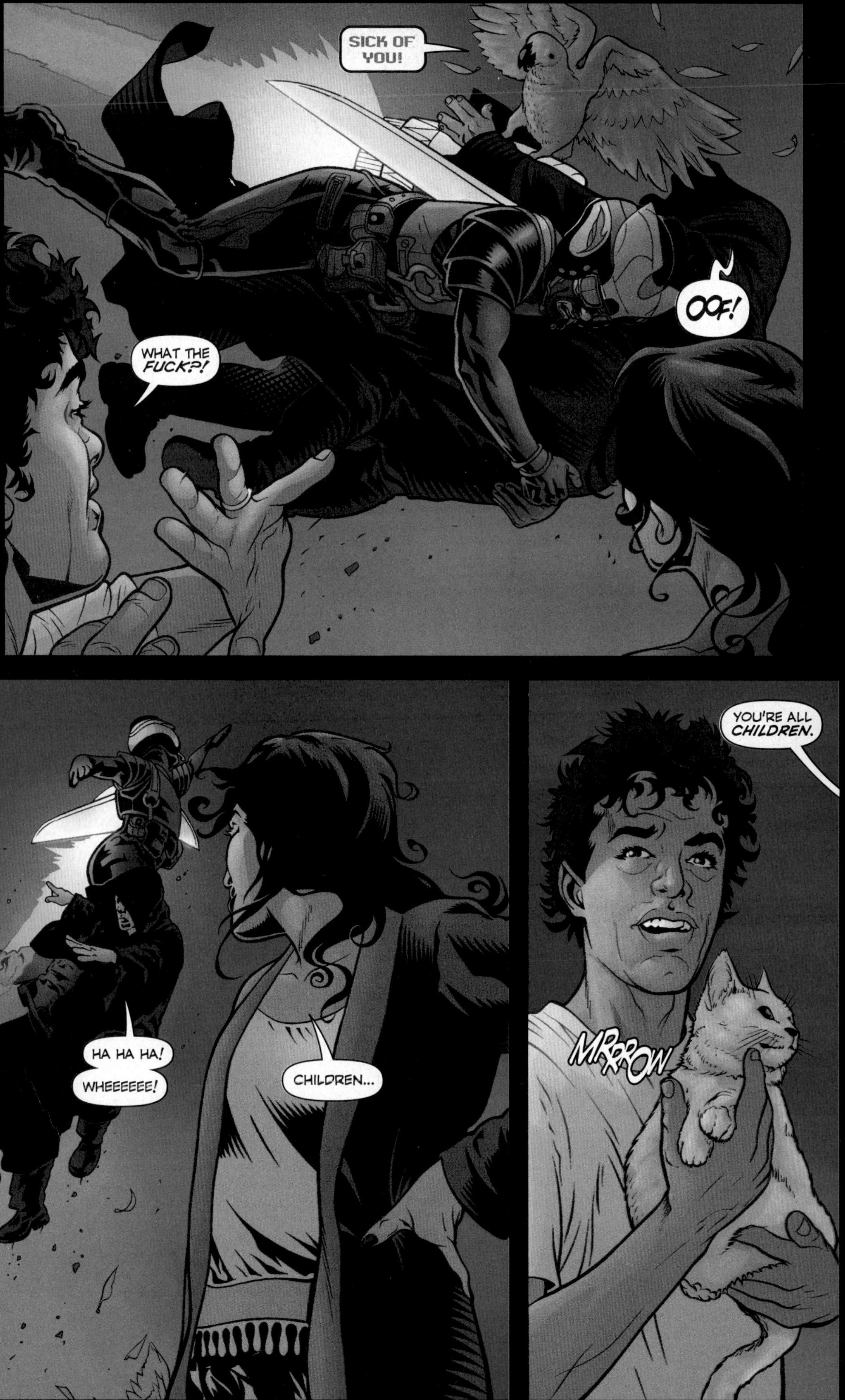
SICK OF YOU!
OOF!
WHAT THE *FUCK?!*
HA HA HA!
WHEEEEEE!
CHILDREN...
YOU'RE ALL *CHILDREN.*
MRRROW

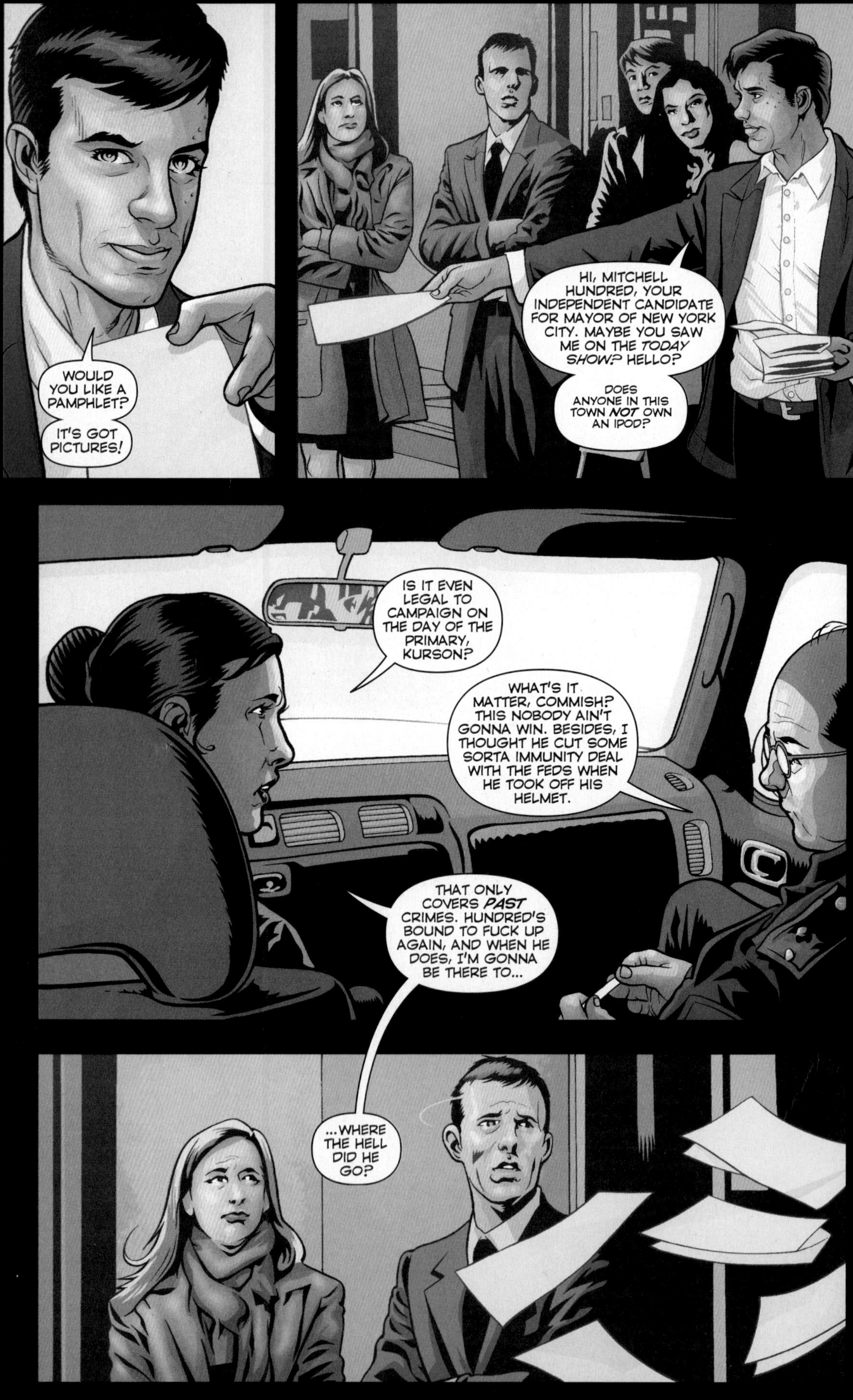
WOULD YOU LIKE A PAMPHLET?
IT'S GOT PICTURES!
HI, MITCHELL HUNDRED, YOUR INDEPENDENT CANDIDATE FOR MAYOR OF NEW YORK CITY. MAYBE YOU SAW ME ON THE *TODAY SHOW?* HELLO?
DOES ANYONE IN THIS TOWN *NOT* OWN AN IPOD?
IS IT EVEN LEGAL TO CAMPAIGN ON THE DAY OF THE PRIMARY, KURSON?
WHAT'S IT MATTER, COMMISH? THIS NOBODY AIN'T GONNA WIN. BESIDES, I THOUGHT HE CUT SOME SORTA IMMUNITY DEAL WITH THE FEDS WHEN HE TOOK OFF HIS HELMET.
THAT ONLY COVERS *PAST* CRIMES. HUNDRED'S BOUND TO FUCK UP AGAIN, AND WHEN HE DOES, I'M GONNA BE THERE TO...
...WHERE THE HELL DID HE GO?

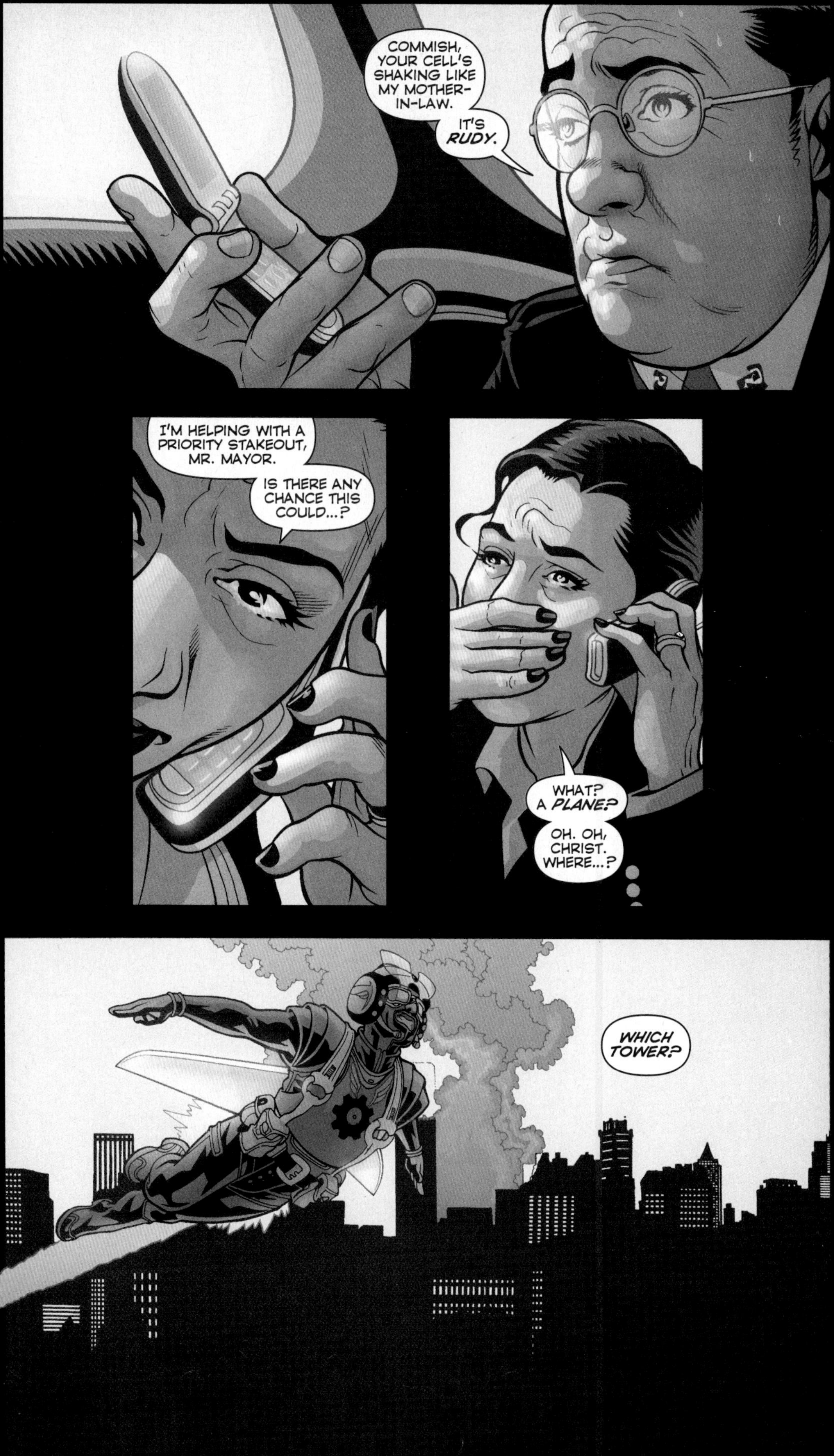
COMMISH, YOUR CELL'S SHAKING LIKE MY MOTHER-IN-LAW.
IT'S *RUDY.*
I'M HELPING WITH A PRIORITY STAKEOUT, MR. MAYOR.
IS THERE ANY CHANCE THIS COULD...?
WHAT? A *PLANE?*
OH. OH, CHRIST. WHERE...?
WHICH TOWER?

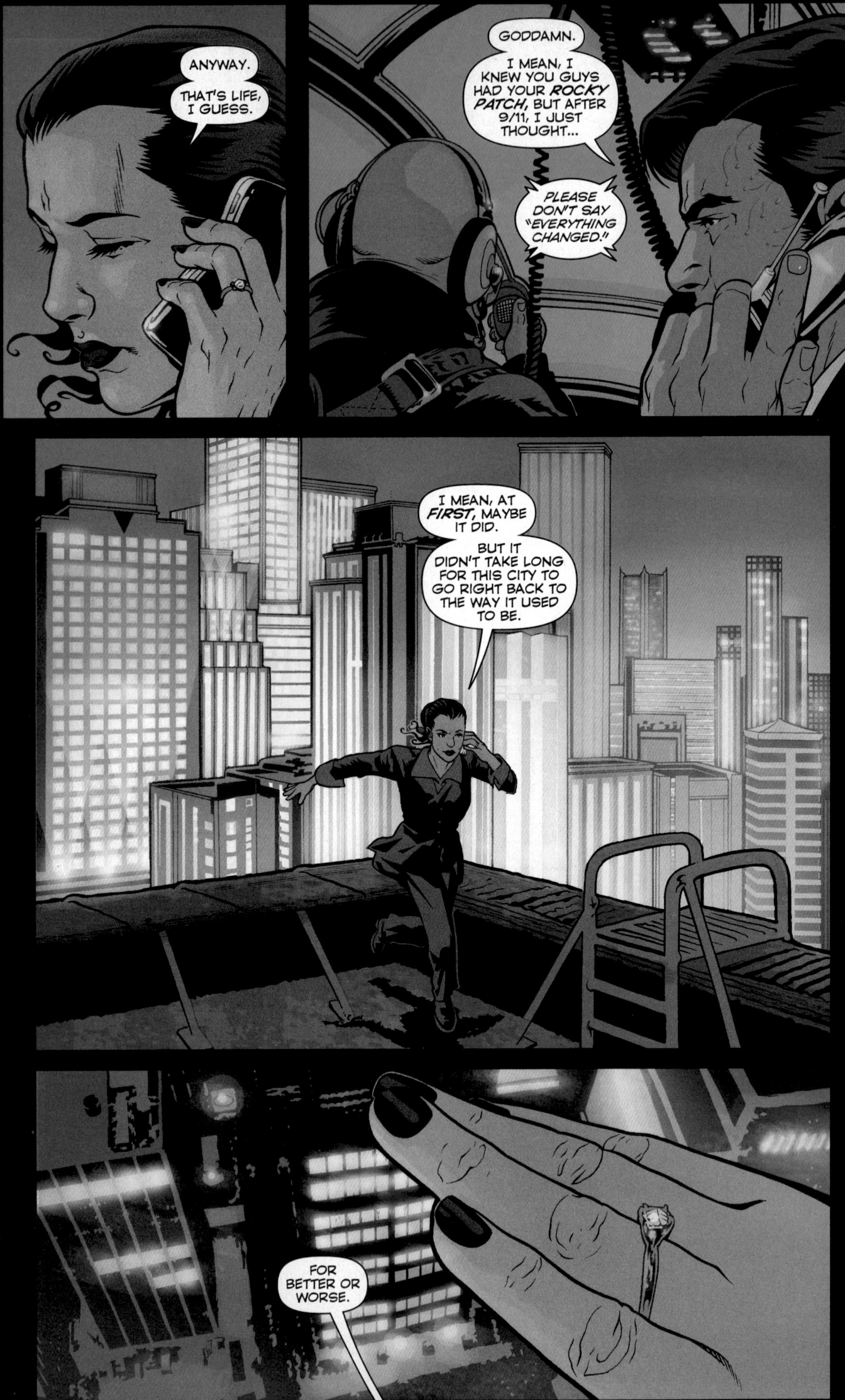
ANYWAY.
THAT'S LIFE, I GUESS.
GODDAMN.
I MEAN, I KNEW YOU GUYS HAD YOUR *ROCKY PATCH,* BUT AFTER 9/11, I JUST THOUGHT...
PLEASE DON'T SAY "EVERYTHING CHANGED."
I MEAN, AT *FIRST,* MAYBE IT DID.
BUT IT DIDN'T TAKE LONG FOR THIS CITY TO GO RIGHT BACK TO THE WAY IT USED TO BE.
FOR BETTER OR WORSE.

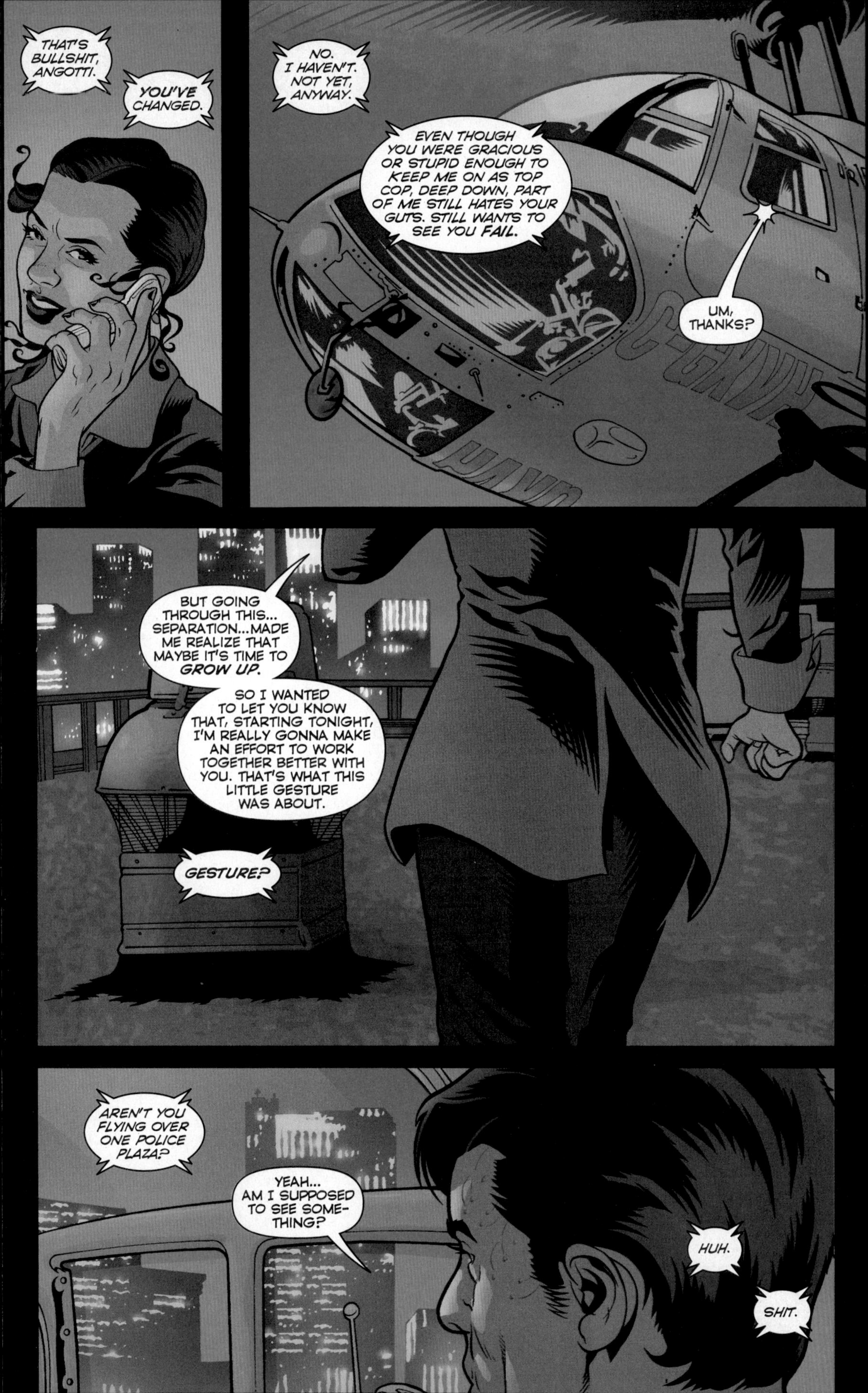
THAT'S BULLSHIT, ANGOTTI.
YOU'VE CHANGED.
NO. I HAVEN'T. NOT YET, ANYWAY.
EVEN THOUGH YOU WERE GRACIOUS OR STUPID ENOUGH TO KEEP ME ON AS TOP COP, DEEP DOWN, PART OF ME STILL HATES YOUR GUTS. STILL WANTS TO SEE YOU FAIL.
UM, THANKS?
BUT GOING THROUGH THIS... SEPARATION...MADE ME REALIZE THAT MAYBE IT'S TIME TO GROW UP.
SO I WANTED TO LET YOU KNOW THAT, STARTING TONIGHT, I'M REALLY GONNA MAKE AN EFFORT TO WORK TOGETHER BETTER WITH YOU. THAT'S WHAT THIS LITTLE GESTURE WAS ABOUT.
GESTURE?
AREN'T YOU FLYING OVER ONE POLICE PLAZA?
YEAH... AM I SUPPOSED TO SEE SOME-THING?
HUH.
SHIT.

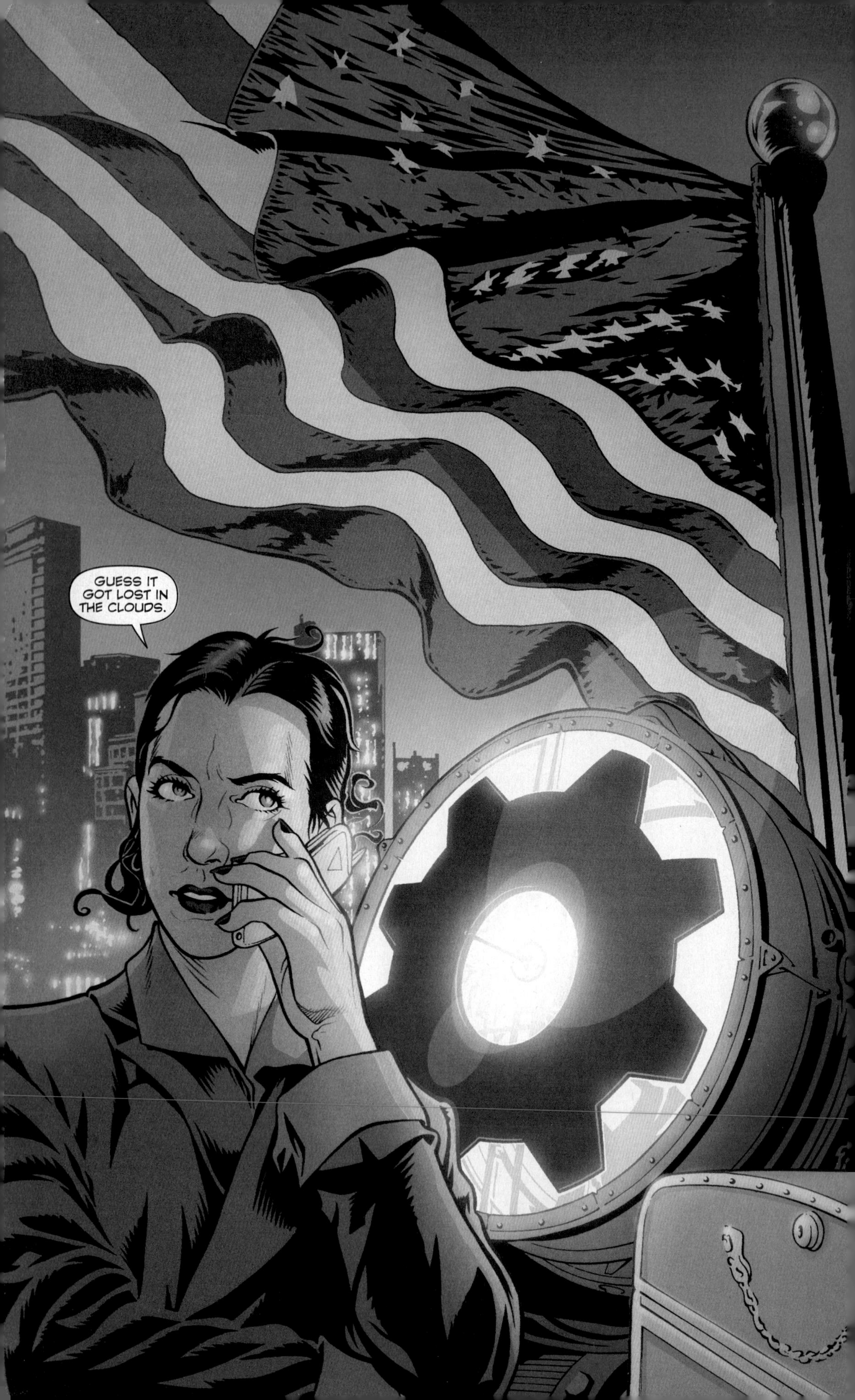
GUESS IT GOT LOST IN THE CLOUDS.

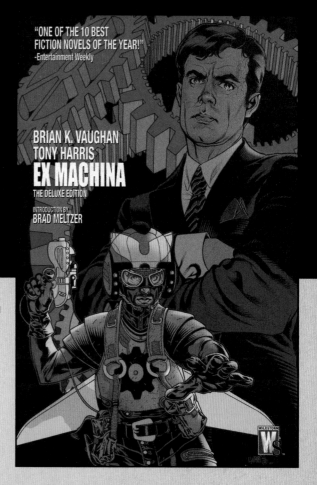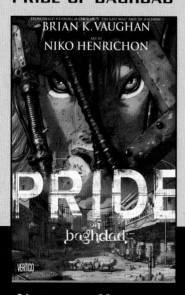

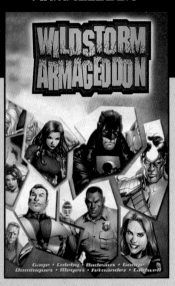